MY
LONGEST
NIGHT

Geneviève and her little brother Claude several weeks after the Liberation of Normandy. Geneviève's dress was made out of material from Lieutenant Wingate's parachute. *Author's Collection. Editions Robert Laffont: Service Iconographique.*

MY LONGEST NIGHT

A Twelve-Year-Old Heroine's Stirring
Account of D-Day and After

Geneviève Duboscq

Translated by
Richard S. Woodward

ARCADE PUBLISHING • NEW YORK

Arcade Publishing books may be purchased in bulk at special discounts for sales promotion, corporate gifts, fund-raising, or educational purposes. Special editions can also be created to specifications. For details, contact the Special Sales Department, Arcade Publishing, 307 West 36th Street, 11th Floor, New York, NY 10018 or arcade@skyhorsepublishing.com.

Arcade Publishing® is a registered trademark of Skyhorse Publishing, Inc.®, a Delaware corporation.

Visit our website at www.arcadepub.com.

10 9 8 7 6 5 4 3

Library of Congress Cataloging-in-Publication Data is available on file.

ISBN: 978-1-61145-721-6

Printed in the United States of America

Author's Note For The
English Language Edition

Since the publication of this book in France—especially since it became a bestseller—a few people have questioned some of the facts I relate. In France, there are some who maintain I did not give their deeds sufficient credit. In America, some veterans of the 82nd Airborne Division, who fought so bravely in La Fière, have no memory of our house and therefore doubt my family's brave deed. The simple fact is that for them La Fière is a small cluster of houses near the causeway over the river, whereas our house, which is still part of that township, is several miles north and across the river. That geographical confusion dims neither their bravery nor diminishes Papa Maurice's heroic efforts from June 5th to 7th, 1944. Those who have been upset by my book seem to have forgotten that I am not posing as an historian nor as an expert in military affairs. This is my personal story. I was a little girl when the events described took place and I have recreated these as accurately and faithfully as I could, relying not only on my vivid memory but on the corroboration of several witnesses who lived through them with me.

I dedicate this book
to all the veterans of the Allied Armies
and in particular to the paratroopers
of the 82nd and 101st Airborne Divisions
who gave their lives to free us,
to Philippe Jutras, a veteran of Utah Beach,
Curator of the Sainte-Mère-Eglise Museum,
to Robert,
to all my children,
and, of course,
to Papa Maurice and
my beloved mother.

Preface

The railroad line between Paris and Cherbourg stretches straight as an arrow from the capital to that major port city. Along the entire route—which was inaugurated three generations ago by the Emperor Napoleon III—the French National Railroad had constructed a series of pretty little houses, given rent free to the families whose job it was to raise and lower the grade-crossing gates and to make sure the tracks in their area were clear and in good shape.

Our house was Grade Crossing 104, which, as its name implies, was the hundred and fourth such post on the Paris-to-Cherbourg line. It was a pretty little house, regularly repainted in soft ocher by the railroad company, and it was surrounded by a profusion of flowers and climbing vines that my mother had planted. It was itself a proud, bright flower in the midst of a barren, marshy landscape. In fact, few people as poor as my parents were in those days could boast of living in a house so tidy and smart.

There were four rooms: the kitchen and my parents' bedroom on the ground floor, and on the top floor an attic and second bedroom. What a crazy floor that top story was! The architect who had drawn up the plans for 104 had for some unknown reason laid it out so that we children had to cross the attic to get to our bedroom. What was worse, the attic was big and airy and faced the marshes, but since it had never been completed it served absolutely no purpose. Our bedroom, on the other hand, was tiny, and looked out on the

Aerial view of Grade Crossing 104. *Imperial War Museum Collection. Editions Robert Laffont: Service Iconographique.*

tracks. So my little brother and I were literally shaken in our beds by the frequent passage of trains thundering by directly beneath our window. The trembling seemed to emanate from the earth itself, but since it was part of our existence it never really troubled our sleep.

Grade Crossing 104 was five kilometers from the village of Sainte-Mère-Eglise, a Normandy town perched in the vast lowlands and marshes that typified our region. Twice a day I had to make that trip, on my way to school and back. The morning trip was pleasant enough, and even the first part of the return trip in the evening: three and a half kilometers through calm and peaceful countryside. But the final leg of the journey was another matter altogether. Once I reached the railroad, I had a kilometer and a half along the narrow path beside the roadbed, with only the marshes on either side. The narrowness of the path itself, the unpredictable wind that gusted throughout the region, the frequent passage of the thundering trains, which spewed their half-burned cinders and menacing jets of steam—all constituted the many dangers I had to face every day. But at the end of that nocturnal, hazardous walk there lay our house, Number 104. I thought of it as my daily reward.

We also had the use of another house, set on higher ground in the midst of a thirty-acre field. This second house had in earlier days been a sheep pen, and so we called it the Sheepfold. It deserved its name. The part which had housed the sheep was enormous, with room enough for hundreds of sheep. As for the humans, they had

Grade Crossing 104. *Author's Collection. Editions Robert Laffont: Service Iconographique.*

to get by with a kitchen on the ground floor, which doubled as a main room, where my parents slept, and a small bedroom on the floor above.

It was hard to say which of the two houses I preferred. I liked them both. Life at the Sheepfold was rougher than at 104. The latter, like all the Grade Crossing houses, had both a pump and a cistern. In times of severe drought, we would go and fetch our water in the Merderet, a little stream that ran through the marshes, which always dried up in summer. At the Sheepfold water was often a problem, and many times we had to share the watering trough for the cattle and horses that my parents were paid to look after. Whether we stayed in one house or the other depended on my parents' professional obligations, for they needed both jobs to keep body and soul alive.

Part of my father's job with the railroad was to check the state of the tracks between Grade Crossings 104 and 103. When the marsh wasn't dry, my father would take us with him in a flat-bottomed boat as he inspected the state of the line. For years the high points of my life were these little cruises, on a boat without sail or wind, and whose captain, my father, was called Papa Maurice.

The Sheepfold, which has stood empty for over twenty years. *Author's Collection.*

MY
LONGEST
NIGHT

September 3, 1939

The day war was declared, it was the church bell of Sainte-Mère-Eglise that rang out first. Never had I heard bells ringing that way. I'll remember it as long as I live. I knew at once that it was a bell of warning or alarm. I could see the belltower from my bedroom window at the Sheepfold, and I was looking, transfixed, at the church.

Amfreville's belltower responded immediately, followed several seconds later by those of Fresville, Neuville-au-Plain, and Chef-du-Pont. It was a strange, slow melody, even sadder than certain autumn evenings when dusk falls. To me, church bells are happy. Of course, they do ring at funerals, too, but those I had learned to recognize. No, this was no funeral; it was a new and menacing sound, a dismal chant filled with storms and desolation that lay heavy over the fields and fen. Why? What did it mean?

That day Mama had left me—the big girl of six and a half that I was—in charge of her one-year-old baby brother, who lay sleeping in his crib. Poor Mama. As the bells began to ring, I was looking at her through the window. She was wielding a sickle, doing her best to cut the tufts of thorny bushes that grow, in random patches, in the meadows, like weeds in a garden. Cattle that ate them could damage their stomachs. Some people called them "cursed thistles," but around here we simply referred to them as "cow killers."

Mama was the sole custodian both of the large herd of beef cattle and the thirty acres of meadow on which the cattle grazed. She had

The Château d'Amfreville. *Author's Collection.*

her hands more than full, and, in addition, two small children to take care of. My father managed to spend every penny he earned drinking with his buddies. So my mother was working, as usual. The ordinary, everyday work of an ordinary, everyday day. As for Papa Maurice, he was nowhere in sight. But we knew what he was up to: he was downing his daily portion of hard cider or Calvados.

My mother had been up at the crack of dawn, as she always was. Before she had left for the Leroux dairy farm, where she and another woman split the job of milking some twenty cows, she had come and laid my baby brother in my arms. He was fast asleep, and I had hardly dared breathe for fear of waking him up.

Little Claude was not just my brother, but also my protégé and my refuge. He was the only person in the world—aside from my mother—with whom I felt at ease. I watched him sleeping, attentive to his every breath, fearful yet impatient for him to wake up, so that I could see him open his eyes and smile and begin to babble.

When she had finished milking the cows, at about nine o'clock, my mother came back to the house. Climbing the steep wooden stairs that led to my room, she had come to claim her baby. While she offered him her breast, I went down and lighted the fire in the big fireplace. It was breakfast time. Our breakfasts were very simple. Two pieces of bread sliced out of the six-pound loaf, grilled over the fire, and dipped into hot milk. After breakfast, work time: for my mother, out into the meadow; for me, cleaning up the house. My older sister and brother, Denise and Francis, had jobs at Leroux's, doing general chores during the summer vacation.

Yes, today was an ordinary day. Outside, everything was still. Off to my left, along the fence that bordered the road, the tall elms cast almost no shadow. It was noon. To my right, beyond the trees that marked the end of the meadow, the marshes began, through which the railroad ran as far as the eye could see. This swamp was still dry; winter was a long way off. I could see some cows and horses grazing there—not ours, I knew. Could it be that Papa Maurice was watching them too, leaning up against the gate crossing of 104—that old wooden gate like all the gates in the countryside—making sure that none of the horses or cattle strayed onto the tracks as the train approached? Or maybe he was pacing up and down the tracks, keeping an eagle eye open for any rails that might have expanded with the heat.

An image of peace and serenity. Nothing bad could happen to us. Life was hard, very hard some times, but it was ours. Why should it change? And who would have the power to change it?

The bells were still ringing. Why? Why were they ringing so loud and long? I had to find out. Glancing at my little brother, and seeing that he was still fast asleep, I left the house and ran toward my mother. She might know. She heard me coming and straightened up. I could see she was crying as she folded me in her arms. I buried my head in her breast and asked her why the bells were ringing that way.

"It's an alarm," she said. "It's awful. They're ringing to tell us war's been declared."

"War?"

"War is when men go out and fight each other. Kill each other."

I'd heard of war before. But in my mind wars took place far away, in a corner of France where neither I nor my mother would ever go. So what would that change for us?

"You'll have plenty of time to learn what war is," she said sadly. "We're going to become poorer and poorer, more and more unhappy."

Maybe so. But I hadn't noticed that we were unhappy. I wasn't a spoiled child, like some city kids who never knew what it was like to work. I already had my responsibilities, my allotted chores. I had seen hard times before, and knew I would again. But still that was no reason to despair, was it?

My mother was crying; I had to cheer her up. At least try.

"Come on, Mama, give me a big smile. And stop working. You'll see. It'll be all right. Come back to the house with me, I'll make you a cup of coffee."

"I can't, Geneviève. I can't stop now. I still have a lot of fences to check before dark. The cattle have broken some of the barb wire, and I have to string new ones."

"Too bad! You can't believe how cute the baby is today!"

I knew that would do the trick: a faint smile came over her lips, and she followed me meekly to the house. As she was sipping her coffee I came over and sat on her lap.

"Don't be sad," I said. "Why don't you teach me a new song."

As far back as I can remember, I always loved to sing. So much so that I sometimes think I learned to sing before I learned to talk. My mother knew how much I loved it—a passion she shared—and so she taught me a new refrain every day, or, on those days when she didn't have time, a new couplet added onto yesterday's song. Like me, my mother had a very pretty voice. And both of us derived equal and endless pleasure from our singing exercises. I practiced all day long, in the house after my father had left for the day, on the road, when I went with my mother to market or on my way to meet my sister Denise on her way home from school. Sometimes I even broke into song in the middle of my classes, before I could catch myself.

It was our one luxury, one that cost nothing and did no harm to anyone. But that day my mother had trouble indulging it. She looked so sad.

"Do you really want me to teach you a new song," she said, "even despite the war?"

Mama had once told me how one of the kings of France, Louis XIII, had placed our country under the protection of the Holy Virgin. In case of danger, it was to Her we had to pray. She could not refuse our prayers. I knew there was a pretty song that talked about it.

"Teach me that song about the Virgin Mary and France," I said.

"All right. But pay close attention to the words. I'm only going to sing it once. I have to get back to the fields."

Then she began to sing, very softly, enunciating the words very carefully. And I repeated each line after her:

> *Holy Mother,*
> *Our sole salvation*
> *Lend us your loving hand.*
> *Save our nation*
> *Save our beloved land.*

Certain memories remain forever engraved in your mind. Nothing will ever erase from mine the memory of this first day of the war, and that song whose words are indeed naive but full of meaning. It was a prayer, a real prayer. My mother smiled and patted me on the cheek. Then she went back to her work, leaving me once again alone with my little brother. But not for long.

My father arrived home earlier than expected. His cap was askew, his eyes glazed, his expression more ferocious than usual as he stumbled across the threshold. He grabbed the door frame to keep from falling down. I knew what that meant. It meant I ought to make myself scarce, and I edged toward the staircase, hoping to sneak upstairs before he saw me. But it was useless. Papa Maurice caught sight of me and roared:

"Trying to hide, are you! Come over here!"

I had no choice but to obey. I knew what was in store for me. No one could have protected me. My mother had come back from the fields. But what could she do? Standing just five feet, and weighing only 100 pounds, she was no match for her husband.

"Come over here," he said again.

Submissively I walked over to him. He raised his hand. The first slap caught me square in the face. Again, the huge hand, bigger than a washerwoman's paddle, struck me full force. A trickle of blood ran down from my lips.

That was enough. As he brought his hand down again, I moved my head away at the last second and his hand crashed into a corner of the massive oak clothes closet against which I had been leaning.

Papa Maurice let out a howl of pain. Then he collapsed into a chair and launched into a diatribe, only partly coherent, about the evils of war. "Madness!" he thundered. "Total madness. Shouldn't be allowed to exist, I tell you!" But I knew it was only a lull in the storm, so I quietly sneaked upstairs to my room. There I knew I would be safe. My father was scared stiff of that staircase. Even in his worst moments, he remained painfully aware of the danger that the ascent of those thirteen wooden steps represented for him. He would have cracked his skull on them. Happily for me, he never made the attempt. So I knew I was safe until the next day.

A little while later, Mother brought the baby up to me. Then she left for the Leroux farm, to milk the cows again, as she did each evening. As payment, she came home with two liters of fresh milk.

Night was falling. I thought back on my day: the church bells ringing their sad alarm; my mother crying; the baby asleep; father coming home drunk. These would be my memories of that first day of World War II.

On that day, I was six years and five months old.

September 1939-June 1944

Jean Leroux and his wife, Madame Marguerite, were the important people of the region. Their farm, *Noires Terres,* was vast and imposing. I used to go there often with my mother, whom the Leroux's had known for many years, from the time before she was married. They always found some work for her on the farm, which assured us of our daily needs. It was work most often paid for in food rather than money–not all that different from the relationship between noble and peasant in the Middle Ages, with the difference, of course, that the work here was voluntary. But many of the labors performed were not all that different than they must have been in medieval times. Both the men and women of the region threshed the grain by hand with rhythmic strokes, for hours on end, seated on the stone floor of the farm courtyard; they were armed with flails, instruments made of two pieces of wood, one long and one short–not unlike the wooden handles of tools–and joined by leather cords about ten centimeters long, which gave them flexibility. It was hard, painful, and trying work, much as it must have been hundreds of years ago.

The buildings that composed the Leroux farm formed a four-sided complex, and I used to walk wide-eyed through the various buildings. One entered the complex through an archway nestled between a stable and cattle barn. On your right were the barns and storage sheds. At the far end of the courtyard was the master's dwelling, only one story high but so vast there must have been ten or a dozen rooms, at least. I thought how nice it would be to live in such a house.

The fireplace at the Sheepfold was built in such a way that we had been able to install, beneath its mantel, a wooden bench where little Claude and I could sit on cold winter evenings. The bench was to the left of the fireplace, the right side being reserved for the chicks born during the off-season, for to sustain our needs we raised both chickens and rabbits. Fastened to the back of the fireplace was a heavy hook which held the big pot in which my mother always kept soup simmering. One winter evening I arrived home from school after a long, icy walk, and sat down at my usual place on the little bench by the fire. I rubbed my hands close to the fire, and had just begun to feel warmer when all of a sudden the hook that held the soup pot came loose, and the pot full of boiling soup spilled all over me.

I screamed. I was burned so badly that I had to spend the rest of the winter in bed. A whole winter of endless days in the house alone, with only my little brother for company. To help the days pass my mother gave me a doll. It was my first doll.

The doctor came to the house twice a week to change my bandages. I hated his visits, for the operation was very painful, and I could never hold back the tears.

"If you cry," the doctor said, "I'll take your doll away."

He wasn't so dumb. I had one toy, one real toy, a doll such as every little girl on the face of the earth dreams of having. And he knew I wasn't about to let him take it away from me.

Leaning over me, he began to remove the bandages. I closed my eyes and clenched my teeth. Not a sound escaped my lips.

My doll was my dream; pain was part of life. If I wanted one, I would have to endure the other.

In the meantime, we had more or less grown used to the presence of the Germans. For the most part that war was far away, and the news of what was happening, brought to us by word of mouth, often seemed vague and filled with rumors. Anyway, war was a serious matter not for children's ears, so in our presence the subject was rarely discussed. And yet we knew more than the grownups realized. We knew that war was, as Papa Maurice had said, total madness, but that it was also very complicated. For instance, we saw that some Frenchmen, our own people, not only sported but proudly wore armbands with a swastika on them. They worked for the Germans, and had the job of patrolling the tracks. They not only invited themselves to lunch whenever they felt like it, but they also ate the best food. They thought that was only normal.

As for the French who continued to fight for our liberation, we didn't know who they were. We didn't even know they existed. The Resistance? We kids had never heard of them. The members of the Resistance laid very low. We all knew about a man named de Gaulle, the general who spoke on the radio. We heard the grown-ups whisper his name. We didn't have a radio. And even if we had, what good would it have done us? Neither 104 nor the Sheepfold had electricity. Our radio was prayer. Every night before we went to bed we prayed for the pilots to bomb Germany, we prayed for this man de Gaulle, we prayed for the soldiers who were dying anywhere in the world, and most of all we prayed for victory.

Meanwhile, while waiting for victory to come, we had to survive. They say that necessity is the mother of invention, and before I was ten I had learned the truth of that maxim. M. Leroux had given us permission to glean his land, after the harvest was in, and that was how we managed to get enough grain of one sort or another to feed our chickens and turkeys during the winter. I also used to go after school to pick two big baskets of dandelion greens from the Leroux farm, which our barnyard friends devoured with great relish. During the summer our fowl managed very well for themselves by scratching about in the fields around the Sheepfold.

However the rations provided by the government were insufficient to fill even our most basic needs, so we had to figure out some alternate ways to better our lot. Then the idea came to me one bright summer day: we would go poaching! Little Claude was by now big enough to accompany me on my expeditions, and so,

The Merderet River: the X marks the spot where Geneviève fed the pike near the bridge on the railroad tracks. *Author's Collection.*

whenever we had a free moment from our chores, off we went, hand in hand, exploring the region around La Fière. La Fière! . . . meaning "the Proud": what a fancy name for a tiny village of only a few houses which in winter stood just a scant few inches above the water that inundated the surrounding swamps. Legend had it that "La Fière" came from a German or Anglo-Saxon word meaning "ferry" and really did not mean "proud" at all. Apparently one could trace its origins back to the Norman pirates of old. And the fact was that, in the written records of the fiefdoms of Normandy, a certain Gauthier de Sainte-Mère-Eglise and Thomas de la Fière each held a knight's fiefdom under a grant from the Lord Lithaire. But all that was long, long ago, and nothing about the region was even vaguely reminiscent of the fierce pirates or warlike knights who once held forth here. On the contrary, the utter calm, the various birds of passage, the peacefulness of the countryside made La Fière a tiny corner of paradise. In 1943, it was our favorite region for exploration. From there, we reconnoitered into the neighboring villages. On this particular day our foray took us to a stream that had all but dried up. And yet it was strange, this stream: a real gold mine, for it was swarming with eels. And eels are delicious. I knew at least three ways to prepare them: fried in the skillet, smoked in the fireplace (in which case you eat them guts and all), or salted. My mouth was already watering, and I made up my mind to bring home this unexpected bounty.

My father's boat was only a stone's throw away, and I knew he always kept a pail in it, to bail out the water after a rain. It was just what we needed to catch the eels. I scooped up a bucketful of water and examined the contents: just as I had hoped, it was swarming with eels.

From that point on it was all downhill. The bucket was heavy, the river bank steep and high. Every step we took we sank waist high in the mud. We had to find help. Abandoning our treasure was out of the question. A willow tree bent down and lent us a helping hand so that we could pull ourselves out of the mire. As for the pail, there was no way we could hoist it out of the mud without our sinking back in ourselves. So we covered it with some large leaves from one of the wild plants that grew in profusion at the edge of the swamp; its sap is a magic balm against the sting of nettles. With the leaves as protection, the eels would not suffer from the summer sun.

We ran toward the Sheepfold, covered from head to foot with a coating of foul-smelling mud. Seeing us arrive, out of breath and smelling to high heaven, my mother let out a cry of alarm. Then she washed us off, combed our hair, and dressed us in fresh clothes while I told her of our miraculous discovery. She didn't believe a word I said: it seemed too good to be true—or honest. But we insisted for so long that she finally agreed to come and see for herself. She saw, and was convinced. With what seemed like barely an effort, she pulled the pail from its prison in the mud and carried it home easily. There she spent the afternoon cleaning and cooking or salting the manna that had come to us, not from heaven above but from the muddy waters below.

When the provision of eels was exhausted, I went back to the river bank and explored other pools near the one where I had made our initial discovery. But miracles only happen once. There were no more eels. Where they had gone I didn't know, but it was certain they had abandoned the drying pools. Still, there were other fish I might catch. Seated in Papa Maurice's boat, I wondered how I might move them from their watery home to my mother's skillet. My prayer, that day, resembled no other. Yet the Good Lord must have heard it and smiled, up there on His saintly throne, for He wasted no time coming up with a solution to my problem. It wasn't the one I hoped for, but it still wasn't all that bad.

I had figured out how to open up my father's padlock, which kept the boat secured to a willow tree at the river's edge, and how to close it again without anyone being the wiser. Thus I could push the boat into the Merderet and navigate at will without asking permission. One day I set off to explore a section of the Merderet that I had never visited. For a while I poled, using the heavy pole that was in the boat, but I soon grew tired of that difficult method and resorted to moving slowly up the stream by grabbing the high grass at the river's edge. I kept my eyes glued to the surface of the water, hoping for the miracle. My arms grew more and more tired, but suddenly the miracle occurred: beneath the water, cleverly concealed by some poacher anxious to add to his own larder, lay some reed fish traps.

If there is enough for one, I reasoned, there ought to be enough for two or three. And even five. The Merderet is so situated that from almost any spot on it you can see in all directions for miles around. No one, not a soul in sight. The stream was calm, the sun shining brightly. The only sounds I could hear were the singing of the birds and the slap of the water against the hull of the boat. I leaned over, plunged my arm into the water and came up with two traps whose contents I emptied nonchalantly into the bottom of the boat. The traps were swarming with fish and eels both. Lots of good lunches and dinners coming up! I brought the boat back to its usual spot, tied it up and returned home with my arms literally filled with fish, which I proudly dumped on the kitchen table.

Then an awful thought crossed my mind. What if these traps had been laid by Papa Maurice himself? What if he were to catch me poaching on his eels in his boat? The answer came to me immediately: he'd kill me on the spot!

One night when he was not in his cups I asked him several discreet questions about fish traps. When he had not been drinking, Papa Maurice acted more or less normally. He was kind and thoughtful with everyone–except me. But when Papa Maurice was sober he didn't resort to physical violence with me. He answered my questions, and from his answers I learned what I wanted to know: the traps had not been laid by him. So I could poach to my heart's content.

From that day on, Mama was able to add fish to our menu twice a week. I had become an honest-to-God little poacher. My mother never guessed how I came by the fish, and she was wise enough not to ask. The pleasure of seeing the food arrive on the table was enough for her. As for Papa Maurice, he didn't say a word. Not even a grunt or grumbled comment in his mustache. He simply must have thought that his wife was managing especially well.

My little game went on this way for several months. As a precautionary measure, each time I poached the poacher's traps, I was careful to take only every third or fourth one. That way, I figured, my poaching had a better chance of going unobserved. There were fifteen traps in all. One more, one less: what did it matter? The poacher who, unknowingly, was feeding our family would never notice, and even if he did he had plenty for himself. What did I have to fear?

The fact is, poachers are an observant breed. That's their job. While he never caught me in the act, one day he did notice some vestiges of what looked like his traps in the bottom of Papa's boat. He hid in the high grass and waited, thinking to surprise my father. The fellow poacher was André Cuquemelle, who lived with his wife and two sons in a pretty house at the other end of La Fière. He gave me a good spanking and scolding. Then, more amused than angry, he gave me a lecture to boot.

"You poor dumb child!" he said. "Don't you realize you could have drowned a hundred times!"

He pointed out to me the dangerous aspects of my poaching expeditions, adding: "I don't care how clever you are. You can't even handle the pole to push the boat along." And he made me promise never to poach again, at least in the stream.

Bye, bye fish; bye, bye eels. What could I poach now? I knew: wild rabbits, which cost nothing and were just as good to eat as our tame rabbits. I asked my brother Francis to make me some rabbit snares and to show me how to lay them. From then on, every day on my way to school I would check the hedges where I had hidden my snares. But rabbits, I decided, were a far smarter breed than eels: for weeks my snares lay empty. Then at long last, I discovered that I had caught a beautiful rabbit by the neck in one of them.

My joy was short-lived, however. I took the rabbit that I had killed in my arms. He was beautiful, his coat soft and silky, and he was dead. I suddenly burst into tears. I brought my rabbit back home. Still sobbing, I laid it on the kitchen table. My mother took me in her lap and did her best to console me. But nothing she said helped. With all the wisdom of my ten years, I knew in my heart I was a criminal. Ever since, I've never been able to take any animal's life.

I went to school every day, and in my tenth year discovered the French language—a language I had hardly known when I started school, since at home we spoke a local *patois*—and I fell in love with it. French history also was one of my favorite subjects, and I often dreamed of the strange quirk of fate that had, through a misalliance, made me a poor child. My paternal grandfather was from a very old, powerful, and wealthy family. Unfortunately for him, however, he fell in love with one of his family's employees and planned to marry her. His father tried to dissuade him, and threatened to disinherit him if he persisted. But nothing would deter him; he married the girl, and his father not only disinherited him but refused ever to lay eyes on him again. My grandfather and his wife lived in great poverty, for all his father's friends also refused to help him in any way or to hire him for any post. His wife shared his fate bravely, and despite all their financial difficulties they still managed to have a swarm of children. My father was their last, their "baby." By the time he came along, their meager resources were reduced to almost nothing. They were so poor by then that they couldn't even buy him a pair of wooden shoes. He could never go to school. To this day, he doesn't know how to read or write. Yet in his own way Papa Maurice is a kind of genius. He has a remarkable memory; he taught himself how to count, and he can do figures in his head faster than anyone I've ever met. Whenever they put him to the test, he beats anyone in the whole region.

My teacher was Mademoiselle Burnouf. A confirmed spinster, she was thin and kind, and she rarely if ever raised her voice, even when provoked. She was affectionate and attentive to our needs, and when—as so often happened—my mind wandered away from the blackboard and classroom into other wonderful worlds, she would gently bring me back to earth.

I had another friend, too, named Madame Mantey. She was much older than Mademoiselle Burnouf, but just as nice. I met her by chance one day in, of all places, the cemetery.

Each morning I would bring to school a tin pail containing my lunch, which I downed as fast as I could all alone in the school yard. The other children either went home for lunch or ate with one of the local people, under an arrangement made so that children who lived in the more distant villages could profit from a hot lunch. Like me, many children lived several kilometers away. I had always refused that solution, preferring my freedom and solitude to the comfort of a regular meal. That way, I always had two hours to myself each day. I wandered idly through the streets of Sainte-Mère-Eglise, which at that hour was virtually deserted. I loved the village's quiet charm, and my favorite building was the old church, which had been built in the twelfth and thirteenth centuries and had managed to last through wars and troubles without so much as a scratch.

One day I wandered into the cemetery, where I discovered a

tombstone of pink marble topped by an almost life-size angel. I read the inscription: it was the tomb of a little girl who had also been named Geneviève. I sat down on the ground in front of the tomb and thought to myself how lucky she was to be dead. No one could hurt her any more or make her suffer. The night before my father had beaten me, and although I usually took his beatings in stride, for some reason this time it had affected my morale and I was feeling sorry for myself.

I didn't hear the old lady approaching. She touched my shoulder. I jumped. The lady didn't ask me any questions, but sensing that I was sad she simply sat down beside me and began to talk, softly and slowly, about everything and nothing. I realized after a while that it must be almost time to go back to school, and told the lady that I had to leave or I'd be late.

She asked me if I would walk with her back to her house, which was near the school. She was old, very old. Worn out by the walk that had taken her farther than she had planned, she at one point put her hand on my shoulder. I gave a cry of pain. The old lady stopped and asked me:

"What's the matter, child?"

"Nothing, Ma'am. I hurt my shoulder, that's all. It's nothing. You can lean on the other shoulder if you like."

"Does it hurt a lot?"

"No, not really."

"I'd like to take a closer look. Come into the house with me."

"I can't, Ma'am. I'll be late for school, and Mademoiselle Burnouf will be angry with me."

"Don't worry about that. I'll go back with you and explain why you were late."

I followed her into her kitchen, where she asked me to take off my sweater, blouse, and undergarment. What she found left her open-mouthed. Papa Maurice has a very heavy hand sometimes. My torso and rib cage were black and blue, and my father's whip had left ugly red welts throughout my upper body. Two wounds, one on my shoulders and the other on my hip, were open and running, partially infected.

Madame Mantey cleansed my wounds and bandaged them gently. She seemed to know what she was doing, and told me that she had been married to a doctor, who had died long ago, oh, some twenty-five years now. Pointing to my wounds, she asked:

"How did you get them? Who did that to you?"

I hestitated for a long moment, then told her in a rush of words. The night before I had arrived home late. Papa Maurice had asked Mademoiselle Burnouf to note in my book the exact time I left school. He gave me thirty minutes to make it home, not a minute more. Yesterday it was my own absentmindedness that had done me in. When I was about halfway home, I realized that I had forgotten to buy bread. So I turned around and went back to the village. As soon as I did I knew that I could never make it home in time, and that Papa Maurice would be waiting to punish me. Depending on how late I arrived, he inflicted one of two punishments, both of which he had made up. Generally he made me kneel down on two pieces of irregularly shaped flintstone, and cross my hands in front of me. He'd then place a brick in each of my hands, and as soon as the weight of the bricks, or my own fatigue, made me lower my arms, he'd pick up his bull's whip and thrash me across the back, as though I were a galley slave. He always made me bare my torso before he beat me, which was where the scars and welts came from.

The old lady listened to me in silence. Then she raised her eyes, and I could see tears streaming down her cheeks. "Listen," she said to me, "I'm going to teach you to pray in a very special way." I believed that this method of praying was responsible for the fact that I was never punished this way again—except once, when I had forgotten to do it properly.

The old lady accompanied me back to school, which was just across the street. Mademoiselle Burnouf met us at the door and said to me:

"Go to your seat. And don't make any noise. The other children are doing their exercises."

I did as she told me. Then Mademoiselle Burnouf closed the schoolhouse door, and I couldn't hear what my new friend told her.

But from that day on Mademoiselle Burnouf changed her attitude toward me. Not that she hadn't been nice before, but now she was even more attentive and patient. I was sure that Madame Mantey had given her a full description of my unhappy home life with Papa Maurice. Yet Mademoiselle Burnouf never talked about it, and I appreciated her discretion. From that day on, she often invited me to have lunch with her, in winter filling me with a good hot soup or a special dessert she had made herself. She didn't have to ask me twice. At home we now lacked almost everything in the way of food, and certainly delicacies of this kind. I did my best to work harder in French, and forced myself not to dream of the birds I wanted to imitate in song and of the trees I wanted to climb with the agility of a squirrel.

Some evenings, when Papa Maurice had not been drinking, I would climb to the top of a tall elm tree near the house–postponing as long as possible the time when I went to bed–and from my high post contemplate the surrounding world.

One night when I was up there a hundred feet above the ground, Papa Maurice passed underneath, and I called out to him:

"Hey, Papa. I'll bet you're too old to climb all the way up here where I am!"

"You're on, young lady!" he called back. And with an agility I would never have thought him capable of, he clambered up the tree till he reached me at the top.

"And what are you doing way up here, all alone in the dark?" he asked.

"Waiting for the stars to come out," I said.

Similar to the chicks hatching from their shells of darkness, the stars never ceased to fascinate me. I spent hours studying them.

"Do you know they have names?" my father said.

"Names? You're joking! Don't you see how many there are?"

"Well, maybe not all of them. But some of them do. Look, see that bright one over there? That's the North Star. Sailors use it to navigate by. And those are the Big Dipper. And over there's the Little Dipper."

"Is there a star called Geneviève?"

"I don't think so," Papa Maurice replied, dead serious.

"That's too bad. I would have liked that."

In the growing darkness I could see a smile cross my father's lips. He put his arm around my shoulders and pulled me against him. For a moment my head rested on his strong chest. It was the first gesture of tenderness he had ever showed me. Timidly, I told him so. His reply was one I couldn't figure out. And what was more, he said it in French, not in *patois*. It was also the first time I had ever heard him speak French.

"You know, child," he said, "between you and me nothing will ever be possible. I'm close to you solely to add to your burden."

What had he meant? What burden was he referring to? His strange admission went straight to my heart. Here we were, snuggled together on our unstable perch at the top of this great elm, watching the stars. Papa Maurice and his daughter. My emotion made me shiver. Papa mistook it for my reaction to the cool night, and made me get down from the tree. I protested that I wasn't cold and asked if I could stay up there a little longer with him. But he wouldn't hear of it.

"Get down, I said."

I got down.

Madame Mantey's conversation with my teacher soon bore its fruits. Each evening before I left school she checked my basket to make sure I hadn't forgotten anything, and went over the list of errands I was to run. She only wrote in my time of departure after she had finished this examination. As a result, I was never beaten any more for having forgotten my errands or for arriving home late. Which didn't mean that from one day to the next my life turned into a bed of roses. When he had too much to drink, Papa Maurice's imagination knew no bounds. He found many another pretense to punish me. But in the course of all this I had gained two real friends. I felt less alone, less lost than I had felt before.

Not long after this incident we moved from the Sheepfold back to 104. As always, we moved by boat from one house to the other. It was the quickest and easiest solution. Both houses were furnished with all the basics, so all we had to do was transport our immediate possessions. We loaded everything into a wheelbarrow and rolled it to the bank of the Merderet, which ran just beyond the line of trees that marked the northern border of the Sheepfold property. There Papa Maurice was waiting for us with his boat. We loaded everything into the boat, which he poled upstream about a kilometer. One of us children would always go with him, to unload the boat at a spot not more than two hundred meters from 104. There we would all reload the wheelbarrow and make the final stage of our journey to our new abode. The whole move took less than a day, and by evening we were settled into our new quarters and new routine.

Only a few days after our return to 104, in the late summer of 1943, the Germans arrived for a visit. We had seen plenty of German soldiers on the troop and munitions trains that passed by, but these Germans arrived by plane. The handsome metal bird swooped down out of the bright blue sky and landed near our house. That day I fell madly in love for the first time in my life: not with the Germans, but with the glorious machine that had brought them. Gently I caressed its gleaming wings and fuselage. One day, I promised myself, I too would fly among the clouds. I who had watched the birds dip and soar in glorious freedom would be jealous of their powers no more.

But the plane had not landed a few scant meters from our house to bring pleasure to a ten-year-old peasant girl. I watched the haughty Germans, resplendent in their impeccable uniforms and highly polished boots, emerge from their plane one by one. They didn't strike me as particularly friendly. But then why should they be? What did we represent for these blond, gray-eyed men? We whose lives were spent in back-breaking work eking out a bare existence from the land, whose main function was raising and lowering the level-crossing gate as the trains filled with soldiers sped past? Nothing more than slaves, ants in a conquered anthill: nothing but poor French peasants. Our role was to be polite and deferential, and to respond to their questions with a "Yes, Sir," "No, Sir."

I watched my father respond to their questions, and was surprised at how polite and deferential he was. I'd never seen him so friendly and courteous. Anyone who didn't know him would have assumed, from his fawning air, that he was a milksop or, worse, a coward, ready and willing to collaborate to save his skin or keep out of trouble.

But I knew Papa better than that. For all his faults, he was no coward. In fact, he really was an old bandit. No one ever put anything over on him. He hated the Germans. But he also knew that he was David to this arrogant Goliath, and that in such an unequal contest the only weapons were guile and cunning. His deference was only a trap, and the Germans fell right into it.

One of the German officers, clearly the spokesman, pointed out toward the swamp and said: "We're going to build an airfield here."

One could understand why this vast, flat plain struck the German engineers as a perfect spot for an airfield. Papa Maurice knew they were perfectly right in their assessment. He squinted and nodded, as though he agreed completely, and said: "I know these swamps like the back of my hand. I'd be happy to take you through them if you like."

The German accepted his offer. Then my father set about quietly and with utter seriousness explaining to the Germans that six months out of the year the swamps were flooded.

"Terrible, these floods," he shook his head as though remembering the annual catastrophe. "And the worst part about it is, we can't do anything about it. Not a damn thing."

He lied with amazing calm. He was risking his neck, and he knew it. During the winter, the Merderet did in fact overflow its banks, but no one had ever thought to try and prevent it. Actually, the brackish water of the Douve, into which the Merderet flowed, brought with it at high tide alluvial soil, and sometimes kelp, that enriched the soil of the pastures.

Yet if anyone had wanted to prevent the floods, there was a simple enough way to do it: dig the bed a little deeper and build up the banks. Papa knew that very well, but he carefully refrained from mentioning it to the Germans. He began to take them on a tour of the area, leading them to those places that were the wettest. He took his trusty shovel along, and every so often would stop and dig down in one or two carefully chosen spots. Almost immediately, the holes would fill with water. The Germans wanted to see everything: the "Big Swamp" near the Château d'Amfreville and Fresville, the "Little Swamp" near La Fière, and the higher ground in the vicinity of the Sheepfold. Papa Maurice knew all of them equally well. With the same servile courtesy he had displayed from the start, he led them into the muddiest parts of the swamp he could find. Within no time, their gleaming boots were thick with mud, and their dashing uniforms spattered with mud up to their epaulettes. And this was in summer!

The Germans refused to admit defeat. For a whole week they took soil samples from dozens of spots, which they would send back for analysis. Papa Maurice was with them from dawn till dusk, constantly offering his help, constantly sabotaging their efforts. Whenever they chose a spot to take a sample, he would smile and say: "Allow me. You'll get your uniform all dirty." And inevitably they let him do the dirty work.

Before putting the samples in the plane, Papa would offer to wipe off the sample cases, and would take them into the kitchen of 104, where he would say to my mother:

"Add a little water to these bottles." Then he would take the doctored bottles out to the waiting plane.

Papa Maurice's little game paid off. The Germans finally gave up the idea of building their airfield. But they figured that someone else—namely the Allies—might get the same idea, and so they decided that the swamps had to be rendered useless. Marshal Rommel, who had been put in charge of the German defenses against a possible invasion, gave the order to flood both the Big and Little Swamps. In great haste, the inhabitants of the swamps gathered their goods and chattel and moved to higher ground. The German soldiers methodically closed the floodgates that, beneath all the bridges over the Merderet, controlled the flow of the stream. These gates were generally never closed except in years of serious drought. But in the summer of 1943, by the order of Marshal Rommel, the countryside around us changed almost overnight. By the end of the week, the swamps were completely flooded. The water lapped at our cellar door, and everywhere we looked all we could see was a peaceful, gray lake. Only the railroad line stood above the shimmering water, like a highway over the sea.

When we asked the German soldiers why they had closed the floodgates, they answered: "To prevent the Allies from landing." Which meant the Germans were afraid of an Allied landing. Which meant that the Allies were planning an invasion. The logic was irrefutable, and refreshing. There was reason to hope again.

Winter settled in. I still went to school every day, but now entirely by a route along the tracks. Our principal, Monsieur Leblond, made us practice air raid drills. He would take us out of the school and lead us along back roads in the direction of La Fière. Whenever he blew his whistle, we all had to dive into the ditches beside the road. Unfortunately, the ditches were filled with nettles, which stung. But Monsieur Leblond, a true philosopher, explained to us that a few nettle stings were far preferable to a single bomb or piece of shrapnel.

As for my friend Madame Mantey, she no longer lived in Sainte-Mère-Eglise. Because of her age and growing infirmity, she could no longer take care of herself, and moved up north to spend the rest of her days with her children. I often thought of her, of her kindness and the strange and useful secrets she had taught me. But I was never to see her again.

Winter slowly gave way to spring. On April 9, 1944, I celebrated my eleventh birthday. I felt I had said goodbye to my childhood. Now I was a big girl, almost a grownup, and I felt closer than ever to my mother, who still worked day and night, with never a word of complaint, to provide for her family. I tried to become more serious, and more focused. I even tried to daydream less.

In this part of the world, children were too poor to enjoy the luxury of adolescence. We passed directly from childhood to the world of adults. The event that marked that transition was First Communion, a big event in our lives. Father Roulland, the priest of Sainte-Mère-Eglise, had set June 25th as the date of our First Communion. Only two months for me to prepare. I studied my catechism every day, with the help of my mother, who in the course of our memorizing, slipped in her own measure of basic education. Be slow to judge others, but quick and harsh to judge yourself. Kindness is the highest virtue. Even Papa Maurice deserved our kindness, and our understanding. "Don't believe everything people say," she said to me. "Even about people who drink too much. People poke fun at them, point at them in the street. They shouldn't. Alcoholics aren't criminals. They're sick. They shouldn't be blamed or reprimanded; they should be helped."

It was hard, but I tried. I didn't hate Papa Maurice. I've never hated anyone. On the contrary, I tried to understand why he disliked me so much. But I never managed to figure it out. For me, Papa was a baffling character, sometimes terrifying and sometimes admirable, especially when he pulled the wool over the eyes of people who thought they were better or stronger than him. But I had no idea that he was also capable of courage.

On Sunday, June 4th, Father Roulland reminded his parishioners to remember to buy their candles for First Communion. The candles were for sale at Mademoiselle Lepresvost's, and the biggest and prettiest ones were prominently displayed in her window. She had all kinds and sizes, to fit everyone's pocketbook. The problem was that for most of the families of the region, even the most modest candle was too expensive. As for us, it was out of the question to think of buying a candle. As usual, we would have to seek alms.

This custom, still practiced in some parishes, had the children of poor families visiting the landowners, soliciting alms to buy their candles. In fact, there used to be three times in the course of the year when alms-seeking was permitted. On January 1st, you could go to the farms and wish the proprietors a Happy New Year, and they would give you some coins in exchange. On Shrove Tuesday we used to be able to go begging for eggs; and, finally, there was the candle-begging custom. The only one of the three that still existed was begging-for-eggs. And good riddance to the other two as far as I'm concerned. But I still couldn't have my candle unless I went begging in the streets. Poor I was born, and poor I would remain. Our poverty was incurable. It was not something you could dismiss or hide. It was there, always, and now I would have to display it for the world to see, while the children of the wealthy had only to cross the threshold of the store and buy whatever candle they wanted. Whenever I thought of it, my heart was filled with rage. The Church didn't seem concerned about the problem. The Church of Christ, who loved the poor more than anyone, allowed the poor to strip themselves of their dignity and beg in the streets for the right to receive one of its sacraments. Every time I thought about it I burst into tears.

My mother did her best to comfort me.

"Think of it as a penance you're offering our Lord," she said to me. "It will teach you humility."

I kept thinking that with a little bit of organization, Father Roulland could have avoided our having to offer that penance. And as for humility, I already knew what it was. But there was nothing I could do about it, so I might as well think of other things.

That Sunday night, on my way home from vespers with my mother, I suddenly started to sing at the top of my lungs. It was a song I had learned from hearing others sing it, a new song that people hummed or sang under their breaths. It was a prayer, but a profane one, a prayer to the English:

> *When English planes*
> *Fly overhead*
> *Our hearts leap up*

With joy, not dread.
Fly on, fly on
Night after night
Our hearts go with you
On your flight!

I thought my mother was going to drop dead.

"For goodness sake, child," she said, "stop that! Do you want us to be shot?"

I burst out laughing.

"Why? There's nothing to be afraid of. There aren't any Germans in the swamps. This is the most peaceful place in the world."

"Never mind. I don't want to hear you sing that song. You're so absentminded you might start singing it on your way to school, just as a German patrol came by."

"That reminds me," I said. "I can't go to school tomorrow. I have to go beg for my candle."

"Tomorrow morning," she said, "I have to do the washing. But in the afternoon I can go with you. We'll leave right after lunch."

"Where will we go?"

"Over toward Pont-l'Abbé. I know some of the farmers in that area. They'll be only too happy to help us." And then she added: "That way your feelings won't be hurt. No one from near home will know you've gone out begging."

I put my arms around her and squeezed her tight, then gave her a kiss on the cheek. When we got home she began to pluck an old chicken, one too old to lay anymore. Our food for days to come, poor animal. Or so we thought.

Monday, June 5, 1944

It was cold out. It wasn't raining, but threatening clouds covered the sky. This same cheerless weather had been lingering on for several weeks. Sometimes it was so cold you'd think it was All Saints Day rather than two weeks away from summer. I was helping Mama do the laundry. It didn't take long to fill up the two big wash tubs; we had a good pump.

To keep busy, and to make this better than just an ordinary day, I decided to go fishing for eggs. This slightly odd form of poaching was something I had invented myself. Since the beginning of the war, the wild fowl and game of the swamp—ducks, marsh hens, teals—were no longer hunted. The Germans and the French authorities had confiscated the peasants' guns, including their hunting rifles. Confiscated in name only, for how many crafty peasants had carefully concealed their guns under their mattresses or in woodpiles, waiting for better days when they would use them again. Better days were coming. But for the time being it wasn't worth it to waste good bullets on small game, at the risk of being shot yourself. So the wild fowl had learned to relax. As long as men killed one another, they could relax. The small trees, or more precisely the bushes that bordered the embankments, were teeming with nests of all kinds. My job consisted of removing the eggs from these nests.

I have my own special way of egg hunting. I dress very lightly, in a bathing suit but with a solid pair of shoes, and I wade into the water and cautiously search the bushes. Although the brambles are covered by more than a meter of water, they can still prick you. At least they aren't as bad as those bushes with black thorns; if they prick you, they always give you a sore or even an abscess. In my poaching, I always keep a sharp eye out for them.

Seeing me pick up my basket, my mother said to me:

"Don't tell me you're going to splash around in that cold water in this kind of weather!"

"I'm taking along a warm coat to put around me when I finish."

My mother shook her head. "I don't like to see you taking so many risks. One day you'll catch your death of cold, and that will be the end of my dear little Geneviève."

Now it was my turn to shake my head.

"Don't worry. God doesn't want me. If He did, I'd be gone long before now."

My mother smiled and tugged on my pigtails.

"That may be true, but you still take too many risks. It's not right."

"I'll be careful. I promise."

"I'll fill a thermos bottle with warm milk that you can take along. Every little while take a sip from it. And don't forget to make sure the eggs are fresh before you take them. No use keeping the older ones from hatching."

My mother was right. The week before I had brought home a basket full of eggs half of which were ready to hatch. That day, the omelette was on the thin side. Mama explained to me what I should do in the future. All I had to do was take one egg from each nest, break it and see whether it's fresh or not. If it is, allez-oop! all the eggs from that nest into my basket. If it isn't, I don't take any. One egg missing from the nests I left alone would not prevent the mother hen from hatching the rest of her chicks. It was a simple method: all I had to do was remember to apply it.

On the average, I managed to bring home between sixty and a hundred eggs from each expedition. And since I poached two half days a week, we always had a plentiful supply on hand. Given the quantity of wild fowl in the area, I never ran out of new nests to poach from. Still, I always kept close to the embankments along the railroad tracks, where the water was not so deep. When I felt that I could no longer stand up on the bottom, I held tight to the bushes.

It was a strange day. Really cold as sin. Mama was right: the water was icy. I let myself down slowly into it, until it covered my chest. I had left my overcoat and thermos on the bank by the path, and the idea of using them later on made me feel better. Yet I enjoyed being alone here in the water. Nothing but water as far as I could see. The water lapping around me, like a liquid belt. I caught myself thinking how nice it was to have a mother like mine, who thought of everything, even sending me off with a thermos full of hot milk.

Despite the abundance of nests, it always took me several hours of searching, and many trips back and forth to my basket, before it was full. The problem was, the eggs were so small! More than once I happened on a nest just as the little marsh hens were pecking their way through their shells. Chilled to the bone, yet full of awe and wonder, I saw the little balls of black down emerge from the tiny eggs. The adorable little creatures swim within minutes after they're born. Life went on, as if nothing special was happening. Here there was no more war, no more Germans or Allies, no more anguish, no more terror. There was only life itself. From my heart a prayer arose: "Thank you, O Lord, for having kept me from destroying these little chicks. And pardon me for all those I kept from being born." And then as an afterthought: "And anyway, Lord, it's not my fault. If this war hadn't gone on so long, we wouldn't be so hungry."

I envied these little fledglings. They would never suffer from the cold, and the swamp would provide them with plenty to eat. Their own waterproof feathers gave them a coat that was soft and comfortable. Yes, it was true that animals' children are happier than those of men. Why? I didn't know, but I remembered Jesus' words when He said: "Look at the birds in the heavens . . ."

I've always loved birds, and they've loved me back. I'm even sure they understand me, that I can communicate with them.

One day I was returning by boat from the Sheepfold. I was about in the middle of the Little Swamp when all of a sudden something struck me in the chest and knocked me backward. I'd been so busy maneuvering the boat pole that I hadn't been paying any attention to what was going on around me. I fell back on the pile of wood that made up the major portion of my cargo. I shook my head and finally managed to pull myself together and sit up on the edge of the boat. The pain in my chest was so great I couldn't keep from crying. When I'd cried myself out, and could breathe a little easier, I looked carefully around to see what in the world had struck me that blow.

At the far end of the boat I saw a duck lying there. That was what must have hit me. I was sure he was dead. Stepping gingerly over my woodpile, I picked up the poor bird, felled by the violence of our collision. Almost automatically, I massaged its chest, as though I were applying some kind of artificial respiration. Much to my surprise, after a few moments the bird opened its eyes. I set him down on my woodpile and stared fixedly at him in silence. Mister Duck stared back just as intently. He cocked his head right, he cocked his head left, as though trying to get a better view of me. He looked so funny that I said to him:

"I must tell you, Mister Duck, that you're going to be fined for not following the rules of the sky. You know as well as I do that you're not supposed to run into people. I'm going to fly myself someday, so I know what I'm talking about. Aren't you ashamed of yourself, making a little girl cry like that?"

The duck, a splendid adult ringneck, then made a most surprising and unexpected move. He edged over, across the woodpile, to where I was sitting, jumped onto my lamp, climbed up into my hands, that were still clasped across my chest, and put his beak alongside my neck. His feathers against my cheek seemed as soft as a caress. We stayed in that position without moving for several minutes. We must have formed a strange tableau for anyone who might have looked out over the swamp and seen us. The marsh waters shimmered in the sun; the clouds drifted lazily overhead; the air, soft and luminous, vibrated in the warmth of early morning. The first day of the world could not have been any more beautiful. I suddenly felt overwhelmed with such a sense of well-being that, as usual, I began to sing. The duck didn't stir. I could feel the rapid beating of his heart against my own.

When I had finished my song, I took him in my hands and said to him:

"You're a lucky duck, you know. If you hadn't been so nice you might have finished the day in Mama's kettle. But now I have to leave, I have work to do. Go back to your family. Next time I cross the swamp I'll call you: 'Hey, Mister Duck!' and I hope you'll come and see me."

Again the duck cocked his head right and left, as though taking it all in. After having caressed his soft plumage once again, I set him on his way and resumed my journey toward 104.

A few days later, retracing my route in the opposite direction, I did indeed call my duck, never expecting to see him. Within a matter of seconds he reappeared, but not by himself: he had his whole family trailing behind him. A whole bevy of drakes and ducklings settled around my boat. Only Mister Duck himself was bold enough to venture on board. Without being asked, he came over and once more sat on my lap, and responded to my petting with obvious satisfaction. Which of us was the more contented I'd be hard put to say.

From that day on I was adopted. Whenever I crossed the swamp on any mission I always called out to "my" birds. The first several times, only the ducks responded. But then little by little others joined them: teals, marshhens, and lots of other birds whose names I didn't know. They even escorted me when I disembarked and walked up the hill to the Sheepfold. I had taken to bringing a supply of grain with me—borrowed from the chicken coops of the Sheepfold—which I distributed to my newfound friends. Each time that they responded to my calls I felt once again the same sense of joy and exhilaration that I had experienced the first time. And yet I still felt guilty, as though by my continued poaching I had betrayed their confidence. But I had a good excuse: we were so often hungry, whereas they, my birds, hatched three or four broods a year, and there was plenty of food for all.

Such were the thoughts going through my mind that morning in early June as I filled my basket with eggs. When I got home, Mama massaged me briskly with a concoction that was partly Calvados and partly eau de Cologne, in which she had soaked a plant that looked to me just like nettles. Within minutes my chilled body was warm as toast again, and this delicious sensation lasted for several hours. I told Claude about the birth of the baby marshchicks that I had seen, and he laughed and clapped his hands as I described how they looked. Often I took Claude with me on my poaching expeditions, but today I had decided it was too cold. Actually he had decided; when we had talked about it, he had said:

"Too cold today for little boys!"

After a hasty lunch, Mama and I set off on our quest for alms. She fastened a basket to the handlebars of her bicycle, so that along the way we could gather food for the rabbits. Since there were two of us and only one bicycle, we took turns pushing it, the way we did on market days at Sainte-Mère-Eglise.

Passing La Fière, we headed toward Pont-l'Abbé-Picauville. We reached a place called La Patte d'oie de Cauquigny, where we paused for a moment to look back toward our house. From there it looked so small. You could see the full extent of the marshes over which there always hovered a light haze, with only the railroad tracks themselves and our solitary house standing above the water. I've always loved haze and fog, which go with my solitary nature and penchant for daydreaming. Mama called me back to the real world.

"Dreaming again, child? If you don't want to get home too late, you'll have to dawdle another day." Then, suspecting the reason for my absence, she added: "Asking alms to buy a candle isn't so terrible. If you like I'll go with you to the farms and ask for you."

I thanked her with a broad smile, and my heart was lighter as we set off again. We'd already covered four kilometers, but still had a long way to go before the first farms. Meanwhile our basket was slowly filling up. As she went down into a ditch beside the road to pick some dandelions, Mama cried out:

"Come here, Geneviève."

I climbed down and she pointed to a fat, black cable.

"Telephone wires," she said. "If I really thought the invasion everyone's talking about were coming soon, I'd cut that cable. The Germans in Sainte-Mère would be cut off from those in Pont-l'Abbé, and I bet that would cause them no end of trouble."

"Do you think the Allies are really going to come?"

She stood up, looked at me strangely, then said:

"I don't know why, Geneviève, but my bones tell me they will. And very soon."

We'd been hearing of the invasion for so long I didn't know whether to believe it any more. But Mama speculated as we continued on our way, not about whether it would come but where. Cherbourg was her guess. It was a big port. But there were lots of Germans stationed there, so if the Allies did choose it, the battle would be bloody, very bloody.

We reached the first farm. As she had promised, Mama went with me to the farmhouse and explained the nature of our visit. The farmer's wife responded with a generous coin, which in itself represented one-third the price of the biggest candle in the window. As she handed it to me she said, in a voice filled with sadness:

"I know that God pays special attention to the prayers of little children. I have a son who's a prisoner in Germany. On the day of your First Communion, don't forget him in your prayers. That way he'll come home safe."

I promised her I would, and I could see, as she thanked me, that her eyes were filled with tears. I understood that war is a special Calvary for mothers. While their sons are off killing one another, mothers of all countries sit home and wait—wait endlessly, and suffer endlessly too.

The second farm my mother took me to was huge, similar in appearance and construction to the Leroux's. But this one was less isolated, only a stone's throw from the road between Sainte-Mère-Eglise and Pont-l'Abbé.

The lady who opened the door had known Mama for a long time, and invited us in for a bowl of steaming coffee and a big piece of toasted bread cut from one of those twelve-pound loaves known as "tourtes." The pretty young girl who waited on us, I decided, must be the lady's granddaughter.

After one more farm, we had money enough for me to buy the largest candle, and Mama noted, with a twinkle in her eye, that I seemed to be walking more sprightly than I had been on our way here. My poor mother would never understand how shy I was, no matter how hard I tried to overcome it.

Starting home, Mama couldn't seem to take her eyes off the telephone cable, which at certain points was visible on top of the grass alongside the road.

"I'll never forgive myself for not bringing a pair of pliers or wire cutters," she muttered, more to herself than for my benefit. "It would be so easy to cut that cable."

"I know what we can do," I suggested. "The next house we come to I can go knock and borrow what you need. I'll promise to return it as soon as we're finished."

"Aren't you afraid, child? If the Germans caught us they'd shoot us on the spot."

"I'm not afraid, Mama. Anyway, we'll be careful. You always said you should follow your first impulse. So let's do it. I'll go fetch a pair of wire cutters."

She simply nodded in reply, and off I ran. An old lady opened the door.

"What can I do for you, child?" she asked.

I blushed and said in a rush of words:

"Well, you see I broke some spokes on my bicycle and if I could cut them it would help me to get home faster. You wouldn't have something I could cut them with, would you? Some tool like a wire cutter maybe? I'll bring it right back. My bike's out there on the road, not far at all."

The lady looked at me strangely, as though she didn't know whether to believe me or not, and finally said:

"I don't know what tools I have left. It's been so long since I used any. Let's go down cellar and take a look."

We had to cross a wide courtyard filled with weeds, which took a while, because the old lady had great trouble walking.

"You're not from around here, are you?" she said. "What brings you to this part of the world?"

"I'm going to have my First Communion at Sainte-Mère-Eglise," I explained, "and I've been visiting the farms asking alms to buy my candle with. As soon as I fix my spokes, I'll be on my way home."

"Why didn't you ask me? I would have been glad to give you some coins for your candle."

"Thank you, Ma'am. But my mother told me I should only go to the big farms."

"She's right, of course. But I still wish you'd come to see me. You wouldn't have gone away emptyhanded, I assure you."

"But I'm not going away emptyhanded," I said, "since, thanks to you, I'll be able to fix my bike."

In her cellar she showed me all sorts of tools, most of them about as old as she was. Hanging on the wall I spotted a big pair of wire cutters, the kind used to mend fences.

"That's just what I need," I said, pointing to it.

"Then take it, child."

"I'll bring it right back."

"I'm sure you will."

Clutching my prize, I raced back toward the road. Even if she had been curious, the old lady had such trouble walking she could never have caught up with me. I felt guilty about borrowing it under false pretenses, but actually my bicycle did have several broken spokes that I would cut. And besides, there was nothing very wrong about cutting that cable. The Germans were our enemies, weren't they?

Mama was waiting for me, sitting on the side of the road, facing the ditch. She motioned for me to sit down beside her. We sat there for several minutes, a welcome rest after my race from the house. Mama examined the cutters I had brought, then glanced down at the cable itself, which we were sitting on. Almost effortlessly, it seemed, she cut the cable, proving that despite the rust the cutters were still solid. Then she stood up, rather suddenly, and walked a few paces down the road, motioning me to follow. Again we sat down by the ditch. Again she cut the cable, and I took the loose piece and tossed it behind a hedge.

Having completed our first act of sabotage, Mama hid the wire cutters under the grass and dandelions in the bicycle basket, and we strolled innocently down the road about a hundred meters or so. Again we sat down on the edge of the ditch and repeated our little operation. Mama had decided that we would make a dozen or so such cuts of two meters each, so that the Germans couldn't repair the cable by simply pulling and splicing it together. This way, they would have to replace the entire length.

As we were preparing for our fifth cut, a handsome rabbit, that we had surely awakened from his afternoon nap, bolted away from under our feet. Startled, we both jumped back as though caught in the act. Mama glanced around, then said:

"Let's move a little farther down the road. I'm sure the rabbit's built its hole where we surprised it. Let's not disturb the family."

Mama was right. There was the rabbit hole, and I could see several little gray rabbits romping about. War and sabotage were no concern of theirs; several meters farther along, we made our double incision once again.

When Mama thought we had done enough damage, she cut the spokes of my bicycle wheels, concealed the wire cutters in the basket, laid out the broken spokes in plain view on top of the grass, and asked me to pedal back to the old lady's house to return her cutters. Meanwhile she started down the road at a rapid pace, moving as far from the site of our sabotage as possible.

Despite the cold, the old lady was waiting for me, seated on her kitchen steps. With great show, I placed the spokes we had cut on the stone steps, then took the cutters from the basket and returned them to their place in the cellar. When I got back to her, the old lady handed me an envelope.

"Here, child," she said, "take this. It's a little something for you. On the day of First Communion, use it to buy yourself some nice treats."

I looked at the envelope with obvious embarrassment.

"I'm afraid I can't accept, Ma'am. Mama made me promise to accept only what I needed for my candle. If I come home with any more, she's going to scold me."

"Take it anyway. If your mother's upset, tell her to take it up with me. I insist. And don't worry about me," she added with a broad smile, "I'm not as poor as I look." She drew me to her and embraced me. "Now run along, child. It's going to rain. If you stay here any longer you'll be soaked before you reach home."

I hopped on my bicycle and sped away. Mama must have been walking really fast, or maybe I spent more time with the old lady than I thought. Anyway, I didn't catch up with her until I came to the bridge over the river into La Fière. I stopped my bike, got off, and handed her the envelope; I told her that I hadn't wanted to accept but the old lady had insisted. I could see that Mama disapproved. I felt myself growing red under her harsh gaze. Timidly I tried to clear myself:

"Really, I tried my best not to take it. But she wouldn't take no for an answer. And she said if you didn't believe me, then you ought to go ask her yourself."

Mama didn't answer. She opened the envelope, and exclaimed, as though horrified by what she had found:

"What in the world will we do with all this?"

"All this" was a hundred-franc banknote, the largest note in circulation. Really angry now, Mama turned on me:

"We're poor, but we're not beggars. That woman was totally unreasonable, and you were wrong to have accepted."

"Let's not argue over a silly banknote," I said. "I know what we can do with it. We can give it to the priest the day of First Communion. And that will be the end of it." Actually, it was still customary in the countryside for those taking First Communion to make an offering to the village priest. This was poor country, so generally it was a modest amount, but for once Father Roulland was going to be spoiled. So much the better.

We walked along in silence. I know my mother. When she doesn't say anything, it means she's upset. I took her by the hand.

"Tell me why you're upset. I don't understand. That old lady was very sweet to lend us her wire cutters. She wanted to make us happy by giving me this envelope. You have to believe me: she didn't want to hurt us."

My mother looked at me, understood the depth of my sincerity, and smiled. A sad little smile.

"When you're a little older you'll understand," she said. "It's a question of honor." Then, after a few more steps: "A question of dignity."

I frowned and squeezed her hand. "I know," I said very seriously, "but the old woman has her honor and dignity, too. When the rich give to the poor, aren't they making an offering to God? She simply wanted to make Him happy." Then, without transition, I took a hop, skip and jump and said: "I wish I could see the Germans' faces when they see what we did to their cable!"

This time my mother's smile was broad. Then her face became very serious:

"I want you to swear to me that you won't mention that to anyone."

"Not even Papa Maurice? Or Claude? Papa will be proud of us."

"No, he won't. He'd be furious. Maybe even beat us."

"You're right. No point giving him any reason to be angry."

"So you promise? You won't say anything, not even to Claude?"

"I promise."

Suddenly the heavens opened and the rains fell, just as the old lady had predicted. A fine, icy rain that lashed at our faces. We were still a kilometer and a half from the house. By the time we arrived we were both shivering. The greenish waters of the swamp were lapping at the embankment by the house.

"If the Allies are coming," she said, "I hope they don't come by sea."

"They'd never be crazy enough to come in this kind of weather," I said.

She shrugged her shoulders, staring pensively out over the marshes. "You never know," she said at last. "Only time will tell."

The Night of June 5

When we got home we found a fire burning in both fireplaces, and it was nice and warm inside after the chill of the day. The kerosene lamp was smoking slightly, so Mama lowered the wick before she even took off her wet clothes. Papa had had the good idea of lighting both fires, one in the kitchen and the other in their bedroom. Several weeks before, the Germans had recruited him for night duty, guarding the railroad bridge between grade crossings 103 and 104. So he slept in the mornings, and spent his afternoons puttering. This week he'd spend all of his time scraping, cleaning, and repainting his boat.

Since he'd been on guard duty, he'd had no time to hang around with his drunken cronies, and we were all reaping the benefits of the new regime. I even had the illusion—which of course did not last—that he might reform and never drink again. Only children of an alcoholic parent fully realize how lucky are those children whose parents don't drink.

It was only seven o'clock, and despite the season it was already dark. More like autumn than early summer. For supper, Mama heated up a big bowl of warm milk, in which Claude and I soaked a fat *tartine* of toasted bread. Then off to bed. But before I went, my mother asked me to put the chicken into the big kettle to cook. That way, if Papa stopped at the house on his rounds during the night he could warm his bones with a bowl of broth.

I went down into the cellar to fetch some vegetables, but a gust of wind blew out my lamp and I had to grope in the dark to fill my basket. The vegetables were from the Sheepfold's big garden. Every day, some member of the family would go over there to check the cattle, feed the chickens, and pick some vegetables. Tonight Francis was sleeping over there, for it was a quieter place to study, and he had exams coming up. He also took care of milking Blanchette, our big fat cow. Blanchette is ours—that is, she was loaned to us by the man who owns the herd of cattle. He didn't pay Mama for taking care of his cows, but in exchange all of Blanchette's milk was ours. In these hard times, that was a considerable help. Our milk, cream, and butter all came from Blanchette's generous output.

Papa headed off toward the bridge, to relieve the guard at nine o'clock. The guards, such as they were, consisted of shifts of ten men, all of whom were huddled together like sardines in a small sentry box the Germans had built next to the tracks. None of them knew what they were guarding, or whom they were guarding against. The Germans had recruited them, so there they were—a motley crew of all sizes, ages, and descriptions. The oldest was Monsieur Touze, who often stopped off at the house on his way home to Sainte-Mère-Eglise for a cup of coffee. Others, like Gabriel —whom everyone called "Gaby"—were still in their teens.

I'd been asleep for about an hour when the loud roar of motors woke me up. It had been ages since I had been awakened by a passing train. But this wasn't a train: it was something quite different. Little Claude was awake too.

"Do you hear that, Geneviève? That sounds like planes."

I got up and looked out the window. Claude was right. They were planes, and they were flying very low. I could see their huge shadows against the clouds. It wasn't the first time planes had flown over our house. In fact, for a long time they'd come over almost every night, and we'd say a prayer for them. Although the noise tonight was louder than usual, I thought nothing of it and climbed back into bed. And yet, why were they flying so low, and why were there so many of them tonight? Suddenly I remembered my mother's words that afternoon: "If the Allies are coming, I hope they don't come by sea." Could they really be coming? No, not in this awful weather. It was just some planes flying over our marshes as they always did, only this time a little lower than usual.

Claude slipped into my bed and whispered in my ear: "I'm afraid, Geneviève. Are you afraid?"

"Don't worry. Those planes make a terrible racket, but in a few minutes they'll be gone. Go back to sleep . . ." I'd barely finished my sentence when I heard Mama's voice from below:

"Stop talking and go to sleep, you two!"

I got out of bed, walked through the attic to the head of the stairs and called down: "It's not us making all that noise. It's the planes." And then I said: "Claude's afraid. Can we come downstairs?"

"All right. Come on."

Neither of us was really afraid any more, but the idea of being able to snuggle in Mama's big, soft bed was just too tempting. But we had hardly reached the bottom of the stairs when Papa Maurice burst into the house, pushing Gaby in front of him. He was obviously so excited he could scarcely get his words out in the right order.

"This is it, woman! They're coming! Invasion! Too damn many planes, don't you see? Has to be it! They're coming! They're coming!"

I had never seen him look so happy. I looked at my mother and smiled, thinking of our afternoon's work with the wire cutters. She put a finger to her lips, reminding me of my promise. It was hard for me not to tell Papa, but I blinked my eyes to tell her I remembered: a promise is a promise.

Mama glanced over at Gabriel and said to my father:

"Where are all the others? What did you do with them?" She then noticed something unusual, and went over to give a closer look. "Your armbands? Where are they?"

"I'll tell you, woman, as soon as I saw those planes passing overhead I said to myself, 'Maurice, get the hell out of here as fast as your legs can carry you.' So I said to all the guys in the sentry box: 'I'm going home to have a bowl of soup. You're all invited. How about it, men, a bowl of steaming broth? How does that sound to you?' And do you know what? Not a taker, except Gaby here. A bunch of stubborn mules. 'Come on, all of you young fellows, it'll do you good to stretch your legs.' 'No,' they said, 'too damn cold out.' So Gaby and I left, saying we'd be back shortly. Shortly, my foot! Anyway, we wrapped our armbands in some heavy stones and tossed them into the marsh. Under two meters of water, that's where they are!"

Papa was radiant, and I was happy for him. He hated to wear that armband, and now he had got rid of it, once and for all. He rubbed his hands together and said:

"And now it's not broth we'll drink. This calls for a celebration. Geneviève, my girl, put some glasses on the table while I go down and get a bottle of cider."

For Papa, any pretense to uncork a bottle was valid. He started for the cellar, but before he had taken two steps the kitchen door was suddenly kicked open from the outside, and standing framed against the darkness was a strangely dressed man carrying a machine gun; he aimed it at us menacingly. Here we were expecting friends, ready to kiss and laugh and celebrate, and instead this fierce-looking man, his jaw set, appeared out of nowhere and was walking toward us.

He kicked the door shut behind him, as violently as he had kicked it open. Poor door, I thought, it isn't used to such harsh treatment. Not a word from him. He just kept looking at us, as though waiting for someone to make a false move. My heart was pounding, and I sensed, in that frozen moment, that if anyone did move he'd kill us on the spot. And yet some part of me was able to study him closely. Where did he come from? His clothes, I saw, were dry, so he had to have come from along the railroad, the only spot in this swampy area where it was dry. "Goodness," I said to myself, "how filthy he is. He could at least have washed his hands and face." For, indeed, both hands and face were black with some-thing that looked like soot.

I wondered how long it had been since the man had arrived: seconds or hours? Yet I felt, despite the obvious menace, that we were all more surprised than frightened. Finally, in perfect French, the man said:

"Friends or enemies?"

I realized what we answered would determine our fate. And then I thought: "What kind of dumb question is that anyway? Who would ever answer: 'Why, enemy, of course!'" How could he take us for enemies, we who had been waiting for the Allies to come for five long years? Assuming, of course, the man standing there was an Allied soldier. In the heavy silence, the intermittent roar of the planes contrasted strangely with the quiet, persistent ticking of our old clock. I thought for a second of Papa's and Gaby's armbands: if they had not tossed them into the swamp, this crazy soldier might have seen all the evidence he needed to decide we were "enemies," and we'd all have been dead. But truth often comes from the mouths of babes, and it was little Claude who ended our paralysis:

"Friends, Monsieur, we're all friends," his high little voice echoed in the room as he walked straight up to the soldier, his hands outstretched toward the barrel of the machine gun.

"Friends," the soldier said, finally lowering his gun. "Really friends?" And he ran his grimy hand through Claude's blond hair.

We breathed again. Following my little brother's example, I went over to the soldier and gave him a big kiss on the cheek. He was surprised, and obviously pleased by the gesture. The whole room relaxed, and in turn my parents, who had been frozen by the fireplace, came back to life and walked toward him.

The soldier quickly took from his pocket a military map and laid it out on the table. He was all business now, the time for amenities over. This time when he spoke, I detected the trace of an accent. I knew people in Canada spoke French, and wondered if he was from that country.

"Show me where the Germans are."

It was the first time that Papa Maurice had ever seen a military map. But he had neither the time nor the inclination to be impressed. He leaned over the table and studied the map for a moment, then lifted his head and asked the soldier:

"Where is my house on the map?"

The soldier pointed to a little black square.

Then, with a little gray stub of a pencil that the soldier lent him, my father underlined several places.

"The Germans are here, at the Château d'Amfreville," he said, "about a kilometer and a half away. And here at Port-de-Neuville, also about a kilometer and a half. At Fresville, too, which is roughly two kilometers from the house. And here, at the Château de La Fière, also two kilometers."

"You mean we're surrounded," the soldier said.

His words obviously surprised Papa Maurice. He looked at the soldier strangely and said:

"What do you mean: 'we'? You're not alone?"

"No, of course not. Don't you hear all those planes? They're full of paratroopers who are being dropped in."

Mama, who I saw had grown very pale, moved over to him: "You mean, Monsieur, that paratroopers are going to come down here tonight?" she said.

"Not 'going to come,' Ma'am," he said. "They're coming down right this minute."

"But that's impossible!" she cried. "You have to stop them before it's too late. They'll all drown!"

"Drown? Why?"

"Come outside and I'll show you!"

Taking him by the sleeve, she led him out to the level-crossing gate. The marsh waters were washing against the embankment only a meter away.

"You must stop them," she repeated. "They'll all be killed if they land here."

"How deep is that water out there?" the soldier said to Papa Maurice as soon as they were all back inside.

"A meter and a half," he said. "In some places almost two. But that's not the worst of it. The Merderet flows through the swamp, and there the water's a lot deeper."

I could see the soldier was trying to figure what to do. Above the house, the endless roar of the planes made it hard to hear. In my mind, I pictured the big white corollas of silk suspended between earth and sky. Hundreds of young men would die beneath our eyes. The trap set by the Germans was going to work. And there was nothing we could do.

Or was there? After all, we knew Americans were tall, so maybe the water wouldn't be over their heads. And even if they landed in the swamp, maybe, unless their equipment loaded them down, they could wade as far as the railroad embankment. It might be only temporary security, but it was certainly better than drowning. But someone would have to steer them toward the tracks. If they landed and started to wade east, they'd all fall into the bed of the Merderet, which is five or six meters deep—even deeper in some places—and they would be lost. The problem was that it was hard to tell where the marsh waters ended and the Merderet began. We knew, but the soldiers never would, even in full daylight.

As though we all sensed what had to be done, we started to act without exchanging a word. Papa headed for the door, nodding for Gaby to follow him, and together they put his boat into the water. As they did, Papa looked up at the soldier and asked him what the equivalent was for *"Venez ici, les gars."*

"Come here, boys," the soldier answered, and I could hear Papa repeating, with a thick accent I suspected, over and over again: "Come here, boys. Come here, boys. Come here boys." He was still saying it as he poled his boat out over the swamp waters.

Mama, meanwhile, had lit a gas lamp, which she turned up as bright as it would go; she climbed up to the top of the level-crossing gate and swung it back and forth, hoping the soldiers who had already fallen into the marsh would see it.

Meanwhile, without anyone telling me, I dashed down cellar and brought up two very dry bundles of wood. They were heavy and I had trouble carrying them, but I made it back upstairs, dropping one next to the kitchen fireplace and the other beside the fireplace in my parents' bedroom. I have always thought of fire as my friend, so I was sure this plan of mine would help save the soldiers. Instead of putting the bundle in flat, I stood it upright in the fireplace. The fires that Papa Maurice had set that afternoon had gone out, so I had to light it. But the wood was so dry it caught almost immediately. Flames shot up the flue, and the heat was so intense it caught the soot which had built up inside the flue as well. Soon bright flames were shooting out of the kitchen chimney. I was sure it could be seen for kilometers in every direction.

Seeing what I had done, Mama climbed down from the gate and came running inside.

"Bravo, child!" she said. "What a great idea! But we should light the other chimney as well."

"I know. But the other bundle of wood I brought up is too thick. I couldn't get it into the kitchen flue."

"Here, let me show you how."

She took the belt off my nightgown and slipped it around the lower end of the wood. She pulled it tight, and the wood slipped easily into the flue. It caught immediately, and within minutes also set fire to the soot inside. Now both chimneys were shooting tall flames into the sky. I went outside onto the track and looked around. A grandiose spectacle. Low-flying planes passed back and forth across the house, and the sky above the marshes was filled with the billowing white of dozens of parachutes swaying gently as they descended. Spewing their enormous flames, both chimneys looked like huge torches held high by some giant—torches that had to be visible for miles around. The trap set by the Germans was not going to work. The soldiers would see the house and head for the higher ground on which it stood. The danger that they might head toward the river was over, or at least diminished. And for any who landed in deeper water, Papa would take his trusty boat and bring them back. These paratroopers who landed in the Great Marsh shouldn't have any real problem, as far as drowning was concerned,

June 5, 1944: American planes dropping paratroopers over
Sainte-Mère-Eglise. *Editions Robert Laffont: Service Iconographique*

for the water was never over your head. The only danger was for
those who might land near Fresville, or the Château d'Amfreville,
both of which were German strongholds. Still, I was sure that when
they saw our well-lighted house, they would head for it. At 104, the
invaders would have a chance to dry out and regroup. Even in the
excitement of the moment, I suddenly realized that the Germans'
scheme to drown the American invaders was actually going to work
against them. For with the marshes flooded, the only way the Germans could reach Level Crossing 104 was via the railroad tracks,
either from 103 to the east or Fresville from the west, and both
routes were too exposed for them to risk an assault.

The soldier—who turned out to be American, not Canadian—

went into the kitchen and asked Mama something. From where I was standing I could see them, but I couldn't tell what it was he wanted. A few moments later he came over and wrapped a blanket around my shoulders. I thanked him with as big a smile as I had ever given anyone. I was happy, happy beyond description. The flames rising from both chimneys were still so high you could see the surrounding area as though it were broad daylight. Some French poet we had read in school had one day asked this question:

> O you, inanimate objects,
> Do you possess a soul?

That night, his words came back to me, and with them I learned the answer: yes, my house does, a warm, maternal vibrant soul. At that moment, our humble house was infused with a rare beauty. Its roof, still glistening from the rain, shone brightly beneath the flames, and every brick and roof tile seemed alive, as though calling the soldiers: here, see me, come over and let me welcome you. Could they hear, and would they respond? This house and this house alone could be their refuge on this fateful night, the safety zone where they could warm up and renew their strength. My dear house, through all these long years have you ever wondered why men built you and then condemned you to such an awful solitude? Did you suffer from being out here all alone? Did you ever feel bad because your interior was lighted only by a humble kerosene lamp? Were you ever jealous of all those other houses, those town houses filled with the laughter of children who, by merely pressing a switch, can light the entire place? Tonight, my house, you have your revenge. You're shining with all your light. Your solid, soot-encrusted chimneys will enable you to play the role of torchlight till morning. You're going to be able to live, second by second, *your night*, the night for which men built you many, many years ago. Be proud, my house. Yesterday, men built you; tomorrow, other men will tear you down. But even if your stones are scattered far and wide, no one can ever steal this night from you, *your* night; no one

D-Day casualty. *Editions Robert Laffont: Service Iconographique.*

can ever take away your glory, your happiness at being here, in this time and place, to receive those whom God has just sent you.

The American came over to me and pointed to a parachute caught in the wires of a telephone pole close by.

"That's the one that brought me," he said.

Actually, the telephone wires must have broken his fall and helped him to a gentle landing, for the long lines from the parachute reached almost to the ground.

"Sir," I offered, "I need your help. In a little while your friends will be arriving. I'd like to say something to them, some words of welcome, in American. I don't think they all speak French like you, do they?"

"No," he laughed, "they don't. Not many Americans speak French."

"Could you teach me a few words of American?"

"What would you like to say to them?"

"I don't know really. Maybe that my name is Geneviève, that I'm happy to see them, that I hope they had a good parachute ride and didn't get too wet, that I've put a big pan of milk to heat on the fire and they're welcome to come and have a cup if they like, that they can also use the house to dry off by the fire." Pointing to the tall flames still dancing above the chimneys, I added: "I would also like to tell them that it's snug and warm inside my house and that . . ."

"Wait a minute," he said, laughing. "You want to tell them too many things at the same time. First let me tell you how your name is pronounced in English: *Jen-e-veev,* although we spell it just like you do. So why don't you greet them by saying: My name is *Jeneveev.* Try it."

"My name is *Jeneveev.*"

"Very good. What else would you like to say?"

"How would you say *chers amis?*"

"Dear friends. But why don't you greet them with 'Hello, boys!' Even before you tell them your name."

I scarcely had time to practice what my newfound teacher had taught me when the scraping sound I knew so well alerted me to the fact that my father was back with his first batch of soldiers. At the grade crossings, the passage had in days past been paved with stones to make it easier for the carts filled with hay to get over the tracks. The prow of the boat scraping against those stones was a sound I had grown up with.

To take up as little place as possible, the paratroopers were standing up in Papa's boat, jammed in like sardines. So tightly, in fact, that I guessed that if I had tossed one of my little brother's marbles in among them, it would never trickle down to their feet. Papa's boat draws very little water normally, but with all this cargo he was having great trouble making it the last few meters from the crossing to the courtyard. Several soldiers jumped out of the boat and pushed it forward. My heart pounding, I cried out to them:

"Hello, boys! My name is Jen-e-veev. How are you?"

"Very well, Jen-e-veev, very well," several shouted back.

My professor began talking to several of the new arrivals, while I ushered others toward the warmth of the kitchen.

Our house had one peculiarity I should mention: it was not horizontal, simply because it had been built on swampy land, and over the years one of the foundations had settled more than the others. The floor sloped rather steeply, and that obliged us to prop everything up—chairs, tables—to make them horizontal. But for once this defect proved to be a blessing, to the delight of my mother. The soldiers were dripping wet, and water poured from them onto the floor. But thanks to the slope it ran right off, down to the drain and back into the marshes from where it had come. I looked around at the room full of soldiers, who were shaking themselves like so many enormous dogs that had been tossed into the swamp against their will. From that moment on, I always thought of them as *our* soldiers.

Mama had her biggest kettle filled with Blanchette's milk, which had been warming for a long time. Never was Blanchette's milk so greatly appreciated as it was that night! Each soldier had a metal cup into which I ladled the hot milk, admiring as I did the incredible amount of gear each of them was carrying. The knives at their hips impressed me as much as did the automatic rifles slung across their chests. In fact, they each had so much gear both in front and back that they reminded me for all the world of the little puffed-up Michelin man in the tire ads. They had pockets everywhere, from which they kept taking the strangest things: powdered coffee or chocolate, which they would mix into the hot milk I had just served them; chocolate bars, which they offered me. I broke off a piece and bit into it: how good it tasted. I had had it before, but not for a long time, because of the war, and I had completely forgotten what it tasted like.

Despite their unexpected bath in the marshes, their faces were still black. When I had first seen them, all I could think was "How dirty the Americans are!" But now I realized that they had blackened their faces on purpose, to be less visible in the darkness.

The heat from the chimneys was such that it would be no time at all before our soldiers were dry. As one of the soldiers was turning a pocket inside out, he dumped out on the floor a little fish, still alive and squirming. Everyone burst out laughing at the sight, and several got down on all fours to recapture it. Finally someone caught it and held it up triumphantly at arm's length. I went over to rescue it from him, but I hadn't the faintest idea what words to say, and my professor was nowhere to be seen. So I simply pulled on his sleeve and said: "Please." Then I added the two words I had heard Papa practicing as he had left earlier in his boat: "Come here."

The soldier understood and followed me outside, where we gently returned the almost asphyxiated little fish to the waters; poor little fellow, it wasn't his fault if he had swum into the pocket of a strange creature who had fallen from the sky.

Back in the kitchen, all the soldiers were turning their pockets inside out to see if they could come up with another fish. But no luck. They acted as though they were disappointed, but just then one of them discovered a tiny green frog inside his cap. Again the laughter welled up, and the soldiers began tossing the poor creature back and forth. I tugged on the sleeve of my "fish-soldier," who immediately understood. He took his buddy outside with him, and again returned the swamp creature to its rightful home.

I could hear Papa's boat again, arriving with a new batch of soldiers, who were as soaked as the first group. I ladled out portions of hot milk, and noted anxiously that the level in the kettle was rapidly diminishing. The twelve liters of yesterday's supply, plus that of the day before, would soon be nothing but a memory. But simmering beside the kettle on the stove was our old chicken. The broth in which it had been slowly cooking for the past several hours would add up to about fifteen liters all told, and to it Mama added

Drowned American paratrooper. *Special Collection.*
Editions Robert Laffont: Service Iconographique.

more water, up to the brim. The chicken was nice and plump, so that even with the extra water the chicken broth would be excellent. Served piping hot, it would warm the next load of soldiers Papa Maurice brought home.

I went upstairs and, groping in the darkness, put on my clothes and shoes. From the window I could see the bobbing little light that Papa Maurice had affixed to the prow of his boat. The new load was arriving. Then all of a sudden I had a crazy idea: overcoming my timidity and my fear of Papa Maurice, I ran down to the landing and took him by the hand as he climbed out of the boat. In normal times I would never have dared do such a thing. But tonight everything was so different! So special! I led him into the kitchen, sat him down and served him a steaming bowl of chicken broth, topped with a spoonful of *crème fraîche* which he loved so much. He gazed at me in silence, clearly astounded, though not really understanding what had come over me. But I understood: tonight something *had* changed. I was no longer the little girl terrified by the very thought of this man. I was a big girl, almost an adult, who had just discovered her real calling: to serve. Serve others, whoever they are, rich or poor, good or mean. My father, at the end of his strength, could hardly walk. Looking at him closely now, I was surprised to see how drawn he was, and how large his eyes looked because of his fatigue. I knew from experience how hard it was to pole that boat. I'd often made the trip to the Sheepfold and back, with the boat full of vegetables from the garden, several liters of Blanchette's milk, and a stack of firewood. The trip out, with the current and the boat light, was always a pleasure; but the trip back, against the current, was always hard. For me, not for Papa Maurice, who is strong as a horse. But today was another matter altogether: even his forces had reached the breaking point. I was glad I dared take him into the kitchen to give him a few minutes' rest and a bowl of broth. It would help him through the rest of the night's lifesaving trips.

A heavy thud, followed by the sound of something sliding down the roof, brought us all to our feet. Papa dropped his bowl and exchanged a fearful look with my mother. Then without a word both ran toward the back of the house. The soldier who had just landed on the roof had probably been knocked out by the shock. My parents knew, from the sound on the roof, from the angle of the roof of the house itself, that he had to have fallen into the fairly deep waters in back of the house. They would only have a few seconds to find him, for if he had been knocked out he would probably drown without ever regaining consciousness.

Papa and Mama returned a few minutes later carrying the soldier between them. The soldiers moved aside to let them pass. They sat him down in a chair in front of the fire, and Mama removed his shoes and some of his dripping clothes, so that she could rub him down with her mixture of cologne and Calvados. In his fall he had lost his helmet, but he did not seem to have broken any bones. Yet nothing Mama did seemed to have any effect on him.

I handed Papa another bowl of broth, to replace the one he had dropped, but he shook his head and headed back out into the night, in search of his lost children. He had not been inside more than a few minutes at most.

Soldiers were also arriving under their own steam, one by one or in groups of two or three, some from the Great Marsh, others along the railroad tracks. Those lucky enough to have landed on dry land remained outside, letting those who were drenched take advantage of the overheated interior to dry off. Nonetheless, I offered them a bowl of broth and they all accepted.

By now the kitchen was so crammed with soldiers that I had trouble making my way back and forth among them. Papa was bringing back still more. The milk supply had long since been exhausted, and the broth was almost gone. But the newcomers would need something warm to drink, to keep the early morning chill from their drenched bones. Mama put on more kettles to heat, and the soldiers mixed their powdered coffee and chocolate as fast as she could prepare it. Despite the hour and the situation, the Americans all seemed to be in a good mood, joking and laughing and offering me everything they had: chocolate especially, but also small tablets on which was marked *chewing gum,* which they explained was not to be eaten but chewed. I found the idea strange and not especially attractive, so I politely declined.

My professor arrived to announce that the soldiers would be launching their attack at six in the morning. I suddenly realized that in the heat of the paratroopers' arrival my parents had forgotten something: something which at that moment struck me as very important. With considerable difficulty, I squirmed my way out of the room and ran down the railroad tracks in pursuit of my professor.

"Monsieur! Monsieur!"

He turned back and saw who it was.

"What is it, Geneviève?"

"My parents forgot to tell you something important. Anyway, I think it's important . . . At the entrance to the Grand Marais there is a *mirador!*"

"What's a *mirador?*"

"I don't know how to explain it. There's a platform up in a tall tree, and there's always a German on guard there."

"An observation post," he said.

"Yes, that's it. But if you don't hide your soldiers before daylight, he'll see you. And there aren't any trees or bushes where you can hide. Only that big stretch of water. If you want to take the Château d'Amfreville, you ought to do it now. Tonight. I know a way through the marshes where the water is never more than fifty centimeters deep. I can lead you there if you like. What do you think?"

"For the moment, I'm not sure."

"Better be careful," I said. "The Germans are real mean!"

My remark brought a smile to his lips.

"Tell me, Geneviève, it's true, isn't it, that the only way out of here is along the railroad tracks?"

"That's right, but not in any direction. You mustn't go towards Fresville. There are as many Germans there as there are at Amfreville. You should head for La Fière."

The tracks, thanks to our chimney fires, were clearly lighted for a long stretch. I gazed down the deserted and somehow threatening tracks and realized that it had been a long time since a train had come by. Doubtless there would be none tonight. I was sure that the Resistance had seen to that.

"What's your father's name, Geneviève?"

"Papa Maurice. Why?"

Without answering, he took me by the hand and led me toward the grade-crossing gate. He cupped his hands and shouted: "Papa Maurice, come here! Papa Maurice, come here!"

From somewhere out in the marshes a voice replied:

"I'm coming! I'm coming!"

My professor-interpreter was standing behind me, and I could feel his strong arms around my shoulders. Leaning against the gate –the poor gate that had been neglected and unused for so many days–we both watched the astonishing spectacle that continued to unfold before our eyes. Paratroopers were still floating down through the night sky, but farther away now, off towards the Sheepfold. The planes made one or two low passes over our house, and I could hear a soldier, with what I later learned was called a bullhorn, speaking to the soldiers below, telling them where the high ground was, directing them towards a more propitious area on the other side of the Merderet.

The lowing, growling motors of the planes made my heart beat faster. I envied the men who were lucky enough to pilot these planes, and told my professor so. I confessed not only how much I loved the planes but also that I harbored the hidden dream of flying a plane myself one day. He ran his hand through my hair and pulled me close against his chest. I savored every moment of this night of nights. Even the little girl I was had learned that yesterday is gone forever and tomorrow is full of uncertainties, so one should live the present in all its intensity. That thought passed through my mind as I stood there looking out over the marshes, huddled in my American's arms. To think I had mistaken him for an enemy when he had first arrived! I had a strong feeling then that all the Americans—our soldiers—would be saved, that none would drown in the waters around us. And that thought filled me with such a strong feeling of joy that I suddenly began to sing.

"That's a pretty song, Geneviève," he said, smiling, and pronouncing my name in the American way. It seemed strange to hear, yet I loved its new sound.

By the light of the flames still rising from both chimneys we could see Papa's boat slowly making its way back toward us. This time it was not crowded, which I concluded meant either that Papa had hurried to respond to the American's call or that there were no more soldiers in the Little Marsh.

"Papa Maurice, can you show me where the nearest German observation post is?"

"I can do better than that," he said. "I can take you there. I think I've fished out all the soldiers. You're in luck: they've had a swim they hadn't counted on, but otherwise they're fine."

Papa Maurice was right: they were lucky to have come away with so few problems. An extra bath never hurt anyone. I thought of my egg-poaching expeditions. They were gone forever. The war was over! The sad, long, awful war was over at last! As soon as I could, I'd go out into the marshes to let Mr. Duck know the good news. Little did I know that not only was the war still not over, but that it had hardly begun.

Both men had crossed to the track and were leaning against the gate on the Grand Marais side. Papa was pointing in the direction of the Château d'Amfreville.

"The closest *mirador* is about two kilometers from here. Takes about three-quarters of an hour to get there. There's another one at the La Fière Château. That one will be easy to take. We can get there along the tracks. There's only a single guard on duty there. What do you plan on doing?"

"We'll be leaving sooner than I had planned. Your daughter tells me that there's nowhere in the immediate vicinity where we can hide once it's daylight. La Fière sounds like the place to move. What do you think?"

"It's true, you're very exposed here. At La Fière your chances are much better. I know this region like the back of my hand. If you like, I can lead you and your men there."

"No, Papa Maurice, you've done enough for one night. Go and get some rest."

"You know, Monsieur, I have an old debt to settle with the Germans. If you take me with you, it would give me enormous pleasure to start with. And if besides I can be useful—"

The American gave Papa a friendly slap on the back.

"I've just remembered something," Papa said suddenly. "The Germans made us construct machine-gun shelters in several spots. We dragged our feet, believe me, so that they never did install the machine guns. But the shelters could be useful to you. Wouldn't that be a good joke to play on the krauts!"

"Okay, Papa Maurice, I'll take you with us."

The officer went back to the house and said something to the men inside. Almost immediately, they began filing outside and lining up in silence along the tracks. Only the soldier who had fallen onto our roof was missing, and my professor went to fetch him.

"Not him!" Mama protested vehemently. "He's in no shape to go anywhere. Leave him with me; as soon as he's better I'll send him on his way to you. As it is, he can't even stand on his own two feet!"

"Sorry," the officer said. "He'll have to come with us."

"Be reasonable, Monsieur. He can't even hold a rifle. The poor boy couldn't possibly defend himself. Leave him with us for a day or two. Otherwise you're just taking him to his death," she pleaded.

The officer did not reply but made a sign to two soldiers who took the poor boy under the arms and trundled him off to where the others were lined up. Mama ran after them and jammed a woolen cap on his head.

"I've looked everywhere," she said, "and I couldn't find his helmet. This won't protect him from any bullets but it will protect him from the cold."

The soldiers were lined up on both sides of the tracks, facing each other, in rows of two. I made my way between the columns, and as I passed I could see the soldiers, obviously amused at seeing a little girl pass them in review, smiling in the darkness. I finally reached my mother, who stood there watching with me as the soldiers turned and left. I'm sure her heart was as heavy as mine. I couldn't take my eyes off the receding column. Our soldiers: when would I see them again? Would I ever see them? My eyes were used to the darkness, but soon night had swallowed them up completely. The house was empty, horribly empty and silent now.

Claude, whose eyes were drooping, slid into bed next to Gaby, while I helped Mama clean up. The soldiers had left a huge provision of chocolate, sweets, and cigarettes. We found them everywhere: on windowsills, the table, the mantelpiece, the shelves. But what good were they now that our soldiers weren't here to share them with us? I felt sick at heart. Our liberators: for them, the war had only just begun. I knew little or nothing about war. I'd never seen so many soldiers as I'd seen tonight, so many planes and paratroopers. For me, the Allies were nothing more than an idea, a far-off hope—until tonight, faint pinpoints in the sky, and the sound of distant motors. Until tonight, I had never met an Allied soldier. No, not quite: I had met one other, and he wasn't even in uniform.

It was an autumn evening in 1943, when we were living in the Sheepfold. I was coming home from Sainte-Mère-Eglise, where I had gone on some errands for Mama. It was a little after eight o'clock—which was curfew time—and I did not have an *Ausweiss,* a pass to be out after dark, so I took a shortcut through the fields to avoid running into a German patrol.

As I approached a farm called *La Couture,* which means "sewing" or "fashion"—strange name for a farm, I remembered thinking—I saw a man on the edge of the ditch that runs along the road. He was stooping down, his back to me. Dressed in a gray jacket, a pair of striped trousers that were ripped and torn and a pair of wooden shoes, he seemed totally preoccupied with what he was doing. My first thought was: another poacher setting a trap. Used to walking silently, in order not to frighten my animal-friends, I sneaked up behind him, bent down and whispered in his ear:

"You're making too much noise. Don't you know people live in the farm up there?"

The man spun around and I could see he was holding a gun in his hand, which he pointed straight at me. Then, seeing who his intruder was, he lowered it and said, in French:

"What are you doing outside at this hour?"

"I'm coming home from Sainte-Mère-Eglise," I whispered. "I took a shortcut because it's so late." I pointed to his gun. "Don't worry," I said, "I won't tell anybody."

The man smiled and put his gun back in his pocket. Then he said to me: "Come and help me." He was burying something and I knelt down and helped cover it with dead leaves and earth. I was dying to ask him what it was, but I was too shy, and besides, I knew it wouldn't be right for a little girl to ask an adult such a question.

A strange hat, made of wool and leather, was lying on the ground beside him.

"Will you give me that?" I said, "as a souvenir."

The man hesitated for a moment, then said:

"If they ever catch you with that, you'll be in real trouble. You and your family both."

I knew what he meant, but I still wanted it.

"Don't worry," I reassured him, "no one will ever know. Not even Mama."

"All right. But be careful."

I took the hat, and the man asked me which way it was to Saint-Sauveur-le-Vicomte.

I pointed towards it, and then walked with him part of the way. The night smelled good. I had tucked the hat in my blouse. Anyone seeing us walking—he in his wooden shoes, I in my galoshes—would have thought we were a peasant boy and girl on their way home. Actually, his accent was very close to ours, yet I could tell it wasn't quite from this region. I thought he looked terribly handsome, although very old for me: he must have been twenty, at least. I was also dying to ask him what he was doing here in Normandy, an angel fallen from the sky, disguised as a peasant. But I didn't dare. And I knew he wouldn't have answered anyway. I left him at the place known as La Patte d'oie de Cauquigny, not far from the marshes. Saint-Sauveur was twelve miles in that direction: he couldn't miss it. Before he left, he took my hands and squeezed them tightly.

"Thank you," he said, "you're a brave little girl."

"Not little," I said, "big."

"Right," he smiled, his teeth gleaming in the darkness, "a brave *big* girl."

He was a few steps away when something occurred to me and I yelled after him:

"How will you ever make it without an *Ausweiss?*"

He turned and smiled: "My papers are all in order." And he disappeared.

When I got home I hurried to my room and slipped the strange hat into one of the two openings of my straw mattress, pushing it in until I was sure it could never be found. I went to sleep thinking of my strange encounter with the man who now was walking in darkness, but who knew exactly where he was going. And I kept my promise; I never mentioned him to anyone.

Two days later, consumed by curiosity, I retraced my route through the fields. When I came to the spot where we had buried something, I scraped the earth and leaves away and soon came upon a parachute. A parachute exactly like those which I had seen tonight, and which now floated like so many enormous flowers on the waters of the marshes. They were the only visible remains of all those soldiers who had spent the night in our house.

What was going to become of them, all those happy, smiling, gum-chewing paratroopers? How I missed them already! How happy they must have been, not knowing where they would land, to have ended up in a warm and welcoming house, with a mother who immediately fed and dried them and treated them as she would have her own sons! How many of them will live to see the sun rise today?

Why couldn't the Germans lay down their arms and give up without a fight?

Why couldn't God have stopped the earth from turning, stopped time, if just for a while? They were having such a good time with us. They needed more rest, just a little more, before they headed off to fight the Germans. I thought of all the wives and mothers and sweethearts and sisters who would read that the great invasion had begun, and who would think of and pray for their soldiers, who were our soldiers too, now. I couldn't stop the tears from running down my cheeks.

Noiselessly, Mama had tiptoed upstairs into my room. She took me in her arms and said:

"Don't cry, child. Go to sleep. Tomorrow will be a long day, and I need my Geneviève well rested." She tucked me into bed. "You were marvelous tonight," she said, "such a help. The soldiers will never forget their little *Jeneveev.*"

"Mama, are they going to die?"

"Don't be silly! The war will be over soon. And we hear that many, many ships will be arriving at Ravenoville and Sainte-Marie-du-Mont. Thousands and thousands of soldiers, all armed to the teeth. Our paratroopers are only the advance wave, whose job it is to secure a number of important points, such as the bridges, so that the Germans don't have time to regroup. But they won't be alone for long. By noon those other soldiers should be here. So the only tough time for them will be this morning. What's one short morning? Besides, maybe the Germans won't even stick their noses outside."

With that, she kissed me goodnight and went back downstairs. I tried to go to sleep but couldn't. I was too worried. True, Papa was with them, and he knew not only every nook and cranny of the whole area but also exactly where the Germans were. For years, too, we had lived without light at night, so we were able to navigate easily in the dark. And Papa was by far the best of the whole family.

For the first time in my life I was anxious for him to come home. He would give us all the news and reassure us that everything had gone smoothly. He would talk and we would listen, full of admiration. And the truth was that Papa had been wonderful. A real hero. I had understood many things this past night, among them that a man can redeem in the course of a few hours a whole lifetime of wrongdoing. Oh, I had no illusions. Papa would drink again, and he would beat me again when he was drunk. But it would never be as important as it had been till now. And despite everything I would try my hardest to love him.

I tossed and turned in my bed, still unable to fall asleep. And I knew that I never would. Too bad! No matter what Mama said, I had to get up and go back downstairs.

In the kitchen, Mama was fast asleep herself, seated on a chair with her head against the fireplace mantel. The soot was still burning in the flues, but much less brightly than before. They had done their share, those two chimneys!

Tiptoeing, so as not to wake my mother, I took a chocolate bar from the table. I wondered how much chocolate I had eaten last night. More than I ever had in my whole life, that I knew! For me that taste had spelled happiness. I bit off a piece, but the taste was not the same. I was the only one awake in the house; the soldiers were gone. Now the taste was bitter and full of worry.

To change my thoughts, I went outside and pumped a bucket of water. Mama would be pleased to have the coffee ready and waiting when she woke up. Gaby and Claude were fast asleep in their bed. An image of peace.

But what about "them"? Where were they? Maybe Papa wouldn't come back. Where had he taken them? Into which fields, behind which bushes, were they lurking, waiting in ambush for the Germans, who probably were also waiting in another set of ambushes for them?

In the midst of my anguish, I suddenly remembered the phone wires Mama and I had cut . . . when? . . . only yesterday afternoon. It seemed so long ago. A world ago.

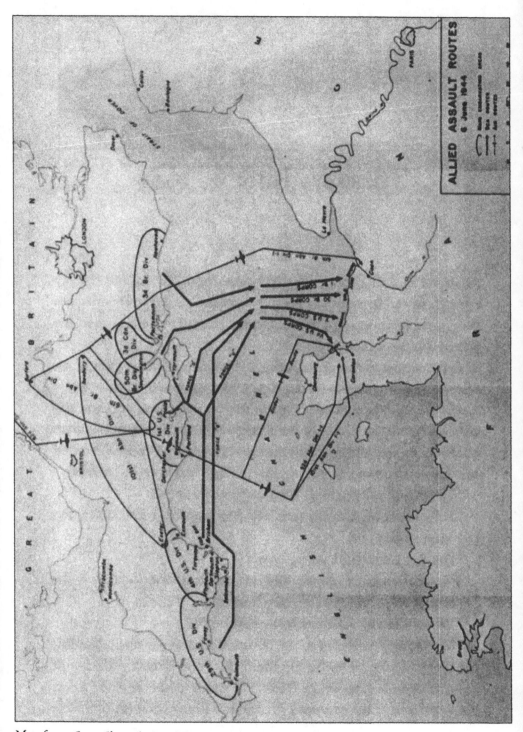

Map from *Cross Channel Attack* by G. A. Harrison. *Editions Robert Laffont: Service Iconographique.*

Tuesday, June 6, 1944

Six in the morning. Day was just beginning to break, and the sky was as gray and overcast as ever. On the calm waters of the marshes the multicolored parachutes still floated, the only bright note in the gray, damp morning.

A sound of footsteps outside. I dashed outside: it was Papa Maurice walking up the tracks, alone, his cap pulled down over his eyes, wearing long rubber boots. Still not a train in sight. Papa was walking on the good side of the tracks—that is, the left side—where he always walked during normal times. He seemed excited. I called out, my voice wavering, asking how things had gone at La Fière.

"Everything's fine, child. Where's your mother?"

"She's asleep next to the fireplace. I've prepared some coffee. Do you want some?"

"You bet I do, child. A big bowl."

We went into the house and sat down at the kitchen table. Mama woke up, and her first words were:

"Where did you take our boys, Maurice?"

"They're at Emile's farm," he said, and I knew the one he meant, not far from 103. "They've already had a good start. I led a few of them to the Château de La Fière. The kraut in the lookout tower didn't even have time to open fire. Didn't know what hit him. The Americans have taken possession of the château. Maurice Salmon is in seventh heaven. We celebrated with a round or two of his best cider. We also heard a general parachuted in somewhere near

Leroux's place—General Gavin, I think his name is. There's another general over at Grade Crossing 103—a General Ridgway, they told me. Our boys have also taken all the bridges—the one over the river, the railroad bridge and the bridge at La Fière. Some bad news, too. All the guys in our guardhouse are dead. Dumb bastards. Old Man Touze, Garcia the Spaniard, and the son of the district chief: those I'm sure of, I saw their bodies. If only they'd listened to me. But as soon as the Americans saw their swastika armbands, bang! It was all over. Emile and his family nowhere in sight. Must have lit out. Can't say I blame them. Anyway, a bunch of gliders have landed in several places in the neighborhood of La Fière. One, with not a scratch on it, right smack in front of the Sheepfold, in fact. I saw Francis. He's fine. Told him not to set foot outside as long as there's still a single German alive in the region."

Papa's eyes shone, and his words came tumbling out so fast it was sometimes hard to follow him. He paused to take a sip of coffee, then went on:

"Not all the gliders made it down in one piece. Two hit trees, and most everybody in them was killed. Poor kids, they didn't stand a chance."

His bowl was empty, so timidly I refilled it, then asked:

"What's a glider, Papa?"

"An airplane without a motor, child. What they do is hook it up to a plane, somewhere over there in England. The plane tows it over its destination, then they cut the lines, and the glider floats down and lands as best it can."

"Can't the men inside steer it? What do they do if they see they're heading straight for a tree?"

"They can steer it to a degree. But not like a plane. And in the dark . . . Anyway, that's what happened to one of them: smacked right into the big oak. Killed everyone."

A thousand questions raced through my head, questions that would never be answered.

"Maurice, when are the reinforcements coming by sea expected to arrive?"

"Today, as I understand it. They're expected at noon, or at the latest this afternoon. They're supposed to hook up with our para-troopers, whose main objective is to take and hold Sainte-Mère-Eglise until reinforcements arrive."

"The sea must be very rough," Mama shook her head, "with this awful weather. I'm afraid, Maurice, I'm terribly afraid."

"You're right, woman: worst weather I've seen in years. But the people who organized this invasion must know what they're doing. Maybe they're even counting on the bad weather to work in their favor. All we can do is hope. Anyway, I have work to do. There are three men missing. Dead or alive, I have to find them."

Little Claude had just woke up and came in rubbing his eyes. The first thing he saw was Papa's armband.

"What's that?" he said. "What's MP mean, Papa?"

"I don't know, child."

He rummaged in his pocket and pulled out a little book which he handed to me.

"It's a dictionary," he said. "Everything you want to know is written in it. Take a look, Geneviève."

I leafed through it, not quite sure how to find what I wanted, but finally I came across MP: Military Police. As I translated it, I could see Papa's chest puff out. Only then did he appreciate the honor they had bestowed on him by giving him that armband. His eyes were moist as he looked at me and said:

"You're lucky, you know, child, to be able to read like that. I wish I could."

"I'll teach you if you want, Papa. The way I'm teaching Claude."

"No, I don't have the patience. If I could learn it in a day, I'd give it a try. But since I know I can't . . ."

"But you can learn, Papa. I didn't know you could speak French so well until last night. And you were speaking English, too. See how fast you learned? It's not so hard to learn how to read. A little bit every day, the way you turn over a little of the garden each day in the spring."

"Maybe, maybe . . . But right now I have other things to do. Go wake up Gaby. I'm taking him with me. If any of those three soldiers are wounded, I'll need his help to get them back."

I did as he said. Since last night, I felt less intimidated by him than I had before, but I was still pretty scared of him. I watched them head off, keeping close to the tracks so as to be less visible to the Germans stationed at Port-de-Neuville. Papa made Gaby lie down in the bottom of the boat, in case the Germans did see them and opened fire.

I knew that he was heading in that direction because it was the one area of the marshes he hadn't explored last night. I was sure he would find the missing soldiers.

I watched the daylight grow and wondered what the next twelve hours would bring. I remembered what my American professor had said to me last night: "The war's over. You'll never see war again, neither you nor your children or their children after them." And I couldn't help remembering, too, what Mama had said they had told her, during the previous war: that it was the war to end all wars. And all the history books talked about at school was war after war. So why should they lie to us and tell us there would never be another? Maybe it would be better if we all died together at the same time. I'm only eleven years old—eleven years and two months to be exact—but I mean it when I say I'm not afraid to die.

And yet I knew I wouldn't. I knew that our soldiers would die in my place. Those soldiers, come from a far-off land, who last night had set foot for the first time on our soil, might never live to really see it. Why did God allow such things? This morning, God, you're no friend of mine!

At catechism, Father Roulland told us: "Hell is a terrible place where sinners, after their death, suffer a thousand deaths." He had lied, too. Hell is right here on earth, and this day, with dawn breaking, will crack open the door to hell, of that I was sure. Those who are about to suffer a thousand torments, a thousand pains, are young and handsome. So why, Father Roulland, did you have to resort to lies?

The sound of a cannon not far off startled me from my sad daydreams, and almost tumbled me into the marshes. The dear old gate crossing saved me once again. But I couldn't tell what was going on. Who had opened fire? I had the impression that it had come from Amfreville.

The sun was up by now, and I dashed along the tracks as a second shot resounded. Almost immediately, a house built right on the bank of the Great Marsh caught fire. Poor Jeannette! I knew that for months they had been preparing her trousseau, piece by piece, in preparation for her marriage in a month or two. All gone up in flames. But maybe, I thought, they had had the foresight to pack up and leave. As these thoughts raced through my mind, I heard a third cannon shot, and this time the little farmhouse at the far end of the Great Marsh, that belonged to Martha and Manuel, also went up in flames.

After the Germans had flooded the marshes, Manuel used to come every day to count the cattle in the surrounding area. During his morning rounds he would always stop off at our house and share a bowl of coffee with us. I wondered whether he was dead now. And what about his wife?

Again the cannon roared, and this time it was the second story of the Château at La Fière that literally exploded. Mama, who had come out onto the tracks where I was standing, said that she had seen the windows flying in every direction. Our elevated position allowed us to get a clear view for miles around. I wondered if Maurice Salmon was all right. For several years he had lived in the château, and as long as I could remember he was our friend. He was thirty years old, very tall and extremely handsome, and he made such wonderful cakes. Two years ago, for Francis' first communion, he made a huge cream cake. He promised he'd bake the same kind for me when I made my first communion. If he were still alive, that is.

Just to think of that cake made my mouth water. And then the notion of eating such a sumptuous cake under the very eyes of the Germans made it all the more delicious. Papa Maurice had gone all the way to Bacilly, without a proper pass, where his uncle owned a grist mill, and he had brought back twenty kilos of white bread for us and several kilos of beautiful flour. And now maybe Maurice was dead.

Bullets were flying thick and fast, and Mama herded me back indoors. I was fascinated by the singing noise the bullets made as they sped past and lodged harmlessly in the marshes or, sometimes, in the woodpile in our back courtyard. Despite the danger, Mama had made up her mind to go over to the Sheepfold and milk Blanchette, as she always did when we needed milk. She never used the boat, which was too hard for her to maneuver, but always walked along the tracks as far as 103, where a path leads to the farm.

Before she left she made me promise not to let Claude outdoors under any circumstances. I nodded, but I could see in her eyes that Blanchette was only a pretense, that the real reason she wanted to go over to the Sheepfold was to see for herself what was going on, and how "our" soldiers were making out. I watched her silhouette disappear in the distance, and I felt a great surge of admiration for that slight, frail lady, who seemed oblivious to the battle raging around her. Her step was as firm and energetic as always.

Time moved by very slowly. The whine of bullets and boom of cannons continued unabated. I busied myself by cleaning up the house. I knew that Mama would be pleased when she came home to see that I had relieved her of some of her housework.

"Woman! Come here and give me a hand!"

Papa's voice. Despite my promise not to leave the house, I ran outside and saw Papa's boat arriving at the gate on the Little Marsh side. His boat was carrying a strange cargo: the wooden ladder from La Bergerie was set lengthwise from bow to stern and on it a parachute had been folded up to serve as a mattress. On this improvised stretcher lay a man, a paratrooper who smiled at me as I ran up to the boat.

"Where's your mother?" Papa wanted to know.

"She went over to the Sheepfold to milk Blanchette. She said she'd be back soon. Do you want me to help you?"

I had suddenly realized that Gaby had not come back with them.

"What happened to Gaby, Papa?"

"He's back there with another soldier who's hurt, but not as badly as this one. As soon as we've got this one into our bed, I'll go back and fetch them."

As he was tying up the boat I couldn't help hear him muttering between his teeth:

"The kid's too small, and this guy weighs a ton. She won't be able to lift him with me."

"I'm stronger than you think, Papa, no matter what you say about me. You'll see."

"All right, let's give it a try. When I say 'lift,' take the two ends of the ladder and raise it enough so we can get it over the edge of the boat. Then we'll carry him as gently as we can in through the courtyard. He's a big number, this guy. And he's hurt bad. Don't you dare drop him!"

"Don't worry!"

I was talking big, but I was frightened out of my wits. I knew I was thin and not very strong. Four years without enough to eat had made me little more than skin and bones. But I knew that faith could move mountains, so why couldn't my faith give me the strength to lift this man on the ladder?

We managed the first step, which was to lift the ladder out of the boat, and, step by step, advanced towards the courtyard. It was an uphill climb, to make matters worse, and I could feel the ladder bending in the middle. What if it were to break! No, I knew that Papa had made it, and that it was good and solid. Little Claude opened the door as we arrived, and, taking careful little steps, I managed to get over the threshold. Behind me, Papa's voice said:

"Set the ladder down on the floor. But only when I say 'now.' Careful not to pinch your fingers. There . . . careful. 'Now!' Very good. You see, child, when you set your mind to it, you can do all sorts of things!"

I had a sharp answer on the tip of my tongue, but I caught myself in time. "If you only asked me nicely," I could have said, "you'd see what I could accomplish." Wasted breath. The fact was,

Papa was in a good frame of mind, or at least had other things on his mind that kept him from picking on me. Be grateful for small favors.

I turned around and took my first good look at our newcomer. He smiled at me, and like so many of our other soldiers, I saw that he had a sparkling set of teeth. He smiled, but I quickly saw that it should have been a painful grimace. Not only was his leg broken, but it was badly broken, in several places. The bones were protruding through his boots. I had never seen such a terrible fracture. What could we do? How could we take care of it?

Just then, Mama appeared, and I breathed a sigh of relief. She'd know what to do. I noted that her milk pail was empty, which struck me as odd. But I realized that Blanchette should have been the last of my worries. Mama sized up the situation immediately. Without exchanging a word, she and Papa bent down over the broken leg. Papa took out the soldier's knife and, with Mama's help, carefully cut away the boot, centimeter by centimeter. When they had managed to remove the boot without even having touched the protruding bones, they proceeded to cut away the trouser, starting from the knee down. When finally the remains of the trouser leg were no more than a pile of formless scraps on the floor, the leg appeared. If you could call it a leg: it was an enormous mass of swollen flesh, covered with cuts and bruises and patches of dried blood. The bones had broken through in three different places.

Until today, we had lived for years with little or nothing, and grown used to it. Suddenly I understood for the first time what it was to really lack not only goods but knowledge. We had no bandages, no disinfectant. Worse, we hadn't the slightest medical knowledge to cope with such a fracture. How should it be set? *Could* it be set? And what about that awful, swollen leg? I suddenly realized, too, that poverty was not only material; ignorance was another, deeper poverty. And it was here, to this house, the poorest of the poor among God's creatures, that He had sent his hurt and wounded children. I had to admit I was having more and more trouble understanding this God. I doubted I would ever understand Him.

Poor or not, Mama kept a cool head. She took from the closet an old sheet, which she began to cut into strips about ten centimeters wide. Then she rolled them up into bandages. She asked me to help her, which I did, but since I had never seen real bandages I couldn't figure out what she would do with them.

Meanwhile, Papa had put the water on to boil. As it was coming to a boil, I started to remove the kettle from the stove, but Mama stopped me.

"Leave it there, child. I want it to boil for several minutes."

"Why?"

"Did you learn at school about germs?"

"Of course we did."

"Well, boiling water destroys them."

"But there aren't any germs here in the country. I thought germs were only in the cities."

"You're wrong, child. Germs exist everywhere. Even in that water. The water is rainwater, which first ran down the roof, dirty from the passing trains, into the gutters, which are also dirty. The filter at the top of the pump cleans the water but it doesn't kill the germs. That's why I want to boil the water for several minutes."

Finally Papa removed the kettle from the stove. I watched his every move: I realized I had so much to learn. He poured a little boiling water into a salad bowl, then added several drops of chlorine bleach. He swished that water around in the bowl to make sure every square centimeter had been cleansed.

"Just in case any stray germs are hiding in the salad bowl," Mama explained.

"I understand," I said, "but I still don't see how you're going to take care of his poor leg."

"As best we can."

Kneeling down on the tile floor, she began to wash his cuts and scratches, ever so gently, a little bit at a time. She had added to the pure water half a glass of Calvados, and when she did I couldn't help smiling to myself. For once, the Calvados was going to serve some useful purpose. Now, if only Mama could use up Papa's whole supply . . .

Papa had gone outside, and a few minutes later he returned with a plank of wood about twenty-five centimeters wide and roughly as long as the soldier's leg. It was the first time I had ever seen a splint put on anyone. After having washed the entire lower leg and cleansed the wounds, Mama asked Papa Maurice to lift the leg carefully, and together they slid the plank underneath it. Then, with the remaining rolls of bandage, Mama fastened the splint to the bottom of the leg.

That was as much as they could do for the time being. Now we had to get him into bed. They both took one end of the ladder and carried him into their bedroom. They placed the ladder on the edge of the bed; then Papa Maurice began to pull the parachute, little by little, from under the soldier, and he was moved slowly towards the middle of the bed. I was amazed at the gentleness with which Papa performed the whole operation: I never thought him capable of it.

From the time we had first lifted him from the boat, the soldier had never once groaned or cried out, though he must have been in terrible pain. Now, to dull the pain, Papa brought him a large glass of Calvados. The intention was good, but that didn't prevent the soldier from making an awful face when he took the first swallow, and from refusing to drink the rest of the glass. But Papa didn't insist, probably concluding that the American just didn't share his passion for applejack.

Both he and Mama went back out into the kitchen, leaving me alone for the first time with the newcomer. I tried to remember the few words my professor had taught me the night before.

"My name is Geneviève," I said, pronouncing it the American way. "Your name, please?"

"George," he said. "Lieutenant George Wingate."

I raced into the kitchen with the news. Both my parents were busy burning the dirty bandages and cleaning the floor.

"Papa, Mama, the wounded paratrooper is a lieutenant. His name is George Wingate."

"I know," Papa said, "he told me on the way back in the boat."

"Where did you find him?" Mama asked.

"In Bernard's fields," he said. "He seemed happy to see me. Yet the first thing he asked me was not to turn him over to the Germans."

"What a funny idea," Claude said. He had followed every step of the operation since we had first arrived with Lieutenant Wingate, wide-eyed and fascinated.

"You're right, boy. I'm for the Allies, but it's not written on my face, you know."

"Tell me, Papa," went on Claude, who didn't miss a trick, "why did you break the middle rungs of your ladder?"

"You noticed that, eh? Good for you. It made it easier to carry him, that's all. It was a long way from Bernard's to where I had left the boat, near the bridge."

"What made you go over there, I mean, to Bernard's?"

"Better find the living than the dead, I decided. If he had landed in the water, he'd have long since been dead and gone. So I decided to check out the fields around the marshes first. And as you see, I was right."

Claude laughed and clapped his hands in glee.

"Good for you, Papa! My Papa's terrific!"

Obviously pleased, Papa lifted Claude into the air and planted two fat kisses on his cheeks. Claude blushed with pleasure.

Before he returned to pick up Gaby and the other soldier, Papa went back into the bedroom to see how "his" paratrooper was doing. We followed close behind, and gazed down at the lieutenant, marveling at his size and his light brown hair. His eyes, I had noted earlier, were almost black. Now he was fast asleep, and we spoke in whispers in order not to wake him up.

"How did you ever find him?" Mama asked.

"The same way I did last night. By calling out, 'Come here, boys. Come here!' And he heard me and replied. It's as simple as that."

My parents had an old-fashioned bed with high legs, a sturdy box-spring and a thick mattress stuffed with goose down. The quilt was also stuffed with down. "You're a lot better off here," my father's tender gaze seemed to say, "than in that field where I found you."

There was virtually nothing left to eat in the house, except for all that chocolate the soldiers had left behind. But I had long ago learned that there's nothing like a good cup of coffee to calm a hungry stomach, so I heated up some for Papa before he left. He didn't even take the time to sit down, but drank it standing up before he headed for his boat. I quickly filled up the thermos with more hot coffee, and I ran out and placed it in the prow of the boat.

Before he left, Papa asked Mama: "I gather you went to the Sheepfold this morning?"

"Yes. I milked Blanchette. But I have to confess I didn't bring any home. I gave it all to the soldiers hidden in the bushes and hedges. Poor lads, they haven't had anything to eat or drink except for that chicken broth Geneviève and I gave them last night. I hope you don't mind."

"No, why would I? By the way, do you know where their food is?"

"No, where?"

"At the bottom of the marshes, woman. So are their munitions. So what I've decided is, as soon as I've brought this second fellow home and found the third, I'll fish all their food and munitions up."

"But you'll never be able to! There must be tons of it."

"So? I'll make as many trips as I have to." And he concluded, in response to Mama's astonished look of disbelief: "It'll be easy."

There seemed little to say, since his mind was clearly made up. He asked Mama to bring him the long-handled brush and a wool scarf. I suspected Mama wanted to ask him what in the world he needed them for, but she simply went and got them. And once again the brave little boat set out across the marsh waters.

The next paratrooper Papa brought back was even bigger than the first. A giant: an adorable, blond giant who laughed at everything anyone said and who limped ashore using the scrub brush wrapped with a scarf as a crutch.

He was over two meters tall, and his big blue eyes sparkled with good humor. His jaw was constantly busy, filled with the eternal chewing gum, and as he walked into the house the thought crossed my mind that he was the sunshine coming in, after a long absence. My parents helped him across the room and settled him in a chair by the fire, which was burning brightly. He had a terrible sprain, and his ankle was swollen so badly it had forced his boot to crack in several places. Gently, carefully, Mama cut away the boot. I marveled at her ability and patience to do it without actually cutting him.

The giant had not come alone. He had wanted to fish up one of the lost boxes from the water where it had fallen, and he and Papa had brought it home with them. He asked us to open it: it was filled with all sorts of army rations. So much for the question of being out of food. Our problem was solved, at least for several days.

"My name is Geneviève," I said, again using the American pronunciation.

"Mine is Kerry," he smiled. "Kerry Hogey."

Claude sat down in front of him and asked if he wanted to play a game of cards.

"Give the poor man a chance to get comfortable," Mama admonished.

But Kerry was already at home, and with a loud laugh accepted the challenge. So there they were, giant and child, engaged in a heated game of cards, half in French, half in English. Thank God for the pocket dictionary Papa had brought home with him.

Again Papa set out, this time in the direction of Fresville. He returned early in the afternoon, the boat loaded with wooden boxes of rations and metal trunks containing ammunition. No paratrooper this time. Mama watched him approach the gate. His face was somber, the face he brought home on days things had been going poorly with him.

"You didn't find the third . . ." she began timidly.

"There's a parachute floating in the Merderet, at the point where Three Rivers joins it."

That was the only explanation he offered.

Even assuming that the parachute had belonged to a man, I thought it was remarkable that only one man had been lost. And perhaps even he had made it safely to shore in another direction. We would never know.

Papa began unloading the boat. Where would we store all these cases? The soldiers were camped in the vicinity of 103, about a kilometer and a half away, and probably wouldn't be coming back here. That meant we'd have to take their food and ammunition to them. But how? They must have been dying of hunger. The gunfire in the direction of Sainte-Mère-Eglise had not intensified, which probably meant that the reinforcements had not arrived.

Suddenly Papa had another brainstorm. He went down cellar and came back with his trusty wheelbarrow; he loaded it with several boxes and headed down the tracks towards Grade Crossing 103.

In a little while he was back, his wheelbarrow empty. They had thanked him, and told him that if he could find the rest that had fallen into the water, he should retrieve them and store them in our courtyard. They would come and take them as they were needed.

Papa also brought back the terrible news that Madame Brisset, the governess of the La Fière Château, had been killed by the shelling. She had a daughter, Bernadette, who was just my age. What, I thought, was going to become of poor Bernadette?

Papa seemed to be tireless. Mama found it almost impossible to make him sit down for five minutes while he swallowed a handful of biscuits and downed another cup of coffee. Once again he was off in his boat searching the marshes for any sign of the missing cases.

The Germans stationed in the Château d'Amfreville continued to fire in our direction, but we were beyond their range. Still, Kerry pried open one of the metal boxes and in the space of a few minutes had assembled a machine gun. He hobbled out to the gate and kept Papa covered as he poled his way across the marshes. It was all well and good that the Germans in Amfreville could not reach him with their fire, but who knows whether others weren't lurking near Port-de-Neuville, waiting to ambush him or anyone else who ventured too close.

Mama carried out a pail of boiling hot water, in which she had put a handful of rock salt. She motioned for Kerry to soak his foot in it. Kerry protested, but she wouldn't take no for an answer; and with his usual laugh he yielded and put his bad foot in the pail, still keeping his sights trained on Papa's boat.

I waited, my heart pounding, in fear I would see Papa attacked, totally exposed out there on the water, but nothing happened. The Germans must have abandoned Port-de-Neuville. Papa could fish for his boxes in peace.

Mama insisted that Kerry come back inside and get some rest, and led him into their bedroom where he discovered Lieutenant Wingate, whose presence he had ignored till then. Both men liked each other immediately, and I could hear them conversing, mostly about my parents, and even though I couldn't understand too much I could tell how impressed and grateful they both felt.

Gaby joined them, and tried to strike up a conversation, but it was limited by the language barrier between them. Meanwhile Mama and I prepared lunch, using the wild eggs I had gathered yesterday (is that possible? was it really yesterday?) to make a delicious omelette. George managed to do it justice despite his obvious pain. He too, I realized, had not eaten since leaving England the night before. We washed it down with the sweet cider Papa had never had a chance to drink last night when he arrived home. Our Americans seemed to like it, and asked for a second glass.

Mama had insisted that Kerry eat lunch in bed, and again he had protested. But she shot a menacing look at him when he started to get up, and he fell back, laughing uproariously, and soon all of us were laughing, so loudly it almost drowned out the gunfire outside.

Outside, war was raging. But it would never come in here. Inside we were drinking American coffee, out of Mama's best porcelain cups, which her father, a sailor, had brought back from some trip long ago. Here all was peace and harmony, and as though we all felt it, there was, suddenly, a moment of silence. Precarious silence. Then, suddenly, Gaby burst out sobbing.

Mama was stunned by his outburst, and took him in her arms.

"Why are you crying?"

Between sobs, he managed to make us understand how happy he was to be here, how good he felt with us, but that he didn't know where his parents were or what had happened to them.

"I have to go find them," he said.

"That would be silly," Mama told him. "You're a good son, and that's fine. Your instincts are perfectly right. But just think: if you hadn't listened to Papa Maurice and left the guard house with him, you'd be dead now. And if you try and make the village—which is ten kilometers away and now one big battle zone—you'll never get there. And your parents will never see you again. So wait until things settle down."

Claude climbed up on Gaby's lap and said to him: "C'mon. Me and you and Kerry will play cards."

Gaby ran his fingers through Claude's hair, trying to make up his mind. Distress was etched on his face, and suddenly I knew that we, too, had a member of our family who was separated from us and from whom we would have no news till the fighting was over: my older sister Denise, who worked on a farm far away. Beautiful Denise—who also loved to laugh and filled our lives with sunshine—when would we see her next?

Our two Americans had fallen asleep. Kerry had overestimated his strength. His stint out at the gate, covering Papa's journey, had worn him out. We tiptoed out of the room.

Meanwhile Papa continued his endless trips back and forth between the site of the lost cargo and our courtyard, which by now had begun to look like a depot. If the reinforcements arrived today, they probably wouldn't need either the food or ammunition. But if for any reason they didn't, the cases could spell the difference between victory and defeat, life and death.

Between La Fière and Amfreville the fighting grew more intense. La Fière had been the first village in France to be liberated. Our soldiers had occupied it last night, and it was clear that they had no intention of giving it up. But the Germans were equally determined to dislodge them, and other houses I used to pass every day were pounded to rubble: Lawyer Jean's, for one; Monsieur and Madame Cuquemelle's, for another.

The sound of cannons booming also grew louder from the direction of the sea, over by Saint-Hubert and Saint-Germain. I had a feeling things weren't going all that well on the beaches. And if that were true, how long could our paratroopers hold out by themselves? I asked myself all kinds of frightening questions, but I never had any answers.

Today, like so many days before, was gray and cold. Normally, the birdsongs of my friends the ducks and teals in the marshes, which began at daybreak, continued well into the morning. But this morning they were all quiet, and I was sure they were huddled in their nests wondering what all the noise was about. My special friend the green woodpecker who used to wait for me every morning on our doorstep, to walk part way to school with me, all the way to 103 usually, had not shown up. No, they would not be singing today. I wondered if they would ever sing again.

Kerry woke up and resumed his guard position by the gate, still covering Papa on his endless route back and forth across the marsh waters. Papa had not slept at all last night either, and I couldn't figure how he managed to keep going. As for Lieutenant Wingate, he seemed to suffer terribly, and was running a high fever. I could see that Mama was very worried.

She announced that she was not going back to the Sheepfold today. Francis would take care of Blanchette and the chickens. Her place was here, next to her patient. Through the half-opened door, I could see her changing cold compresses on his forehead every few minutes. Both Claude and I had been told not to enter the room any more. Mama was afraid we would disturb him, in spite of ourselves. I saw how he was suffering and wondered how he could be so brave, could keep from crying out the way he did. I remembered when I had spent the better part of one winter in bed, as a result of those terrible burns I had suffered, so I knew how he must feel. That morning Claude had taught him a few words of French, which he had repeated with a delightful American accent that had made us all laugh. Using the pocket dictionary, I decided I would write out some English sentences for him to correct when he felt better.

Later in the afternoon, Mama said to me:

"Where's Gabriel?"

"I saw him go outside a while ago. He may be in the bathroom, or maybe with Papa in the boat."

"He's not in the bathroom, and I know Papa doesn't want him with him in the boat. It's too dangerous. Papa doesn't want the responsibility."

In fact, Gabriel had decided to leave, to go find his parents. Mama found a little note on the tracks thanking her for all her kindnesses and asking her forgiveness for sneaking off like a thief in the night. He hoped to be back soon with good news.

Night fell. Mama brought in several bundles of hay, which were generally used in the rabbit warrens, and spread them out on the kitchen floor. Tonight they would serve as her mattress. She also rigged up a hook to hold the bedroom door open—the natural slope of the house caused it to close automatically—so that she and Papa could check on our wounded visitors through the night. With some reluctance, Mama gave Claude and me permission to kiss Lieutenant Wingate goodnight. His flushed face, and the sweat on his forehead, revealed the extent of his suffering. I brought my lips close to his ear and whispered, in English:

"I love you, George."

He didn't answer, but he stared at me intently. Then tears came to his eyes. He raised his hand, as if to run it through my hair, but he didn't have the strength and the hand fell back on the sheet. I begged Mama to let me sleep with her, so that I could keep watch over George, too, but she would have none of it and chased me off to my own bed. I even resorted to my "doe-eyed" look, which generally made even the hardest hearts melt. I'm told I have pretty green eyes, flecked with gold, but even this tactic failed.

Upstairs, Mama asked me to make sure that Claude said his prayers, since she didn't have time tonight to stay with us. I got down on my knees with him, and together we prayed.

Dear God, we pray tonight first of all for our two new Americans, who are in pain and need Your help. Especially George, who's hurt very bad. And please look out, too, for our parents, for without them we'd be in real trouble.

We crawled into bed, and Claude fell asleep almost at once. But I couldn't sleep, and I also had the feeling I hadn't said enough prayers, so I got out again and knelt at the foot of my bed.

Dear God, it's me again, and I'm afraid. Not so much for myself as for all those men out there fighting each other. And please take care of Bernadette, who doesn't have a mother any more, so who's going to tuck her into bed at night now? And God, I have a feeling the next few days are going to be very hard, so we'll need You even more than ever. And don't forget Bernadette.

I realized I had been up for forty-two hours. Yet I wasn't tired, and felt that if I had to I could go on even longer. But even as I was thinking that, the little girl of the marshes sank into sleep, her last thought being a question to herself: I wonder what tomorrow will bring?

Wednesday, June 7, 1944

The scraping of the little boat against the grade crossing embankment woke me from my dreams. It was barely daylight. Quietly, so as not to wake Claude, I slipped from the bed and went to the window. Just as I thought: Papa was already hard at it, his boat filled with boxes. How long had he been up? I threw on some clothes and, holding my shoes in my hand, tiptoed downstairs, making sure not to make the steps talk. Usually I could make them squeak when I went downstairs, but the staircase led to my parents' bedroom, and I didn't want to wake up our guests.

Mama was already awake, the coffeepot was on the fire, and she was busy gathering the bundles of hay that had served as her bed. I tiptoed up to her and said:

"How are they this morning? Did George sleep well?"

"They're both awake," she said. "You can go in and kiss them if you like. Just be sure not to wear them out with your idle talk."

I ran toward the bedroom door. George looked better this morning. Rested, more relaxed. He seemed to be in less pain, too. I took his head in my hands and looked at him intently. Neither of us exchanged a word, and I wondered how, given the language barrier, we could ever really communicate. Yet our eyes were in a sense more eloquent than words.

Kerry smiled when he saw Mama bring in a tray with two bowls of steaming coffee and biscuits from their K-rations. He helped me raise George to a sitting position, and Mama slipped an extra pillow behind his back. He drank the coffee but refused the biscuits. Mama offered him a second bowl. "No thank you, little mother," he said in English, which sent me running to the pocket dictionary. The only problem was that I didn't know how to spell "mother," so it was hard to look it up. Sensing what I was looking for, Kerry took the dictionary from my hands, and as he did the piece of paper on which I had scribbled some English phrases yesterday slipped out. Kerry picked it up, read it, and showed it to the lieutenant. With his incredible accent, George said to me in French:

"*Bravo, Geneviève, c'est très beau!*"

"Not *très beau*, I corrected, "*très bon.*"

Delighted to be corrected, George smiled and kept repeating, "*très bon,*" not "*très beau.*"

I was so pleased to see him feeling better that I clapped my hands with delight and was laughing when Mama came back into the room. She grabbed my hair and pulled my head back, saying:

"I thought I told you not to wear our patients out."

She lead me out toward the kitchen, putting a sudden end to the English lesson, but not before I had managed to blow a kiss back to George, who laughed at Mama's mock-serious scolding.

To atone for my sins, I decided to sneak out and pick a big bouquet of water lilies, which grew in abundance just at the base of the tracks. Only, to pick them I'd have to wade into the water up to my waist.

Fifteen minutes later I was back at 104, soaked to the skin. Actually, I'd come within an inch of my life, for the bullets were whizzing all around me as I picked the flowers, but I was too intent on my task to be really scared. My mother didn't know whether to spank me or kiss me. I didn't even tell her that I had to crawl back on all fours. Anyway, she undressed me, dried me off, rubbed me down with her special liquid, and gave me a dry set of clothes, scolding me all the while. I was shivering. The water, as well as the air, was very cold. I wondered whether summer would ever come. When I was dressed, I said to Mama:

"May I please have permission to take a bowl of coffee out to Papa? It would do him a world of good, poor man."

"Absolutely not! You're not leaving this house again. Go up-stairs and call him from the attic window."

Upstairs, I called out to him in English:

"Come here, Papa Maurice, come here!"

He was unloading another cargo from his little boat. "What do you want, pest?" he yelled up.

"I've heated up some coffee. Come and drink it while it's still hot."

"I'll be right there."

After having tidied up the kitchen, Mama, with Papa's help, changed the lieutenant's dressings. Then, standing up, Papa drank his coffee. I pushed a chair toward where he was standing, hoping he would get the message.

"How long have you been out in the marshes?" I asked.

He scratched his head. "Damned if I know," he said. "Since Monday night at eleven, I guess."

"You mean to say you didn't go to bed at all last night either?"

"That's right."

"Why?"

"You see how choppy the marsh waters are? That's a sure sign that the seas are rough. The invasion will probably be delayed until calmer weather. And that means there will be no reinforcements, no food or ammunition for our boys. So they'll badly need every case I can recover from the marshes."

"But Papa, it also means that if you don't stop you'll be dead, either from exhaustion or a stray bullet."

"So what? You wouldn't be all that sad, now would you, child? That way you wouldn't have anyone to punish you. You're lucky I've been busy these past forty-eight hours. Otherwise I might have found time to give you a good whacking."

"I'm not sure I would mind dying, anyway, Papa. Just like you."

"Don't say such silly things, you stupid child!"

He got to his feet, and I walked him over to the door. I pointed to the mounting pile of cases in our courtyard.

"You think they're really going to need all that?"

"I'm afraid so, my girl."

"You think things will be terribly rough for them?"

He nodded, then shrugged his shoulders in a gesture of helplessness and headed back to the marshes. I couldn't get over the man's strength and tenacity. For the first time in my life I felt real admiration for this hard-hearted man.

Mama had decided she was going to make another trip to the Sheepfold, to milk the cows. Actually, her mission had a dual purpose: to check on Francis and the place in general, and to provide milk for "her" soldiers. She had made up her mind that each of them was going to have a liter of milk that day. If necessary, she would also milk the cows in the surrounding farms, for many of them had been abandoned. The poor cows were so swollen with milk that as soon as they saw Mama arriving with her pail they headed toward her in a real stampede.

That day Mama gathered two hundred liters of milk. The officer in charge of the headquarters that had been set up at one of the farms couldn't believe his eyes as he watched this tiny woman rolling a wheelbarrow full of metal drums, each containing twenty to thirty liters of milk. When she made him understand whom the milk was for, he called over a soldier and had him transfer the cans into a jeep. Then off they went, my mother and her newfound chauffeur, stopping by every bush and hedge in which the Americans were concealed to dispense her fresh milk. The paratroopers were ecstatic, especially those whom she recognized as "hers," and greeted her so warmly that she would remember that day for the rest of her life. According to what they told her, we were virtually the only civilians left in the area. Most of the farmers had fled, as had the people who lived in Grade Crossing 103.

Mama explained the plight of Lieutenant Wingate and asked that a doctor be sent as soon as possible. They told her that was impossible, simply because no medical team had been parachuted in with them on Monday. Still, the major promised her that as soon as he could find someone with any medical knowledge, he would send him over with whatever medicines they had at their disposal. I knew it would be more than we had.

It was six o'clock by the time Mama arrived home. The tip of one wooden shoe was missing, and her big toe protruded through.

"Have to put a patch on my poor shoe," she laughed. "I just can't be seen walking around with such awful looking footwear."

"What happened?"

"A piece of shrapnel. Clipped the toe of the shoe right off!"

"What about you?"

"Not a scratch, child. I'm a lucky lady."

"What did you do when it happened?"

"Nothing. Kept on walking, thanking the Lord for taking such good care of me. I took advantage of the occasion to ask Him kindly to keep up the good work. How are our Americans? Were they good boys while I was gone?"

"Very good. The lieutenant's asleep. I think his fever's up again. How is Francis doing?"

"Fine. He goes outside only when he absolutely has to. The Sheepfold is as solid as a rock. And less exposed than we are here. Where's Kerry?"

"Out by the gate, covering Papa again. I made him sit down and put his foot in a pail of hot water. And do you know what, Mama? He's learned to imitate your expression when you're angry. I can't help laughing every time I look at him."

"They're both such nice young men. But I must say I'm very worried about George. I'll feel better after a doctor has seen him. The major said he would send someone as soon as he can."

Mama had brought Blanchette's milk home, and she used it to make a general store of chocolate milk. Kerry's foot seemed on the mend, but George, who was clearly in great pain, drank his chocolate milk in silence. His fever seemed worse than ever.

Mama changed his bandages and cleansed his terribly swollen leg, which still looked horrible. What if gangrene, about which I knew nothing except that it was something we couldn't handle, had already set in? How would we ever save him?

As these thoughts were going through my mind, I happened to glance through the window and saw someone in the distance, near the bridge over the river, heading in our direction. I opened the door and called out to Papa, who was busy unloading boxes from his boat. Papa came over and squinted in the direction where I was pointing. He had the sharpest eyes in the family, but all he could make out was that three men were walking along the tracks, in what seemed to be a slow and painful progression. He went in and borrowed the lieutenant's binoculars, and after having studied the group for a long moment he said to my mother:

"They're wounded, those three. Mind, woman, I'm not going to keep you from doing what you believe is your duty, but don't count on me to help you."

"That's no way to talk!"

"Those three soldiers are krauts!" he said bluntly.

Apparently disbelieving, Mama took the binoculars and looked for herself. Then, without a word, she handed them back to Papa. I would have loved to know what was going through her mind. Whatever it was, her face was calm and serene, but inside I was sure she had to be asking herself all sorts of questions. What was she going to do? She knew that the Americans had orders not to take any prisoners, at least for the first several days. What would happen when the two groups met?

"Can I look through the binoculars?" I asked timidly.

Firmly but coldly he said: "You'll see those three soon enough, child." And with that he handed the binoculars to my mother and headed back to his boat, clearly intending to take another trip into the swamp, but also leaving us to our own devices in this tricky new situation.

Since they were wounded, I reasoned, maybe they wouldn't cause any trouble.

In any case, Mama, as though she had just made up her mind, chased Kerry back inside and sent him back to bed, over his heated protests. There was no question now that the Germans were heading for 104. Where else would they go? There was no one left for miles around.

"What are you going to do?" I asked anxiously.

"We'll see how things develop," she said.

Kerry's rifle was leaning against the wall. Mama picked it up and took it into the bedroom. Lieutenant Wingate was fast asleep, so she first placed a finger on her lips, pointed to the gun, and then to the tracks. She slipped the gun in under the eiderdown, where Kerry would have easy access if necessary, then went out and closed the door. Before she had left, Kerry nodded that he understood. He would cover us, but wouldn't start anything. The three men, who were almost at the house now, looked pretty harmless, but you could never tell.

Two of the Germans were supporting the third, each holding one arm slung over their shoulders. The man in the middle seemed in bad shape. When they reached the courtyard they paused, but Mama made a sign for them to come in. They didn't seem to be armed, and their uniforms were torn and spattered with mud. From where had they materialized? And how had they managed to make it all the way here without being shot? The railroad lines had been in the hands of the Americans since yesterday morning.

One of the Germans, speaking impeccable French but in a voice that was toneless and weary, said:

"The lad here has lost a great deal of blood, Madame. He'll surely die unless you help him."

The young man in question was only about twenty. He'd taken a bullet through the thigh, was bleeding badly, and was obviously in great pain. The other German, considerably older, had been shot in the heel. His wound was far less serious. Mama made them both sit down. Then she said to me:

"Run down cellar and get me a bundle of hay."

The third German went with me and helped me carry back upstairs a huge bundle of hay which we spread on the kitchen floor.

"Now bring me the parachute, which is still on the ladder. We'll use it as a sheet."

The German brought the parachute over and spread it out on the hay. After she had removed his bloody trouser leg, Mama had the badly wounded German lie down on the improvised bed. She washed and bandaged the wound, then slipped a pair of pajama trousers that belonged to Francis on the new patient. She had cleansed his wound with a mixture of water and Calvados, and now she gave him some to drink. His reaction was not unlike George's the day before.

"Drink it down," she admonished. "It's the only thing we have to ease your pain."

The third German, the one who spoke French, was tall and handsome. He must have been about forty, and everything about him indicated aristocracy and good breeding. I was sure he was an officer, though if so he had removed his stripes. I noticed also that the other soldiers had removed their buttons, and wondered what that meant.

Strange times. Here we were, harboring two Americans and three Germans, and the common bond between them was that they were all miserable, wounded, and in pain. I asked Mama if I could offer the third German a cup of coffee and she said of course I could. He accepted it with a sad little smile. He was gazing down at his two companions stretched out on the American parachute in this French peasant kitchen, cared for by a compassionate woman who gave of herself to both camps without prejudice.

Just then, Kerry hobbled into the room. Unarmed. Silence and amazement. Kerry had never seen a German before. But he quickly sized up the situation. Still no one had said a word. Kerry and the German officer were looking at each other intently. Then, spontaneously, the German offered Kerry his hand. Kerry hesitated for a fraction of a second. He glanced over at Mama, who nodded almost imperceptibly. Then the blond giant took the proffered hand. Both men continued to study each other closely and amicably. Inside 104, on this seventh day of June, 1944, there were no longer any enemies: there were only men joined together by their pain and suffering.

Still, I had trouble believing my eyes. It was clear both men liked each other immediately, and there they were by the fireside, drinking together, sharing a cup of American coffee, trying to communicate; according to the rules of war they should have been out fighting, killing each other. But I had long since concluded that 104 was a very special place, one that eluded the rules of the game.

The two other Germans were asleep on their bed of hay. The younger, I could tell, was fast asleep; as for the second, I wasn't sure. Something about him frightened me. Whether it was my lonely life, or something God-given, I have always had a special faculty for reading people's minds, a sixth sense that enables me to foresee trouble. Mama has said that God gave me that gift to keep me from being too proud; and since I could read only unpleasant thoughts, it was humbling to see how ugly and base some people were.

I couldn't tell precisely what the older German was thinking, but I could tell that he wished us ill. I knew, too, that his presence here under our roof was a threat to our lives. Why? How? I couldn't honestly say; yet I was sure that it was he alone who posed that threat to us.

The German officer took several snapshots from his wallet and showed us the members of his family. His mother, an elderly lady with snow-white hair, had the same air of rectitude and decency that he did. In fact, they looked very much alike. In another snapshot, a beautiful young woman was holding two children by the hands, both about my own age. The stone mansion in the background, with its well-manicured lawn, brought to mind a life of well-being, far from the fire and blood that had brought us all together today.

Kerry also brought out some photographs, first of his parents, a good-looking couple who seemed far too young to have a son Kerry's age; another of his fiancée; and a third of a scraggly dog.

Both men, though they spoke no common language, had established an immediate though tenuous bond, something you could almost feel. Yet there was a basic difference in their moods. Despite his wound, Kerry seemed to emanate happiness and conviction; I could sense he belonged among the victorious. The German, on the other hand, was full of sadness, anguish; his eyes, face, and carriage betrayed his inner feelings. For these two, at least, the outcome of the war was no longer in doubt.

Mama concocted a delicious meal for us all, using the vegetables from our garden mixed with meat taken from the American K-rations. It was a strange assortment around the family table: Mama, Claude, and I; Kerry and the German officer. Only Papa was conspicuous by his absence. After the meal, the German woke up his two companions and forced them to take some nourishment. Kerry and Mama went to see to George, but we were not allowed in, which I knew meant that he was worse.

In the distance, the roar of cannons continued, over in the direction of the ocean. We began to wonder what it meant: could it be that the Allies, because of the weather or the stiff German resistance, had called off the invasion and decided to sacrifice the paratroopers who had jumped into Normandy, "our" paratroopers? No, that was impossible. They couldn't abandon their own soldiers; they couldn't abandon us who had waited for them for so long.

I went out to the pump to fetch some water. Mama would be angry if she knew, but I couldn't stay indoors. As I glanced down the tracks towards 103, I had trouble believing my eyes. I could see a car, or some kind of vehicle, bouncing along between the tracks. Several soldiers were seated in the car, but I didn't know how they kept their seats because the car was rocking crazily as it hit each railroad tie. I dropped my bucket and ran for the house, calling to my mother. She appeared and looked at the object of my concern, then broke into a broad smile.

"That's a jeep," she said. "A special kind of American army truck that can go anywhere, even in water I think."

"How do you know that?"

"Because," she said with a sly smile, "I've driven in one of them."

The jeep pulled up at 104, and, with a smile, I greeted them in my stock English:

"Hello, boys, how are you?"

One of the soldiers replied in perfect French:

"Très bien, Mademoiselle, ça va."

Mama took him into the bedroom to see Lieutenant Wingate. A few minutes later he emerged.

"Don't worry, Madame. I'll see to it that you have what you need right away."

Then, turning to the German officer, he said politely but firmly, in French:

"I'll be back shortly. Then, I'm afraid I'll have to take you with me. I'll need you to point out your army's current position."

With that he climbed back in the jeep and headed down the tracks. I gave Mama a quizzical look.

"He's gone to fetch some medicine for George, whose fever's gone up again. I'm sure the medicine will help bring it down." And then she repeated, as though to reassure herself: "The medicine can't help but do the trick."

As she passed the German officer, he seized her hand and said:

"Would you perhaps have a piece of paper and envelope, Madame. I'd like to write a note to my family." His face was sad beyond description. "I know that I'm going to die today," he said, "and I'll never see my family again."

"Don't be silly! Stop saying such things!" Mama admonished. "You're in good health. For you, the war is over. So why do you talk about dying? Your wife would be angry if she heard you."

"In a little while the Americans are going to take me with them while they reconnoiter. I know what that means for me."

"You don't know what you're saying. The Americans are men of honor. They wouldn't shoot someone who's unarmed."

Mama sounded very convincing, but then the German cut in and said:

"You don't understand, Madame. It's not the Americans who are going to kill me."

It was as though Mama suddenly understood the full implication of his words, and she buried her face in her hands. "You don't mean . . ." she began. "You don't mean to say that . . ."

"Yes," he said, "that is exactly what I mean."

He knew that the Germans would see him in the jeep with the Americans, would assume he was a traitor, and make sure to shoot him first. Unless they decided not to make any such fine distinctions and wiped out everyone in the jeep. Either way, he didn't stand a chance.

"I want to write one last time to my family."

Mama laid her hand on his shoulder, fighting back the tears. "My poor boy," she said. "My poor poor boy. How stupid war is. How unbelievably stupid!"

I saw, then, that they were both crying. I quickly cleaned off the table, sponged it, and brought out a pad of paper and some envelopes. Out of discretion, Kerry and the other American soldiers went outside and sat on the courtyard steps. After he had finished writing, the German slipped into the envelope the snapshots that he had shown us a short while before. He also had some money in his wallet, which he removed and handed to Mama.

"For all the trouble we've caused you," he said. "And for them," he said, gesturing to the two German soldiers on the makeshift bed.

He didn't know my mother. She drew herself up to her full height and said, in a voice I hardly recognized:

"Keep your money, Monsieur. If I took you and your comrades in and did my best to care for you, it was out of Christian love. Your money means nothing to me. I wouldn't touch it."

The German was completely stunned. Coming from a woman whose poverty was obvious, this categorical refusal surprised and upset him.

"I didn't mean to offend you, Madame," he said. "Please excuse me. And promise me you'll send this letter to my wife and children."

Mama's face softened immediately. "Don't worry," she said. "I promise." She took the letter and slid it in between the sheets in the linen closet.

The jeep was making its crazy way back down the tracks toward us, and as soon as it arrived the officer jumped out and ran into the bedroom. He gave George two grayish tablets, which he said ought to relieve the pain, and handed several small boxes of the same pills to Mama, after having written the dosage on one of them. Then, pointing to the two Germans, he said:

"You can give the pills to them, too. It won't cure them, but it will ease the pain."

His words were followed by a heavy silence. This American, who seemed to exude confidence and calm, was about to commit an act of total madness. He was venturing out on a pointless mission, risking his own life, that of his men, and the German's too. We had heard what he had said earlier to the German, so we knew he thought his mission was important. But everyone knew that Amfreville, where they were headed, was swarming with Germans. Everyone, I supposed, but this American.

"Let's get going," he said.

Mama stepped in front of the American. She begged him not to go. It was crazy, she said. Weren't there enough dead already? Why take unnecessary risks?

"I can tell you as I'm standing here, the whole village of Amfreville is full of Germans," she said. "If that's what you want to know."

I chimed in too, saying that Mama was absolutely right. We'd lived here for four years and knew just where the Germans were stationed. He'd been here less than two days. Why couldn't he listen to us? His point was that he needed more specific information; he wanted to find out precisely where every German machine-gun emplacement was situated, and the only way to find out was at close range. An argument that might or might not have held water. After all, we were only poor civilians. But I still wasn't convinced.

He looked at us in surprise, slightly shaken by the force of our arguments. But he swept them all aside with one simple sentence:

"We're here to win the war." After all, he was a professional soldier. Then: "All right, men, let's get going."

Seated in the front between two American soldiers, the German looked back one last time at our house. His face was a mask of sorrow. I suspected that if he had wanted to save his own life, he could have told the American everything he wanted to know. I suspected that he knew where every soldier and every gun emplacement in Amfreville was. But he was a German, and had no intention of betraying his comrades. Despite what Mama said to him a little while ago, the war was not over for him.

The engine sputtered into life, and the jeep careened down the tracks in a cloud of dust; then to our amazement it turned off at one point and headed straight into the marsh waters. Mama had been right: the vehicle also went on water.

It had progressed no more than a hundred yards when the Germans opened fire. Stray bullets hit the outside of our house, as we huddled close to the floor. I crawled upstairs while Mama wasn't looking, and peeked out the attic window to see what had happened to the jeep.

The Germans were still raking the area with their fire, but despite it the jeep headed straight for the château, sending a double spray of white water in its wake. At the bridge to the island, where a tributary of the Merderet flows into the larger river, the driver must have realized he had come too close to the German installations and tried to stop. The next thing I saw was all five men diving from the jeep into the swamp.

Kerry, who had also followed the jeep's progress, was furious to see his buddies in real trouble—even though it was of their own making—and to know that he was powerless to help them. He stomped around the room in a fit of rage. Why hadn't they listened to us? What had made them set off on that suicide mission?

"For God's sake! They're all going to be slaughtered!"

I looked around. It was Papa Maurice, back from his latest fishing expedition, who had joined me at the attic window.

"You never should have let them set off to Amfreville in the first place!" He looked at me, livid with anger.

"They wouldn't listen to us," I said.

He was watching the progress of the fighting through the binoculars. Then, suddenly, he handed them to me.

"Here, look for yourself, child," he said.

I asked him to show me how to adjust them, and for a moment his fingers paused in front of my eyes. I couldn't believe what I saw. *The skin of Papa's palms was gone,* worn away in the course of the past thirty-six hours he had spent endlessly poling his boat through the marshes. The skin of his palms must have been stuck to that wooden pole!

My desire to watch the battle vanished. I grabbed his wrist and literally dragged Papa Maurice downstairs. He couldn't figure out what had come over me, but for once put up no resistance. I made him sit down and began preparing bandages for his mutilated hands. Both thumbs and both little fingers were worn away to the bone; muscles and skin had disappeared. I could only imagine how he must be suffering. But he kept protesting, saying it was nothing and I shouldn't make such a fuss about his hands. I had all I could do to cleanse and bandage them, but I finally convinced him that his job was done: he had found and brought back all the food and ammunition that had been parachuted into the marshes, and our courtyard was piled high with his booty. Now I was finding out that I could be as pigheaded as he, a chip off the old block. I glanced up at the bullwhip hanging on the wall: somehow it no longer sent shivers up and down my spine. I decided that from now on I would obey Papa only if *I* wanted to.

Somewhat against my better judgment, but thinking under the circumstances that it would please Papa, I poured him a big bowl full of Calvados. A fatal error. This hardened drinker hadn't taken a drop since Monday noon; during the same period he had eaten nothing and had not slept either. The result was almost immediate: moments after he had drunk the Calvados he passed out and slumped over the table.

Mama and I weren't strong enough to carry him. I quickly spread some straw on the floor, then dragged him over and heaved him onto it. We didn't even remove his boots.

I looked at this man, whom I had always feared and hated, with a mixture of love and admiration. For since the first paratroopers had arrived Monday night he had not stopped, using every last ounce of energy he possessed, until he had collapsed. I leaned down and whispered into his ear:

"Papa, you're a hero. I love you."

I was glad he couldn't hear me. He would have been upset at the very idea of being called a "hero," and would have given me a good cuff.

On the bed above him, Lieutenant Wingate was sleeping fitfully, his fever still high despite the gray pills. When he and Papa awoke, I knew they'd be happy to see each other. The lieutenant considered Papa his "savior," and couldn't stop admiring him. Papa felt just as strongly about the man whose life he had saved. Men are strange creatures, all right. What could this foreigner from across the sea possibly have in common with this illiterate, coarse peasant? Who would have thought that gruff, tough old Papa Maurice could feel so strongly and tenderly about another human being? I had to confess I found grownups hard to figure out.

Whatever it was between them, it was touching to witness, though. As soon as he saw Papa, the lieutenant reached out for his hands, and often they would remain that way, hand in hand, just looking at each other without saying a word. Every time he came back from the marshes, Papa would glance inside at "his patient" to see how he was doing. And if he seemed better, Papa's face was a mask of joy; if worse, it was clouded and somber. It was Papa, too, who insisted on taking George his cup of coffee, and waiting there while he slipped it.

Now, though, Papa was out, at least temporarily, and Mama and I were in charge. For him the war no longer existed; his worries about the food and munitions were over, and his anger at our failure to prevent the Americans from setting off toward Amfreville was calmed by his deep sleep. Thus he did not see, a short while later, the jeep come bounding back along the railroad ties, hurtling past our house in the direction of 103, with only four soldiers in it. We couldn't tell whether or not they were wounded. And their German prisoner: what had become of him?

Suddenly the steady sound of gunfire ceased. Only the smoking ruins of Jean Leroux's house and that of the Cuquemelles' reminded us how close the battle was to our tiny refuge.

Mama moved from one patient to the other, Germans and Americans indiscriminately, dispensing medicine, changing bandages, applying compresses. In the course of her rounds she glanced outside:

"Come here," she called.

"What is it, Mama?"

"I could have sworn I saw a head emerge from the water down the tracks three hundred meters or so."

For several minutes we both stared at the spot she had indicated, but saw nothing. She must have been mistaken. To make sure, I went upstairs and looked out the window, to get a better view of the marshes.

"You're right, Mama," I called down, "you're right."

It wasn't a head I had seen, but first a hand, then an arm reaching up out of the water. My heart began to beat fast: I knew it was our German officer.

I bounded down the stairs two at a time. Mama was looking through the binoculars.

"The poor man must be drowning," she said. And with that she dashed out of the house and headed down the tracks. As she did, the Germans opened fire, but they were too far away, and their bullets splashed harmlessly in the water several hundred meters short. I saw her kneel down over the wounded man, whose body was in the water, and whose head would first slump, then jerk back up, as it touched the water. She tried to help him to his feet, but he was too weak, and she was too small to support him. She dragged him for a few meters toward the house, then gave up. It was hopeless.

I couldn't bear it any longer, so I ran to join her. Seeing me, she screamed:

"Go back, in the name of God, go back inside! Do you want to kill yourself, child?"

I jumped down into the water, which came up to my waist, and kept moving toward her, though it was hard to move swiftly in the water, and I was out of breath by the time I reached them. I had been right: it *was* the German officer who had gone off with the Americans a few hours before. He was in terrible shape. He had been shot in the chest, and bubbles of blood were rising to the surface and bursting with a dry little noise. It didn't take a doctor to tell that he was in critical condition. But maybe, if we could get him to the house, we still might save him.

"The first thing we have to do is stop the bleeding," Mama said. "I'm going back to the house to get a towel. You stay here and keep his head above water. He's not strong enough to do it himself."

She made me sit down in the water, my back against the side of the roadbed, holding the German's head in my lap. "If we hold the towel tight against his wound, maybe we can check the flow. I'll be right back. I don't think there's any danger of the Germans shooting at you now. I'm sure they've been watching us through their binoculars and see we're trying to save one of their men." And with that she sprinted toward the house.

I held the German's head gently on my lap and stroked his forehead. He must have been shot at the point when we had seen all five occupants of the jeep jump into the water. That had been three hours ago. And for three hours he must have crawled and pulled himself painfully back toward us, toward that house where he had been received and cared for. It was a miracle he had made it this far.

Mama was back with the biggest towel she could find. Carefully, we removed his blood-soaked shirt, then pressed the towel against the gaping wound. The German, who had been growing paler by the minute, revived and opened his eyes. He looked at us intently.

"I'm thirsty," he whispered. "Very thirsty . . ."

How could he be so thirsty when his body was immersed in water? Mama sat down and took his head in her lap, while I raced to the house and made a pot of very strong coffee. I was back in a few minutes, gave Mama the cup, and she fed him by little sips. Then, as though the idea had just struck her, she said:

"Maybe if we gave him a couple of the gray pills he'd feel better."

Again I ran to the house to get the pills. It was like a miniature hospital inside, and little Claude was the nurse in charge. He was sitting beside the bed where Kerry and George were lying, every few minutes changing the cold compresses on George's forehead. How he had changed in the past two days, that boy! From a laughing, happy-go-lucky child he had become a serious, silent young man. Pain and suffering and death had matured him virtually overnight. Before heading back to Mama and the German, I paused and gave him a big hug.

Mama shook her head: the towel was by now as red as the shirt had been. There was no chance of saving the poor man. Even if the bullet itself, which had pierced his lung, had not proved fatal, his monumental exertion in making his way back here undoubtedly would. But Mama refused to give up.

"Remember how your father brought George back?" she said. "Maybe we can use the ladder to carry him back to the house."

This time it was she who went while I again held the officer's head. In a few minutes she was back with the ladder. But it was no go: he was far too heavy for us to lift. We tried to slip the ladder under him in the water, but that didn't work, so we set it on the bank and tried to pull him on it, but to no avail. I hated myself for being so frail and weak!

The pills had apparently begun to work: he seemed in less pain than before.

"Stay here," Mama said. "I'm going to take the boat and see if I can find someone who might come and help us." She took the ladder, which itself was not light, and made her way once again back to the house. I knelt down in the water and held the German's head against me. Just then the sun, which we hadn't seen for days, broke through the clouds and bathed the German's face in its glow. But only for a moment; soon it was gone again. At least I knew it still existed.

The soldier's breathing was easier now, and that awful whistling sound that had come every time he breathed in and out when we had first arrived was gone. He opened his eyes and stared at me.

"I feel better now," he said, his voice so faint I could barely hear it. "Doesn't hurt anymore." Then he didn't speak for a minute or two. "Tell me, child, why are you staying here with me? Your mother takes care of the wounded out of Christian love," he said. "She told me so herself. But what about you? You're far too young to know what Christian love is. So why are you here?"

"Shh," I said, "don't talk. You'll wear yourself out."

"No, I'm fine, thanks to the medicine your mother gave me. Do you know how good it feels not to suffer, even for a few minutes? Of course you don't. Anyway, I want an answer to my question: why are you here?"

"I'll tell you why, but on one condition: that you don't talk anymore and wait quietly till Mama comes back with help. All right? I'm here because I saw that Mama couldn't manage alone. She tried to carry you back by herself, but couldn't, so I thought that maybe together . . . Anyway, I have to confess there's another reason too. I owe God an old debt. And being here is the repayment."

"Owe God a debt? Ah, I want to hear all about it."

Again I scowled at him and told him not to talk. I even raised my hand as though to threaten him if he didn't obey. He smiled. I couldn't help thinking how crazy it was: me, a little girl, raising her hand in mock threat and scowling at this man whose life was slowly ebbing away, and he found it funny.

I smiled back. I still had a lot to learn about grownups, but this man, my enemy, and I were closer at that moment than I had ever felt to anyone.

"All right," I said, "I'll tell you the full story." Even if he found it silly, it might help pass the time for him, ease his suffering. "Only remember, no interruptions."

He blinked his eyes in assent.

"One evening, as I was leaving school, I was terribly hungry. Oh, I'm always hungry, it seems; in fact I sometimes wonder how a girl as skinny as me can eat so much and still be hungry . . . Anyway, this particular day I saw a German soldier standing in front of Monsieur Deloeuvre's house, munching on a piece of bread and butter. I stopped and looked at him, and I'm sure he understood from my look that I envied him eating that piece of bread. I suspected he was a cook. He made a sign for me to follow him into Monsieur Deloeuvre's garage, which the Germans had transformed into a kitchen. My, how good it smelled in that kitchen! The soldier made me sit down and he served me an enormous snack, which I gobbled down without being asked twice. When I left he shook my hand as though I were a grownup. I was pleased and proud, both because I had been so hungry and because he had treated me so well. After that, the soldier watched for me every afternoon by the gate, and if he was alone he would signal for me to come in. He even made up special snacks for me. But we never exchanged a word: he didn't speak any French. He seemed happy just sitting across from me watching me eat. Who knows, maybe he had a little sister my age back in Germany.

"That arrangement went on for some time. But one evening when I was quietly eating my snack, we heard the sound of footsteps coming toward us across the courtyard. The soldier seemed scared out of his wits and he gestured for me to go hide in the closet; the top part was used to store the bread, and the bottom the sacks of flour. He made me kneel down between two sacks of flour and he quickly pulled an empty sack down over my head, so that I looked like a third. The closet had Dutch doors, so that while both doors opened left and right, only the top halves did.

"The German officer who had just arrived walked over and opened the closet doors. I huddled there trying not to shiver, trying not to breathe, while he inspected the upper shelves. So I closed my eyes and prayed, and I told God that if only the German didn't find me I'd find the means some day to pay Him back. And the officer closed the closet doors without ever seeing me.

"But his visit had frightened my German soldier-friend, and he no longer invited me into his kitchen. What he did, though, was slip a piece of bread or a cookie or piece of cake into my schoolbag on my way home. This was the way we worked it: he would stand just inside the fence and I'd walk past. When I got to where he was

I'd turn my back to the fence and he'd slip whatever he had into my bag. Things went on that way for several weeks, and then one day the cook wasn't there anymore. I still went by day after day, but I never saw him again.

"And that's the story. One of your compatriots was kind to me when I was hungry, so today I'm happy to give you a little of my time. And pay God back to boot."

The German smiled. Every once in a while I wiped the blood from his lips. I asked him how he felt, and in a voice that was almost normal he said:

"Those pills your mother gave me have practically erased the pain."

"Erased the pain." That was the first time I had ever heard that expression, and I remember it to this day. The German spoke perfect French, not only without accent but with an elegance I wasn't used to. He seemed serene and calm; yet I was sure he knew he was going to die. It was as though he was fully resigned to his fate and accepted the fact that I was there to ease his dying.

"Tell me another story," he said.

"All right. I'll tell you about the time I committed a frightful sin."

"A frightful sin," he smiled. "I find that hard to believe." Again he smiled, and closed his eyes. It was a silly little girl's story, and I hoped it wouldn't bore him.

"It was shortly before Christmas. I was having lunch in those days at an old lady's house, a dear old lady who lived next to the school. A German officer was lodging with her, a tall handsome man who didn't speak a word of French. For the holidays, he received from home a beautiful box, decorated with a lovely colored Christmas tree, filled with all sorts of cookies and candies that we hadn't seen in France for years. It was so beautiful!

"And on the spur of the moment the officer gave it to me. It was like a dream, and that night on my way home I hugged the box to my heart. I had sworn I wouldn't open it. I was going to give it to my family as a surprise. But the road was long and lonely and very cold. So I said to myself: 'Just one little sweet won't hurt anyone.' And then before I knew it I had eaten two, then three, until there was hardly anything left. My mother was furious, and made me go confess to Father Roulland. He told me that I had sinned, and that I risked going to hell. I believed him then, but now I know he was wrong. In fact, I'm sure of it."

"What makes you so sure?"

"Because I realize, Monsieur, that we're already in hell. So from now on I won't pay any attention to all those stories about eternal fire and brimstone."

"Tell me why," he said.

So we continued talking about everything and anything, under the gray sky: both of us oblivious to the cold water, his head on my lap, his eyes closed most of the time but his voice calm and normal. Every few minutes I would wipe the blood from his lips again. I had the feeling I had known him for a long, long time.

The more we talked the more I began to confide in him, telling him about my doubts and dreams, my worries and my hopes. Before long, it was he who was encouraging and consoling me.

"I'm having trouble with Jesus," I admitted. "It's all well and good that He asks us to love one another, but it's pretty clear that it doesn't work, does it? Or when He says: 'If you love me, you will do as I do.' But that doesn't work either. No matter how much I may love Jesus, I'm not even capable of getting you out of the water and safely home where you'd be warm. If He were here, He'd know how. But I have a strong feeling He's not even thinking about us."

"You're wrong, child. He hasn't abandoned us. But His plans are not for me to get better, or even that I make it to your house so I can be next to my fellow soldiers. He has something better in store for me. Later on you'll understand, and you'll see I was right."

"Maybe. There are so many things I don't understand, so many that make me angry and upset. Mama tells me I think too much. What God wants, she says, is faith above all; after all, reason has its place. Only I'm like Saint Thomas: seeing is believing. Oh, it's not that I don't love Him; it's just that I have a few things on my mind to tell Him, that's all. Like why doesn't He come and help us now: He can see how badly we need Him. If He did come walking over the marsh waters, I'd say to Him: 'Oh, there you are! It's about time. Help me carry this poor man, and don't waste any time curing him.' "

"Wouldn't you be afraid of making Him angry?"

"Why? He has a temper Himself! Remember how He chased the moneychangers out of the Temple? How I would have loved to see that! I guess that's one of the reasons I love Him: because He's not all peaches and cream. People who are always pleasant and smiling are boring, don't you think?"

"I do, my child. Tell me, if you had one favor to ask Jesus, what would it be?"

Lowering my head, I looked down into the officer's ashen face.

"One favor? I'd like to place my hands on your chest and say: 'Father, I love You. In the name of that love, may this man be made well again.' "

The German smiled. "That would be nice," he said. Then: "What other favor would you ask if you had another?"

"*La jugeote,*" I said without hesitation.

"What does that mean?" he said.

I realized he couldn't be expected to know all the familiar and local terms we use in these regions. I explained to him that it meant having good common sense.

"I see," he said, "you mean wisdom."

"And I would also ask to keep what I already have: a love of the trees and the birds, my passion for storms and fog."

"Why do you love fog?"

Clumsily, I tried to explain what fascinated me so much about the fog that always floated just over the marshes, rarely lifting. I loved it because it seemed to hide something from me. And when the sun broke through, the rays were like the ramp to heaven—some invisible stairway leading up to the thrones of God.

"You'll find that stairway, child," he said, "I'm sure you will."

"Only if I improve," I said. "I'm as stubborn as a mule, and I daydream too much."

The German laughed. "You have your whole life ahead of you to improve on those two fronts," he said.

"Don't be too sure," I said, shaking my head. "The war's only just beginning. I might find myself in heaven sooner than expected."

"That's true," he said gravely. "These are sad, dangerous times."

"Anyway," I said, "I'm not going to worry about it. God made us, and He'll take us when He sees fit. He wouldn't be so surprised if we showed up early."

"You know," the German smiled, "you talked about getting wisdom, but I think you may already have found it."

Then I went on to tell him about my hopes and ambitions, about my singing voice, about how I always felt like singing wherever I was, even if it was the wrong time and place. "Today," I confessed, "is the first time in my life when I don't feel like it. It's the war, I'm sure. But I'm not the only one: the birds don't feel like singing either."

The German asked me to sing something for him. I said I couldn't. The cold water would make it impossible. My voice would be shaking. "And besides, I don't feel like it."

"I wouldn't mind," he said. "Even if your voice was shaking from the cold I'd enjoy it." Then he opened his eyes and said: "It's true, you must be terribly cold. And I'm sure my head is too heavy on your lap."

I told him I was fine, that I didn't mind it at all. I almost told him that his head wasn't any heavier than the bricks my father made me hold when I had been bad, but I'm glad I didn't. He wouldn't have understood. Anyway, I knew I really had to grant him that request.

"What kind of song would you like, happy or sad?"

"Why don't you simply sing me the last song you've learned. I'd prefer something sad, but . . ."

"You're in luck," I said. "The one I've just learned *is* sad."

Despite the cold, despite the water lapping against my chest, despite the fact that I was so stiff I could barely move, I cleared my throat and began to sing, barely humming at first, then louder and louder. In a few seconds, the miracle occurred; I forgot everything around us—the terrible battle raging, the stray bullets that sometimes whined past, my fear, the cold, the roar of the cannons in the distance, and the growing concern that something might have happened to Mama, who should have been back before now. And I sang.

For me, the man whose life was slipping away before my eyes became my child whom I had to sing to sleep. The strong clear tones of my child-voice rose above the marshes.

> *Daddy darling, Daddy love*
> *Who dwells in heaven above*
> *Look down upon your suffering child*
> *Your homeless waif*
> *And bring him safe*
> *To where you dwell . . .*

The soldier listened, his eyes closed, but I knew he wasn't sleeping. I went on:

> *Since you have gone*
> *I've been alone*
> *In pain and sorrow*
> *So bring me home*
> *Today, tomorrow,*
> *Let me come*
> *To where you dwell.*

"I'm sorry," I told him, "but they're the only two verses Mama taught me."

"So it's your mother who teaches you to sing like that?"

"Yes, we often sing together in the evening. She has a beautiful voice. She copies out the words for me, and I memorize them next day on my way to school. By the time I get home I know them by heart. It makes my trip to and from school seem shorter. Singing makes a lot of things easier to bear."

"I've never heard a prettier voice than yours," he said. "I'm sure you'll end up being a great singer one day. Can you sing me another one?"

"All right, but this one is very long, I warn you."

"I think I still have enough time left to hear it."

"It's a song about war."

I began to hum the tune. Then I began the song, but I knew I wouldn't get through it without crying; it was too sad, and several of the images it evoked appeared in my mind too vividly.

One evening in a rose-colored room
a little child slept.
A smile crept
Upon his lips
For in his dream
He saw a flag unfold.

Mama, he said, where's Papa gone?
To fight the war
In some place far?
Let me go fight it too
I may be small
But I am strong.

I still wasn't crying. I went on:

Then from the wood
All bathed in blood
Her husband came
And called her name.
He fell beside
The tiny bed
Wherein his child
Lay and cried . . .

I couldn't go on. In the following stanza the enemy emerges from the woods and kills the mother too. I tried to explain to the German officer why I couldn't sing that stanza—and why I had never been able to.

"I understand," he said. "Why don't you skip it and go on to the next stanza."

The final stanza depicted the boy twenty years later, praying at his parents' grave:

> *The time to wake*
> *Is not yet here,*
> *O parents dear*
> *But soon I'll make*
> *My vengeance clear.*
> *Sleep, sleep in peace*
> *Without surcease.*

By then the tears were streaming down my cheeks. I could see that my officer too was affected by the song:

"Life is sometimes like songs," I said. "A man is killed. Twenty years later his son will set out to avenge him and be killed in turn, and no one knows why."

"You're right," he said. "War seems to go on and on. And even women and children are no longer spared its horrors."

I realized suddenly that he was no longer thinking of my song but of the two children he had shown us on the snapshot that morning. I didn't know what to say to him. Suddenly he was racked by a shudder. I asked him a stupid question. Here he had been immersed in icy water for almost seven hours, and all I could think to say was:

"Are you sure you're not cold?"

"It doesn't matter anymore," he said. "Don't worry about me, child." Then his voice appeared concerned as he said: "Will your Mama be coming back?"

"Of course she will. She went off in the boat to find a man who can help carry you to the house. She isn't used to poling the boat, so it will take her a while to get to the nearest village and back. But she'll be here soon."

"She's gone to a great deal of trouble," he said. "But she'll never find anyone willing to help an enemy soldier."

"That's not so," I protested. "The Normands are good people. When someone's wounded or hurt, it doesn't matter what uniform he wears. It's not fair for you to think that."

"You've both done more than you should. You've risked your lives to help me. But we have to face the truth. There's nothing more you can do for me now. I'm grateful for all you've both done already."

I realized that he kept referring to "you both," meaning Mama and me. He had no idea I had a father, who could have come and helped us if he had been in shape. When the soldier had arrived that morning Papa had been off in his boat, and their paths had never crossed. It was just as well, for I would have found it hard to tell him that Papa would never have lifted a finger to help this dying man. He had joined the other camp. For Papa, Christian charity was meaningless. For the Germans a few hundred meters away in Amfreville, too, I thought; I was sure they had been observing us. It would have taken them less than an hour to come over here in a boat and fetch their wounded comrade. Without running any risk, either: there were no paratroopers anywhere near. And yet they didn't come.

I gazed down at my German and tried to smile at him, but my heart wasn't in it. Nothing I could do or say would help him anymore. And besides, something he had said began to prey on me: *where* was Mama? Was she all right? She had been gone such a long time!

The German seemed to fall asleep. His head lay heavier on my arm and knees. Then he started up, opened his eyes and shouted:

"Your mother! Your mother!"

"She's coming, Monsieur," I said. "She's coming."

I said that without really knowing. But as I glanced over my shoulder there she was, running toward us down the tracks. If she was running, it meant she was not hurt or wounded!

"Tell her above all not to forget that letter."

"Don't worry, she won't. Now save your strength, she'll be here in a second."

But Mama arrived too late. His suffering was over. He gave one last shudder and died in my arms. Almost at the same moment the sun broke through again; the droplets of water on his face shone brightly and lent his face, for several seconds, a strange sort of beauty.

When she arrived, Mama saw that the German was dead.

She had been gone for two hours; the German and I had talked together for two hours. From the first moment Mama had spotted him struggling to make it back to 104, over five hours had passed.

The two hours of conversation had seemed like a lifetime. A man lived, and then he died. Death in our part of the world was a natural thing. Simple and logical. Part of life. That's what had made it easier for me to remain in the water all that time, talking almost normally, without embarrassment or anxiety, while a man's life ebbed slowly away. I must say, he had helped; not for one moment did I sense that he was afraid.

Mama put her two hands under the officer's head, lifted him gently, moved him away from the embankment, and let his body slip beneath the water. I tried to get up but I couldn't move: I was too stiff. Mama had to lift me up and help me to the house. My clothes—and hers—were soaked not only with water but blood. We needed to wash and change into dry clothes and, above all, to warm our chilled bones. After that long visit with death, our warm, silent house seemed like a peaceful refuge.

I felt drained, and especially sad. Mama took me in her arms and held me tight.

"What matters, my darling Geneviève," she murmured, "is that we tried. The wound was too bad. There was nothing we could do to save him. When the war's over we'll see that his family receives his letter."

Yes, we'll send that letter. That's all we can do now for the poor man who lies beneath the waters of the marsh; for that enemy who, for a few short hours, was closer to me than anyone else.

As soon as we entered the house Claude jumped up and down with delight and ran over to snuggle up to Mama.

"Do you have to go to the Sheepfold this evening?" he pleaded. "I've been alone here all day."

Mama hugged him tight. It was true, he had played the gallant little doctor all afternoon, without relief. She assured him that she wouldn't go to the Sheepfold. Francis could milk Blanchette, and besides, we had almost everything we needed to prepare a half-decent evening meal. We still had plenty of bread and milk, and the K-rations would round out our needs.

Lieutenant Wingate called out softly from the other room, and Mama went in to see what he wanted. I didn't dare join her for fear of waking up Papa Maurice, but she motioned me inside. He was feeling better, and his face showed it. The gray pills had done their job. But both of us remembered what the officer had told us: "They won't cure, but they'll make him feel better."

Mama undid the bandages on his broken leg. It was the first time I had ever seen a wound of that kind, and it was all I could do to keep from screaming. The leg was so swollen it looked as though it would burst. It was all blue and green, and it smelled horrible. I brought the bottle of Calvados, and Mama gently bathed the open wounds. The lieutenant said nothing, but he gritted his teeth and closed his eyes.

There weren't any more bandages. The sheet we had cut yesterday was completely used up. Mama stepped over the straw mattress on which Papa was still sleeping soundly and handed me another pair of sheets. Remembering what she had done, I silently began cutting them into narrow strips. Mama then changed the lieutenant's dressings, and handed me the dirty bandages to throw away. At the rate we were going, we'd soon be out of sheets, and then what would we do for clean bandages?

I decided to take matters into my own hands. I put on a kettle to boil over the hot fire, and then took it down into the cellar, which also served as our laundry room. I poured some strong soap into the water, and one by one slipped the dirty bandages into it. It was almost more than I could stand; the smell and the strips covered with blood and pus were hard to bear. But I knew that I had to. With a piece of wood, I beat them as hard as I could. After a while, I removed them from the hot water and rinsed them thoroughly. Then I put them back into fresh water and boiled them again over the fire.

Mama came out of the bedroom carrying a kerosene lamp and asked what I was doing. I explained it to her, expecting she might be angry. But she simply examined the results, then knelt down and washed them again with a stiff brush. Later that evening I rinsed them, wrung them out, and hung them in the attic. They would be ready to use the next day. It would be a lot of work, but if necessary we would have enough bandages—if you could call these rough, unwearable strips of cloth "bandages"—to carry us through.

The war raged on around us; but here, in this tiny way station, we were isolated, cut off from the world, as if we were the sole survivors of some cataclysm.

Mama prepared dinner for everyone. She asked me to feed the German who had been shot in the thigh. Tomorrow I would go pick some water lilies in the marshes, since they were known to heal cuts. I tried to explain this to him as I fed him, but he didn't understand a word I said. He must have thought I was a terrible loudmouth. But I did make him smile when I came over to him after dinner with a bath glove soaked in eau de Cologne. I scrubbed his cheeks so briskly that he looked like the town drunk. Then I handed him a mirror, and he looked at himself with astonishment, doubtless amazed to find he was still alive.

The old German ate with us, at the kitchen table. He really frightened me, and I couldn't wait to see him leave the table. I didn't know why he affected me so. Papa was still asleep. A day and a half of rest would put him back on his feet. Mama and I organized a regular watch, as we sometimes did in winter. In fact, it was so cold it reminded us of winter. Claude and Kerry were playing Old Maid; Mama was sitting by the fire sewing. I took out my school books and tried to study—even though I had no idea when I might go back to school—but I couldn't concentrate.

Before I went up to bed I brought in a good store of firewood, for both fireplaces, so that Mama wouldn't have to go outside again that night. She noticed that I was unusually pensive, and asked me if anything was wrong. I shook my head. But the fact was that all I could think of was that today a man had died in my arms. And as for Lieutenant Wingate, despite a momentary reprieve he was still deathly ill. I was also aware that those out in the fields, our boys, might be wounded or dying, with nobody to help them. Without fully understanding what was happening, I realized that today, June 7, 1944, my childhood had come to an end. No longer would my mother and I sing together at nightfall; the war, which killed men, had also killed our songs.

Claude crawled in bed beside me and asked me to help him say his prayers. Tonight, we had so much to ask God that I didn't know where to begin.

> Dear God, I know You've had a full day, but please, first of all, don't forget Lieutenant Wingate and all the other wounded soldiers. Then there's our older sister Denise, whom we haven't heard from, and our brother Francis at the Sheepfold. Please remember, too, all our soldiers who landed here only two nights ago and who will have to sleep outside again tonight despite the cold and icy wind.
>
> We pray, too, for all those soldiers who've landed on our shores and who have suffered because of the terrible weather of the past several days, and who may be seasick. Then there are all those people of Sainte-Mère-Eglise whom we love so much: Monsieur Leblond, our school principal, his wife, and son Robert; my teacher, Mademoiselle Burnouf; Father Roulland, who often takes me to task because I don't know my catechism. Please let

him know that often, when I seem to be daydreaming, I'm really thinking of You. Maybe if he realized that he'd be less harsh with me.

Then there are Monsieur and Madame Leroux and all their relatives, about whom we know nothing since the paratroopers landed. Probably Papa Maurice will pay them a visit tomorrow, but meanwhile please take care of them. And all the Cuquemelles—Martha, Manuel, André, his wife, and their son: You know they no longer have any home, so where are they going to sleep? I'm sure You'll take care of them. And Maurice Salmon: will You make sure he is nice to Bernadette, and takes good care of her, now that her mother is dead?

We pray, too, for all the soldiers, from whatever country they come, who don't have a home and family to welcome them and take them in the way Kerry and George do.

Monday, when I went out with Mama begging for candle money, the first lady who gave me money told me that God heard the prayers of children. Well, tonight He had His work cut out for Him.

I fought off sleep, trying to remember who it was I had forgotten in my prayers. I knew there were many more I should have prayed for, but for the life of me I couldn't remember who. Then, just before I fell asleep, I recalled that it was my own parents I had forgotten to pray for. Too bad: God would have to fend without me.

I dreamed: the German officer I had held in my arms was climbing up a beautiful staircase. His left hand was grasping a ray of sunshine as he ascended. In his right hand, he was holding a handsome soldier's cap. He turned around and made a sign to me, far below. I was pleased to see that his uniform was clean and dry and well-pressed, and that it contained not only all its buttons but also all its officer's stripes.

Thursday, June 8, 1944

Dawn was barely breaking when sounds from the ground floor woke me up. Suddenly my dream came back to me, and although I told myself it was only a dream, it somehow made me happy.

I inched out of bed, making sure not to wake up my brother. The two days we had just lived through had left their mark on him, and his sweet little face seemed filled with deep sadness. I pulled the blanket up over him and was on the verge of giving him a kiss on his cheek, but checked myself just in time. "Let the child sleep," I said to myself.

Picking up my shoes, I tiptoed toward the stairs, glancing mechanically out at the marshes. It was still as gray and grim as ever. A fine, biting rain was whipping the windows, and in the waters below, the waves were even choppier than they had been the past several days. I thought of how rough the seas must be, and wondered whether the Allies had really landed or were held up by the weather, the worst I had ever remembered at this time of year. If reinforcements didn't arrive soon, the Germans would have a chance to regroup, and then the paratroopers wouldn't stand a chance.

Mama was as usual preparing coffee, but her good-morning kiss was perfunctory, as though she were thinking of something else.

"What's the matter?"

"The lieutenant spent a bad night. I'm afraid he's getting worse. And his fever has shot up again."

"Can I go in and kiss him?"

"Yes, but tiptoe. I think Kerry's still sleeping."

The lieutenant was drenched with sweat, and fat beads of water rolled down his cheeks. Still, he gave me a faint smile when I went in. But I could see that he was in bad shape: his face was chalky and drawn. I knelt down beside his bed and took his hand in mine. It was boiling. Silently I prayed.

> Dear God, it's me, Geneviève, again. Please help us keep this man alive. I know You have more than You can do, what with all that's going on, but we love him like a member of our own family. Please . . .

I felt Mama's arm help me to my feet, and now tears were rolling down my cheek, which she wiped away.

"Geneviève, I'm going to Sainte-Mère-Eglise. I must find a doctor. We can't wait any longer, or I'm afraid George will die. I'm sure I'll find someone in the village to come and give him proper care. I don't have any money, but I'll promise to pay out of my next salary."

"Why don't you take the money the lady gave me for my communion candle? But Mama, do you think it will really help? You've done everything you can for George. The only thing left is to cut off his leg, and the doctor won't do that here. You'll be risking your life for nothing. Please don't go. Think of Claude and me. If you were to die . . ."

"Don't worry, nothing will happen to me. I'll pray as I walk. When He's needed me I've always responded. Now that I need Him, He'll know what to do."

"When are you leaving?"

"As soon as I've finished my coffee. I'll go milk the cows, but I'll let the soldier distribute it alone today while I sneak into Sainte-Mère-Eglise." She gave a deep sigh. "Those poor boys. They must be in terrible shape after three days and nights without sleep. And in this awful weather. War is so stupid!"

"What do you want me to do till you get back?"

"Make sure our patients have everything they need."

"Mama, I couldn't change the lieutenant's bandages all by myself!"

"Don't worry, I've already changed them. Papa gave me a hand earlier. Keep an eye on your brother and make sure he doesn't go out. And I don't want you to go out either, not even for a minute."

"I wanted to go out on the marshes to fetch some water avens for the German. His wounds aren't bleeding any more."

"No, I want you to promise me not to go out under any circumstances. He's a solid young man and as soon as he recoups the blood he's lost, he'll be fine. The only thing I want you to remember is to give all the patients plenty of liquid."

"Papa's already gone to the Sheepfold?"

"No, he's down in the cellar puttering. He's made up his mind to make a portable chamber pot for the lieutenant. Call him and tell him the coffee's ready."

"But you told me not to go outside."

"Keep to the wall and you'll be all right."

Although the Germans entrenched in the Château d'Amfreville could have used our western wall for target practice, our southern façade was safe enough. If you bent down low and took advantage of the raised level of the roadbed, you could make it from kitchen to cellar in relative safety, despite the occasional whine of a bullet that would lodge harmlessly in the woodpile.

As I started to open the kitchen door, my mother called after me:

"Not a word to your father about my going to Sainte-Mère-Eglise. He might not let me."

"Cross my heart. By the way," I said, coming back to where she was standing, "there's something else I wanted to talk to you about, but I was afraid you'd think I was silly."

"Tell me anyway."

"It's just that . . . the older German soldier frightens me. I don't know why, but I have a strong feeling he's a threat to us."

"Thank you, child. Not only do I not think you're silly, I appreciate your telling me. I've seen enough proof of your 'feelings' to know that you have a special gift of sensing things most of us can't, and if you sense danger I'm convinced it must be there. But for the time being, I wouldn't worry. The German is wounded and can't hurt anyone. As soon as he's better we'll turn him over to the Americans. Still, keep an eye on him, and if you see anything really suspicious, call Kerry."

"I will. I only wish he had been the one who died yesterday rather than the other, nice German."

"Yes, he was a decent and loyal person, or so he seemed. But remember, Geneviève, he was a German, and probably an officer. Yesterday he was demoralized and depressed, but what would he have been like if he'd arrived at the head of a German battalion and found us housing our wounded paratroopers? Try to remember that, child: never judge men by initial impressions. Now, run off and fetch your father for coffee. And not a word about it to anyone."

She didn't have to tell me twice. Silence and solitude were so much of a second nature with both of us that our motto could have been: "Silence and efficiency." Unhappily for Lieutenant Wingate, for the moment our efficiency was at its low point. We had so few supplies and were so inexperienced. Would he die because we couldn't care for him properly? Mama's chances of reaching Sainte-Mère had to be slight, but I knew that she was right to try.

Down cellar, Papa showed me the fruits of his labor. It was all I could do to keep from laughing at the silly-looking chair, which seemed to be walking on stilts. He had cut out the wicker seat and fastened a makeshift toilet in its place. However grotesque it looked, I realized it was quite practical. My parents' bed was an antique and stood several feet off the floor. Thus Papa's chamber pot, which was exactly the same height as the bed, could be moved right next to George and we could edge him over onto it without moving the broken leg.

Papa and I went back upstairs, where Mama served us coffee. As usual, we drank it in silence. My mind was filled with all sorts of questions I wanted to ask them, but I didn't dare. Why, for instance, was the sound of the booming cannons so much louder today? Did Papa know? I glanced over at him. He seemed more upset and depressed than I had ever seen him. Why? I probably would never know, since he rarely shared his real feelings. But then, out of the blue, as though he were talking to himself, he said:

"He's had it. It's gangrene, I know it."

"Yes, I'm afraid you're right," Mama sighed.

Again I looked over at him. Was it possible that this rough, tough man was so taken by Lieutenant Wingate that he was suffering in a way I had never seen, or even imagined he was capable of? That meant he had a heart, and I had never known it till now. Could he ever forgive me for having been so blind all these years? But then I had learned so many things about him these past three days—only three days?—that I had trouble putting them all together. As soon as I could resume my solitary walks through the countryside I'd think about it some more.

Kerry emerged from the bedroom and sat down between them. He seemed to sense what was upsetting them, and instinctively he put his arms around their shoulders and drew them to him in a filial gesture of affection. Tears were rolling down Mama's cheeks. Kerry began speaking English, and though we couldn't understand the words we knew they were words of comfort.

It was still not daylight, but Mama got to her feet, having decided she would set out right away. My heart began to beat wildly as she began to put on her woolen work clothes. Was I right to let her go? Ten kilometers through all that fighting was a long way. Very long. If she were killed, what would happen to Claude and me? How would we cope in this terrible world of war and fighting? How would we take care of these four wounded soldiers?

I looked at Mama and couldn't figure out why she looked so fat all of a sudden. Then I understood that, in dressing, she must have first put on her town clothes, then slipped her working clothes on over them. That way, after she had finished milking the cows at the Sheepfold, she could slip out of her work clothes and leave them there, picking them up again on her way back from Sainte-Mère-Eglise. Papa would never know the difference. But Mama would never have allowed herself to go to town in her rough work clothes. No matter how poor we were, she always looked clean and neat when she went to town. The same went for us, too: there were always freshly washed and ironed clothes for Claude and me whenever we had to go to town.

I was proud of her. She was ready to literally set out through a battleground, risk her life at every step, but she was not ready to confront her husband's anger. Then I found myself thinking that between the two evils—that of Father's anger or the dangers of war—she may not have been all wrong.

When I could no longer see Mama walking down the tracks I left the window. I took in several deep breaths, to try and calm my anguish. I listened to the wild beating of my heart, but slowly it subsided. I felt calm again. Now to work.

I cleared the table and washed the coffee cups, then prepared breakfast for the wounded. Papa and Kerry were busy with Lieutenant Wingate. I served some black coffee and biscuits to the old German, and despite all my efforts I had great trouble keeping my hand from shaking.

The blond soldier thanked me for the coffee and told me how good it was. It should have been: it was real coffee for a change, thanks to the American rations. After breakfast I changed his bandage, and I could see I had guessed right: the wound was healing, and was no longer bleeding. True, he wouldn't be walking overnight, but in a few days, as soon as the danger of hemorrhage was past, we could move him to a sitting position. I took advantage of the older German's moving to a seat by the fireplace to fluff up the straw mattresses they used for beds. The younger German gave me a broad smile, but it quickly changed to a grimace when he saw me approaching with a bucket of steaming hot water and my washcloth and soap.

I did my best to wash him gently, and when I was finished I scrubbed out the bucket, for it was the only one we had. Then I refilled it with hot water and offered it to the older German, who shook his head and then resumed his meditative pose by the fireplace, his head touching the mantelpiece. Since his arrival, he had

steadfastly refused to wash. I wondered whether he was so dis-
couraged that he didn't care any more to make himself presentable.
But Mama had always taught us that the way you look affects the
way you are, so I made another effort, despite the fear I felt in his
presence. He shook his head more vigorously. Okay, okay. Have it
your way.

I knocked quietly on the bedroom door. My father's gruff voice
told me to come in.

"What do you want?"

I could tell he was in a foul mood. Timidly, I asked:

"I just wondered whether you wanted me to help you wash the
lieutenant."

"I'll tell you when I need you. Close the door when you go out.
And leave the bucket."

I knew better than to argue, so I wasted no time heading for the
door—so fast and so awkwardly, in fact, that I managed to bump my
head against the door frame. Almost immediately, a bump the size
of a goose egg sprouted on my forehead.

Claude was coming downstairs as I appeared, and I met him on
the bottom step and hugged him tightly. He saw my bump and, his
eyes wide, said:

"Did he hit you again?"

I told him that it wasn't Papa, that I had banged my head on the
door frame, but I had a hard time convincing him. I sat him down
and gave him some breakfast, but he only nibbled at it. He seemed
silent and pensive.

"What's wrong, Claude?" I said finally.

"Where's Mama?"

"She's gone to the Sheepfold. She'll be home late, since she's
going to track down the cows that have strayed away and milk
them all. Then she's going to distribute all the milk to the soldiers,
who are hidden all over the place, so it will take her a long time." I
was not a very good liar.

But all my chatter had failed to rouse Claude from his daydreams.
I made another effort to cheer him up.

"Papa and Kerry are washing Lieutenant Wingate. Why don't

you go in and help them." Then despite myself I added with a sigh: "They won't mind your being there."

Claude came over and nestled in my arms.

"Will the war be over today?" he said.

"I'm afraid not. The weather's still so bad that the soldiers who are arriving by boat have probably had trouble making it ashore."

"What if they never come?"

"Never? Don't be silly! The generals who planned the invasion wouldn't give up now, after having sent in their paratroopers. That would be dumb!"

"Of course it would," Claude said. "It would be dumb. And I'm dumb to have thought it!"

"No you're not. You're the nicest little boy I know, and I'm happy you're my little brother."

I held him tight against me.

"If only the war would end," he said. "I want so much to go to school with you, Geneviève."

"You will," I assured him. "Just be patient. School doesn't begin until mid-October anyway, so we have plenty of time."

"How many months yet before school opens?"

"Let's see. This is June. Then there's July, August, and September. Almost four months."

"I know those months," Claude said. "Mama taught them to me. But almost four months is a very long time!"

"No it's not. And besides, as soon as they stop fighting we can go outside again, and then we can play all sorts of games with those pretty parachutes. And do you know what? There's a glider over at the Sheepfold, and we can use it for our own plane. I'll be the pilot and you the radio operator, all right?"

"All right. But first the war has to end."

"Don't worry. Because of the war I won't be going back to school till next fall, so I'll spend all my time with you. Now let's get you dressed. You won't be able to wash up this morning; Papa's using the bucket.

"That's all right, I don't mind," he smiled at me maliciously.

Although he had long been able to dress himself, he clung to the habit of letting me help him. We would play all sorts of games, as his arms disappeared into the sleeves of his shirt, or his feet in his trouser legs, and I could always make him laugh wholeheartedly. But today I had trouble even making him smile. He was worried about Mama's not being there. I was happy he didn't know where she had really gone. Or did he? Did he too possess some sixth sense like mine? If so, he had not breathed a word to me about it. I looked at him admiringly, not only because he seemed so mature for his age, but also because, next to me, who was always emotional, he was a model of calm and levelheadedness. Often, as I was about to commit some folly, he would stop me by saying:

"Don't, Geneviève, you'll only get into trouble."

And usually I'd stop, if only to please him. We were so close, in fact, that if anything happened to one of us, the other suffered. We shared everything: our games, our secrets, our joys and sorrows. Papa never beat him, but I was sure that when he beat me, Claude felt it as much as I did. He often tried to keep Papa from punishing me.

"Please don't, Papa, please don't," he would plead.

"Keep out of this," Papa would say, "this is no business of yours."

At which point Claude would retreat, his head bowed, aware that he was powerless to help.

"Geneviève! Come here!"

It was Papa calling. I ran to the bedroom, careful this time not to hit my head. Papa Maurice handed me the bucket. He had washed and shaved the lieutenant, who managed a weak smile when he saw me. His eyes betrayed the extent of his suffering. My heart went out to him: he was so brave. Since last night, the wounds on his broken leg had become even more infected, and filled the room with a terrible smell. Poor George! If only Mama could make it to town and bring back a doctor before it was too late.

After having fluffed up the pillows, Kerry settled his friend in the center of the bed and rejoined me in the kitchen. He made me understand that he wanted to wash up and shave. I scrubbed out the bucket again and filled it with hot water. He stripped down to the waist and began to wash himself. To keep him from catching cold I added some wood to the fire. I kept looking for chores to do, to make the time pass more quickly. I tried, but I couldn't keep my mind off Mama, wondering where she was and whether she was all right. The time seemed to pass so slowly. The ticktock of the old clock only seemed to make it worse. Finally I couldn't bear it any longer; as Kerry watched, puzzled and intrigued, I went over and stopped the pendulum. Papa would doubtless notice it and start it going again, but even so I figured I would have gained a few precious minutes, or even hours. Poor clock: it isn't your fault.

In any case, my anxiety would have some positive side effects: when Mama came home she'd find the house as neat as a pin. I scrubbed the floor till the tiles shone, washed the windows, and even cleaned the fireplace tiles, which Mama generally only cleaned once a week, on Sunday mornings. The old German soldier watched me manipulate the fireplace tongs with a dexterity I could tell surprised him, as I maneuvered the logs to make the fire burn better. But like the trees and birds, fire is my friend too. I often spend hours staring at it, and I'm always the one who picks and arranges the kindling, when we need to revive the embers or start a new fire. There was a real friendship, a real complicity between us.

Kerry, who was still limping badly, hobbled off to the courtyard and came back with a stack of canned rations for our lunch. I had trouble making him understand that we didn't need them today, that Mama had already cut up a rabbit for me to cook. I wasn't a very good cook yet, but I knew enough from Mama to take over when she was gone. I mentioned to Papa that we didn't have any more vegetables and that we'd need a new supply from the Sheepfold soon. He said he'd take the boat over that afternoon and bring back a new supply.

As he was getting ready to leave, he said to me:

"Take good care of the lieutenant. I'm afraid he's not got very long."

His voice was so choked up when he said it I had trouble finding an answer. Then I said:

"Don't be gone too long, Papa. Your lieutenant needs you. It's easier to die when you have someone you love there beside you."

"How would you know anything about that?" he said gently.

"Yesterday the German officer died in my arms. I felt he was happy that I was with him. He even asked me to sing to him."

"How long did it take him to die?"

"I don't know exactly. Mama and I spent four hours with him, but I don't know how long he'd already been in the swamp before Mama spotted him."

"How badly wounded was he?"

"A bullet in the chest," I said shaking my head. "There's not much you can do about that."

Now it was Papa's turn to shake his head. "Goddamn war," he muttered. "Can't take it anymore!"

And with those words he headed toward his boat. I think if a stray bullet had caught him out on the marshes during the next few minutes, he would have died happy, so distressed was he by the knowledge that his lieutenant was dying.

Claude and I were left alone for several hours to care for our wounded soldiers. At noon, I took in some food to Lieutenant Wingate, scarcely believing he'd touch it, and to my great surprise he ate every last morsel. Seeing the look of amazement on my face, he reached for his French phrase book and said, in French:

"Je ne souffre plus."

He wasn't in pain anymore? What did that mean? Papa hadn't given him any painkillers today, that I knew: the boxes were up on the mantelpiece, and no one had touched them.

I was so happy I called Kerry to witness the minor miracle. His plate was empty, clean as a whistle, and George was asking for a second glass of cider. I couldn't contain myself, and ran back into the kitchen where I picked Claude up in my arms and danced him round and round. With my own personal logic, I told myself that since George was hungry again, his body had overcome the terrible wounds in his leg, and that he was going to be all right. The phrase began resounding in my head, over and over again: "He's going to be all right! He's going to be all right!"

All of a sudden my anxiety vanished. Happiness breeds happiness, and so I was now almost sure that Mama would make it home all right. Automatically, my feelings translated themselves into song.

"Geneviève!" Claude cautioned. "You're going to wake everyone up!"

I thanked him with a big smile. He was right: after lunch, our patients generally fell into a sound sleep, which they all needed. Outside, I could still hear the distant roar of cannons; inside, all was calm and quiet. No matter what was happening beyond the walls of 104, here hope was reborn.

I washed and dried the dishes, then put them carefully away. Time still lay heavy upon us, and to shorten it Claude and I began to play cards. We had barely finished our second hand when I saw in the distance the tiny form that I knew was Mama, striding along briskly up the tracks from the direction of 103. Alone. She had not brought a doctor with her. She came into the kitchen, and I could see by the flush in her cheeks and the gleam in her eye that she had had a successful trip. Claude, who long since had guessed that she had gone on more than a trip to the Sheepfold, rushed over and buried his head in her arms. She lifted him up, hugged him tightly, then turned to me and said:

"How's everything here?"

"Better than you know."

"What does that mean?" she asked.

"George. You'll never believe it, but he ate like a horse. He says he feels better, and I think he's telling the truth."

"I know," Mama said.

"What do you mean, you know?"

A mysterious little smile played about her lips. I had a feeling I understood what had happened.

"You didn't find a doctor," I said, "so you made your own special arrangement with the Good Lord."

It was less a statement than a question. Mama's smile was absolutely malicious.

"Not with the Lord," she said. "With the Virgin Mary."

"Tell me. Right away!"

Faith, I should mention, was part and parcel of our daily lives: God, the Virgin Mary, Jesus, and all the saints were as close and familiar to us as were our flesh-and-blood neighbors and friends. That my mother had made a "deal" with the Virgin Mary struck me as perfectly natural. I sat her down by the fire, and while I reheated her lunch I listened to her story.

"There's not all that much to tell," she said. "I never made it to Sainte-Mère-Eglise. The fighting is still going on there. Some American soldiers stopped me on the road that leads to the Couture farm and took me to an officer who spoke French. He asked me why I was trying to get to town and I explained that I was going in search of a doctor for Lieutenant Wingate. He said that was out of the question. 'The place is still filled with Germans,' he said. 'Actually, we don't really know what the situation is at Sainte-Mère-Eglise. We've lost contact with the paratroopers who landed there and don't even know whether they're still alive.' In fact, he said that he feared the worst, since he suspected that the Germans had machine-gunned most of them before they had even reached the ground. Anyway, the Americans were hoping to set up a field hospital very soon, and as soon as they had he would send someone to pick up George, Kerry, and the two Germans. But for the moment there was nothing he could do."

"So?"

"That's all."

"Don't keep us in suspense any longer, Mama! Tell us how you made it back from the Couture farm. That's a long way."

"The American officer gave me two soldiers to see me safely back as far as 103. If I had been alone, I'd have been back long before now, but with those two youngsters it took us forever. Every time they heard a burst of gunfire, no matter how far away, they made me hide behind some hedges or in the ditch until everything was quiet. It took me twice as long to get back from the farm as it took me to get there. The officer also told me that when he sends the medics he'll try and come himself, too. He's the one who gave me the idea of going to the Virgin Mary with my problem. As I was leaving, he said to me: 'Keep up the good work with your wounded boys, Madame. And pray to the patron saint of your village to help you.' He kissed both my hands and added: 'Thank you for all you've done, Madame. And may God bless you.' There were tears in his eyes, and I could see he was terribly moved.

"On my way home I began thinking, and the more I thought the more I realized that he was right. The Virgin Mary is all powerful, and She would answer my prayers immediately!"

"What prayer?"

"Curious as a cat, aren't you? Well, since you've worked so hard and done such a good job with our patients, I'm going to tell you: if the Holy Mother saves George's life, I'll make an offering of the ribbon of the poor at the next feast day."

"Saint Marguerite's Day?"

"Exactly?"

"And what if the war isn't over?"

"Don't be silly. It will long since be over."

The ribbon of the poor. The humblest yet most fervent offering that anyone can make. In our parish of Neuville-au-Plain, two kilometers from La Fière, the patron saint is Saint Marguerite, who in her earthly life was the poorest of the poor. Each year we paid her homage with a high mass and a feast that lasted long into the night. During the mass the parishioners make an offering of a ribbon, usually blue or white, about a meter and a half long and five to ten centimeters wide. The parish priest blesses them, and the families then lay the ribbon on the statue of Saint Marguerite. This rather special votive offering stays there until the wind and rain have brought it to dust again. I have never heard, in this part of the world, of a request made to the Virgin Mary involving the ribbon of the poor that was not immediately granted.

Knowing that no doctor would come, and strong in her invincible faith, Mama had had the presence of mind to turn in her hour of need to the Holy Mother. Thus she had known, even before I had said anything to her, that George was going to get well. It is said that faith can move mountains. Why can't it overcome gangrene?

We tiptoed into the room where both Americans were sleeping. George's face was relaxed and peaceful. His face was no longer bathed in sweat, the way it had been this morning; he was less pale, and his breathing was more regular. But more striking, the awful smell that had been almost impossible to bear was completely gone. Mama and I exchanged a happy, conspirational look. Now I too was convinced: George was indeed going to make it. I didn't know when or how, but I knew that he had reached the low point and that from here on he would slowly get better.

Suddenly, whether because of our presence or simply because he had slept long enough, George stretched and opened his eyes. He was astonished to see both of us standing motionless next to the bed. Taking both our hands in his—a gesture he would not have had the strength to make that same morning—he murmured:

"Mama . . . Geneviève . . ."

A faint but brave smile crossed his lips. Claude joined us, and I lifted him up so that he could see the lieutenant: He leaned over and gave George a noisy kiss on the cheek. Kerry awoke, slipped out of bed, grabbed his broom-crutch, and hobbled off to the kitchen without a word. He was back a moment later bearing a tall glass of cider, which George downed with obvious pleasure.

Outside, the muffled roar of cannons still echoed, coming from the general direction of Amfreville and Fresville. But we didn't care: all that mattered was that George was going to get better.

I asked my mother for permission to go outside in a little while to wait for Papa Maurice at the gate.

"I want to be the first one to tell him that George is better. Papa's so upset about George. I'm sure he went over to the Sheepfold simply because he couldn't bear seeing George die."

But Mother wouldn't hear of it. She repeated that I was not to go out under any pretext. If I disobeyed, Papa would be furious. "Besides," she added, "he may have been drinking."

I shook my head. I knew what she was referring to. In the cellar at the Sheepfold were two big barrels; each of them contained eighteen hundred liters of cider. One was what we call "pure juice," which was strong stuff, with a high alcoholic content; the other, cut with water, served as our everyday drink. A few snorts of the former was all Papa needed to sink into a state of semi-drunkenness, when he became horribly aggressive. Mama was right: there was no point running the risk of upsetting him unnecessarily.

Late that afternoon I heard his thick voice calling me. I could tell he was in a foul temper.

"Geneviève! Come here and help me unload the boat."

Under normal conditions he would have unloaded the boat himself, but since his seventy-two-hour stint in the marshes his hands were swathed in bandages. I went outside, remembering to hug the wall, for the Germans had taken to opening fire as soon as someone emerged from 104, if only for target practice.

The boat was loaded down with food: Papa had picked great quantities of vegetables, plus a pail of milk, a basket of eggs, an old chicken, and a couple of rabbits. The prow of the boat was virtually hidden by two huge bales of hay, which I was sure he had brought back for Mama and him to sleep on. It would be more comfortable than the simple blanket on the floor which had served as their bed these past several nights. He had also brought back an ample supply of wood for the fireplace, at least half a cord, for our supply had dwindled badly.

Silently I helped Papa unload. My tongue was burning to tell him the good news, but I didn't dare. Seeing me pick up one of the bales of hay, he said:

"That's too much for a skinny lass like yourself."

That unusual display of thoughtfulness gave me the courage to blurt out the news:

"We have a surprise for you, Papa."

I could see that I had aroused his curiosity.

"What surprise?"

"George is better," I said, the words tumbling out. "You'll see. This noon he ate everything on his plate."

Without pausing in his labors he said tonelessly:

"The remission before death." He had trouble getting the words out.

I had heard the expression before. Often, shortly before they die, people have a period of several hours, or even days, when they seem to experience a miraculous recovery, as though their body has, for inexplicable reasons, pulled itself together. I knew that wasn't the case with George, but Papa didn't.

"You're wrong, Papa. Mama tried to make it to Sainte-Mère-Eglise to fetch a doctor, but she was turned back. So she made a vow on her way back home, and her prayers were answered. It's as simple as that!"

Papa set the big pail of milk down on the ground and looked at me strangely as though he hadn't really absorbed what I had said. He stared at me hard, with his catlike eyes, and I could feel the fear that I had just conquered welling up in me again. His look was fierce and full of wrath.

"If you're lying . . ." he began, and there was no need for him to finish the sentence.

"Go see for yourself," I managed, trying my best to conceal my terror. "I can finish unloading. Anyway, with your hands you shouldn't be carrying these things."

But he just stood there, staring at me.

"Go on. What are you waiting for?"

Then he let go of the milk pail and ran, faster than I have ever seen him move, toward the kitchen. Later, Mama described the scene to me when Papa entered the bedroom. George was awake, and Papa dashed over to the bed, took the lieutenant's hands in his peasant paws, dropped to his knees, and began to sob, his head buried in the pillow. George gently withdrew one of his hands and patted Papa on the head like a little child, saying:

"Papa Maurice, Papa Maurice . . ."

Papa finally regained his composure and pulled a chair up to the bed; he was sitting there silently, still clutching the lieutenant's hand, until well after dark. He couldn't dare believe that the miracle had really occurred. And yet there it was, right before his eyes.

If further proof were needed, Mama prepared for supper that night a big kettle of cabbage soup, topped with *crème fraîche,* and Papa himself took the steaming bowl in to George, who devoured it to the last drop.

Mama gave us permission to stay up later than usual that night, but Papa didn't even seem to notice. When finally we headed up to our room, Mama accompanied us, and as we crossed the kitchen she noticed that the younger German had tossed his covers off. With the same gentle and maternal gesture that she would have used for her own children, she pulled both the parachute that served as sheet and the coarse woolen blanket back over him. I couldn't suppress a look of love and admiration, which she saw.

"Yes, my child, war is for men. We women are made to love." And then, so softly that I hardly heard it, she added: "And to suffer, too."

Again tonight, Claude left his own bed and crawled in with me. My bed was really too narrow for us both, but when we snuggled close it was all right. And besides, we were warmer that way. That night our prayers were filled not with requests but thanks for George's miracle. But we finished with a fervent prayer for all the wounded soldiers, starting with Kerry but including all those, on both sides, who were in pain and suffering that night. They'll never know, all those soldiers, how hard we prayed for them the night of June 8, 1944.

As I was falling asleep, Claude suddenly asked:

"Geneviève, explain to me how a prayer works. When we ask God for something, how does He make it work?"

"I don't really know," I said. "Or maybe I do. Let me give you one example. When the two German soldiers arrived, I saw right away that the young one—the blond—was losing blood so fast that he would die unless we found some way to stop the bleeding. So I prayed, very hard, and almost before I had finished Mama got up and went outside and picked several wild herbs out on the embankment. She crushed them and applied them to the wound, and in a few minutes the bleeding had stopped. That's how it works."

"Didn't it make you jealous that you'd done the praying and Mama got the credit?"

"Not really. I'm not jealous, at least not anymore."

"You used to be?"

"Yes, but I paid dearly for it."

"Tell me about it."

"All right. But then you must go to sleep. One day, before the Germans flooded the marshes, I was walking beside the river and a piece of bread from my afternoon snack fell into the water. A big fat fish jumped out of the water and grabbed it. I found him funny, so I tossed in another piece of bread. And again he snapped it up. I ended up giving him my entire snack. After that, for several days running, I went back to the riverbank and fed him my snack. But as soon as he'd finished he'd swim away into the reeds. I was jealous that he was so clever and such a good swimmer, and that he'd never stay with me after the snack was gone, so one day I decided I was as good as he was, and I jumped in the water to find him. Only I'd forgotten I didn't know how to swim, and I almost drowned. Since then, no more jealousy for me!"

"That's a terrible story. I can't bear to think that you almost drowned. You'll never do it again, will you?"

"Don't worry! I'd be too afraid to try anything as silly as that ever again."

And on that happy note, nestled in each other's arms, we fell asleep, happy to be alive, happy in the knowledge that George was not only alive, too, but that he was, without any doubt, going to get better.

Friday, June 9, 1944

Yesterday the birds didn't sing. Will it be the same today? I looked out the attic window at the endless expanse of water that surrounded us. Today was as gray and sad as yesterday. What had happened to the sun, which usually at this time of year turns our marshes into a veritable fairyland? The waters shine the minute there's a bit of sunshine over by *Noires Terres,* iridescent, full of tender colors, and the marshes are a beehive of activity: ducks, geese, myriad other water fowl strike up a chorus that lasts most of the morning. Later the sparrows join in, and other melodious creatures of the swamp. Papa said that it was unusual to hear such a chorus, that it was because guns had been banned by the Germans and there had been no hunters for so long that the birds had a sense of security. Now the hunters are back, looking not for game but for other men, but the result is the same: the birds have stilled their voices, terrorized by the unaccustomed gunfire echoing day and night through the swamp.

What will today bring? Will we live to see the end of it? Will the invasion finally occur, and reinforcements arrive to take the increasing pressure off the paratroopers who've been here four days and nights now? These questions ran through my head as I pulled on my clothes that morning.

There was something else: I felt danger, and it was closer than before. I tried to listen closely to the sounds, both in the house and outside, trying to detect what it might be.

I went downstairs with a sick feeling in the pit of my stomach—a knot that I could not control. Four bowls of steaming coffee were lined up on the table, and their aroma filled the kitchen with a wonderful odor. But I knew that I couldn't eat or drink: I was too upset. As casually as I could, I asked my mother, who was buttering some pieces of bread:

"How are our patients this morning?" Then, before she answered, seeing a big mound of what looked like freshly made butter, I said: "Did you make butter this morning? I didn't hear the butter churn." We had a churn which made marvelous butter but which also made a horrible grating noise as the blades turned and meshed. The noise is so loud it could wake the dead, but I had not heard it that morning.

"Yes, Francis had taken the cream off the milk that we hadn't used these past couple of days, and Papa had the good idea to bring it home last night. I churned it down in the cellar, so as not to wake anyone up. As for our patients, George, Kerry, and the blond German all slept like logs. But the older German coughed most of the night."

"So that's why you made the butter!"

"Yes and no. We'll all benefit from it."

I knew that butter was a wonderful remedy to stop coughing. If you drink a hot bowl of milk in which a spoonful of butter has been melted, your coughing will stop ten minutes after you've drunk it. And if you repeat the remedy once a day, the cough will go away. Despite the cold and dampness of the marshes in winter, and of frequent forays into the cold water itself, we never have colds or coughs because of that concoction. In our family, which boasts many sailors on both sides, we call it "spreading oil on water," the analogy being to the maritime habit of using oil to calm stormy waters at sea. In any case, it was a remedy that had worked for all of us without exception through the years.

The Germans must have had to wade through the swamp on their way to 104, and the older one had caught a bad cold. Tomorrow, thanks to Mama's medicine, he'd be as good as new.

"Did he take it without grumbling?"

"Yes, in fact he even gave me what might be taken as a smile."

"Only you have the power to tame an old bear like that one!"

She asked me to help serve breakfast to the patients. If she'd prepared breakfast, that meant she had already changed their bandages.

"By the way," she said, "yesterday you bandaged the young German too tightly."

A bandage can't be too loose, in which case it slips off, or too tight, in which case it prevents proper circulation. She said she would show me the right degree of tightness next time she changed his bandage.

"That way you'll remember by seeing it done."

"By the time the next war comes along I ought to be a good nurse, don't you think, Mama?" I said.

"There won't be any 'next war', " she said. "This will be the last one."

I shook my head. How could she think or say such a thing? No more wars?

"Did you study the history of France at school?"

"Of course I did," she said. "Why?"

I couldn't believe Mama was so naïve. The whole history of France is one long succession of wars, each more murderous than the last. And if you go back and study early history, it's the same thing. I'd read my Bible, and the Old Testament was also filled with awful wars. Hitler was perhaps the devil, but he hadn't invented anything: Joshua had wiped out the city of Jericho thousands of years before.

I was only eleven, but I had already read and seen enough not to believe those rosy stories about the glorious future of the world. Adults are wrong to treat children as though they were inferior, as though all they did all day long was eat and sleep and play. Children have minds, too, and can see what adults try to hide from them. If I were to pile up all the "whys" that I formulated in my head in my eleven years, they'd form a pyramid that would reach to the clouds.

Why do men have to go about killing each other? Why are there wars? Why are there families in which children are loved, and others where they're not? Aren't children all the same, weak and willing and in need of guidance and love? Why are the clouds so beautiful here in Normandy? Why is the earth so sad when the sun refuses to shine? Why do some men live while others die? And, above all, why is my stomach all tied up in knots this morning, warning me of some danger I can't define or pinpoint?

"You seem very pensive this morning," my mother said.

"I have all sorts of thoughts going through my head," I said. "Can I take George his breakfast, then Kerry?"

"You like those two a lot, don't you," she said.

"Yes, and so does Claude."

She nodded toward the two Germans lying on their beds of straw and said:

"And what about them? Do you like them too?"

"I don't know. I don't wish them any harm. I'm happy to take care of them, to nurse them back to health, but like them . . ."

"You ought to, you know."

"They're Germans!"

"Someday you're going to have to forgive them in your heart," Mama said. "So why not right away?"

"After all the awful things they've done to us? All the deaths they're responsible for? You want me to forget all that? Can Bernadette forget that because of them she no longer has a mother?"

"Who's talking about forgetting? We haven't the right to forget, but we can and must forgive. Maybe you have to be a little older to understand."

"I've thought about all that. The only thing that matters is that nothing happens to you, and to little Claude."

"Are you afraid?"

Caught off guard by her question, I blushed to the tips of my ears. Then I said, shyly:

"Yes, I have one of those bad feelings. I sense some danger."

She gave me a long hard look, but said nothing.

Kerry woke up, but when I offered him his coffee in bed he

shook his head. I understood that he wanted to get up and have his breakfast at the table, with us. George was not only looking better but feeling better than yesterday, and as I looked at his face, which had good color, and his eyes, which looked alive again, I silently offered up a prayer of thanks: "Thank You, God, for this miracle."

Mama announced that she was going over to milk the cows again, leaving me in charge. Despite the enormity of the events taking place all around us, there was a comforting regularity to the tasks and chores that filled our waking hours.

Claude finally woke up and came downstairs, and I gave him his breakfast, thinking at the same time I'd invite Papa to have a cup of coffee too. I found him down cellar, hard at work on another strange construction.

"It's for the lieutenant," he said. "I'll give it to him as soon as he's ready to start walking."

I looked more closely and saw that he was making him a pair of crutches. Partly to please him, I suggested that when he had finished the crossbar I'd be happy to pad it with soft cloth so it would be more comfortable under the arms.

"You mean to tell me you know how to sew?"

"Of course I do. Mama teaches me a lot of things. But to tell the truth, I'd much prefer doing carpentry with you."

"Carpentry? You're crazy. That's not a girl's work."

"I don't care. I'd still like to learn it."

"Here, give it a try," he said, handing me his plane. "See if you can plane down that piece of wood."

A bit clumsily, I tightened the plank of wood in the vise and . . . Papa Maurice burst out laughing, delighted to see that I was too short to reach the top of the plank.

"Better start eating more," he said.

I wasn't beaten yet. In one corner of the cellar stood a wooden box that had contained hand grenades. I pulled it over to the vise, adjusted what remained of the top, and climbed on top of it.

"You see, I *am* tall enough!"

Papa Maurice allowed me to make several passes with the plane; then he stepped over and gently lifted my elbow ever so slightly.

"More supple," he said, "with the arm, and more supple with the wrist, too. It'll make the work easier. There, that's the way. Not bad. You do have some talent, child."

He ran his fingers over the piece of wood I had planed down and murmured: "Not bad at all, not bad at all."

"I like wood, Papa."

"You do? That's what I like most in the world. Wood."

"Will you teach me?"

"We'll see, when school's out for the summer. If I have the time. First learn to read and write. That's more important than anything else." I could tell by his tone of voice that his failure ever to learn to read and write still weighed heavy on him, and I quickly tried to change the subject.

"Claude wants you to come up and have breakfast with him. He's been complaining he never sees you anymore."

He smiled and put down his tool. When his son called, he responded.

Over coffee he looked at me and for the first time in my life asked me:

"What do you want to be when you grow up, Geneviève?"

"An airplane pilot," I said without hesitation.

"What a crazy idea. That's not a woman's job either."

"Of course it is. There are lots of women pilots: Maryse Bastié, Maryse Hilze, Hélène Boucher . . ."

"How do you know that?"

"I read books about them."

"I'll never have enough money to pay for your studies too much longer," he said. "You'd better give up the idea."

If I had dared, I would have responded that I wasn't counting on him to pay anything for me. But certain truths are better left unsaid, if you want to keep peace in the family.

"Don't worry about me," I ventured. "I'll make out all right. I'm just as stubborn as you are."

I could see my remark amused him. It was true we were alike in many ways. I have his eyes, his violent temper, his emotionalism, his love of solitude and the outdoors. But what I wanted to avoid at all costs was to resemble him morally. So I fought against it, as hard as I could. Yet I had to admit that during the past few days my image of him had grown less harsh. I had seen him give of himself wholeheartedly, risk his life to save others: he had really acted heroically. I had discovered that he was capable of caring about the suffering of others, and had seen him cry over someone he cared for.

My parents heroes? It didn't surprise me about my mother. Self-denial and sacrifice were so much a part of any peasant woman's role, especially when it came to bringing up children. Heroism quickly becomes a habit. But Papa, the "Old Man," the drunk, whom I had so hated and so misjudged? As Mama says, beware of initial impressions.

I watched this man, this hero, playing with my little brother, and suddenly I was overcome with emotion. I got up and kissed him. He looked at me oddly, trying to figure out what had come over me.

"I like you a lot, Papa," I said.

He blushed and turned his head away. My sudden declaration must have affected him more deeply than I had expected, or than he wanted to show. Had I, without meaning to, discovered the chink in that impregnable armor?

Mama came back, carrying a big pail of milk. It was almost noon, and I had set the table and prepared lunch. Mama complimented me, something she rarely did, apparently because she didn't want me to become spoiled and because she was afraid I wouldn't be able to tell sincere from false compliments if I received them too readily.

We took turns taking care of the wounded, but Papa reserved for himself the task of serving and caring for George, who was without question our spoiled child. Mama helped me hoist the younger German into a sitting position on his makeshift bed, and we slipped a thick eiderdown behind his back, so he could eat comfortably. His color was coming back and he too seemed well on the road to recovery. Kerry and the older German took their lunch at the table. I noticed that they barely exchanged a word. Clearly, Kerry didn't like him any more than we did. His sour face was enough to turn off even the amiable American.

After lunch, Mama helped Kerry back into the bedroom, despite his protests that he wanted to remain with us in the kitchen. But according to Mama's hospital routine, patients rested after meals, and on that she was intractable. Seeing that Kerry was slow to obey, she scowled at him ferociously, which made him laugh with equal intensity. He grabbed Mama and gave her a big kiss on the neck, as though she were his own mother, and disappeared into the bedroom, trailing laughter as he went.

With our four patients safely asleep, we sipped our coffee quietly, and except for the distant rumble of cannons it would have seemed a perfectly normal and peaceful day. But suddenly I sensed that something was wrong, and the knot in my stomach became even tighter. Papa had seen someone approaching along the tracks, from the direction of 103. He didn't seem to be wounded, and he was walking quickly and surely. Papa went into the bedroom, borrowed George's binoculars, and began following the man's progress towards us. Not saying a word but his face mirroring his clear discontent, he came back to the table and continued sipping his coffee.

"What is it?" Mama asked.

"A kraut."

"Is he armed?"

"Not that I can see. But you never know."

"Oh, he can't do us any great harm. Even if his intentions aren't the best, he'll see right away that we're good, decent people who wouldn't harm anyone."

Pointing to the two sleeping Germans, she added:

"Besides, he wouldn't dare harm us. Who'd look out for his two comrades?"

Despite her reassuring words, the knot in my stomach refused to dissolve. I tried to take a good deep breath.

"Should I wake up Kerry?" I said. "He has a rifle."

"You keep out of this," Papa said abruptly. "I can take care of this without any help."

More to keep my hands and mind busy than for any other reason,

I poured some more coffee for both my parents. As I poured Mama's, her eyes met mine, and I could read in them both indecision and anxiety. She too was afraid; yet she was smiling.

Our house is the only one in the area, so there was no way he could pass us by. Papa opened the door and stood there waiting for our visitor, while we huddled a step or two behind. It was, indeed, a German soldier who entered our courtyard, and we could see his face turn red with rage as he saw the stockpile of American ammunition. He walked among the cases, touching first one and then another.

"You there," Papa called out bravely, "come over here."

The soldier gazed at him with undisguised arrogance, but Papa refused to be intimidated. In a voice clothed with authority he said:

"Leave the cases alone and come over here!"

The German seemed to understand French. He hesitated for a moment at the entrance to the little courtyard, but Mama gestured behind her at the two German soldiers who were fast asleep and put her finger to her lips. He couldn't see very clearly what she was pointing at, but finally he did come into the kitchen and seemed amazed to see two compatriots peacefully sleeping there.

Thinking it was a wise thing to do, I offered him a cup of coffee, but he brushed me aside and began shaking the older German roughly. The soldier jumped to his feet and they both began to talk heatedly in their own language. They walked over to the door and looked out at the pile of ammunition, their discussion growing more and more animated. Then the German who had just arrived turned back to us and said in French, his voice filled with anger and hate:

"You will tell me immediately which villages are in the hands of the American paratroopers." He looked at my father as he said it, but Papa didn't bat an eye.

"You out of your mind, boy?" Papa countered. "If you think I'm going to tell where the Americans are, you're crazy as a loon."

"I demand that you tell me without delay!"

The German didn't know who it was he was ordering about. I

knew there were going to be fireworks. After the second order, Papa suddenly jumped on the German, grabbed him with his big peasant hands, and twisted the German's arms behind his back.

"In this house, Papa Maurice gives the orders," he said. "You're going to behave just like all our other guests. And if you don't I'll see you stop giving dumb orders once and for all, if you understand me, my fine feathered friend!"

Suddenly collapsing onto a chair, the German's tone became soft and conciliatory. "Please understand me, Monsieur, I'm a soldier, and all I want to do is rejoin my regiment."

Papa released his arms. "I don't care what you want to do, young man. For you the war is over. You're staying right here."

"No, Monsieur, the war's not over. I can still do my country some good. Please let me go."

"You're not so arrogant now, are you, boy? You're no longer ordering, you're asking. At least that's a step in the right direction. So you think we should let you go? Why? So that you can incite your buddies to open fire on us. What do you take me for, an idiot? Haven't you done enough mischief already? You and the whole German army must have rocks in your heads!"

The German pointed to the cup of coffee I had offered him a few minutes before. "Do you mind?" he said.

Mama nodded. He drank his coffee in silence. Then he helped the older German back on the bed. I watched them, and found it odd how warmly they clasped each other's hands: there was no warmth in either of their hearts, that I knew.

Before we knew it, the new arrival had made a dash for the door and began running as fast as his legs would carry him in the direction of Fresville. Taken by surprise, Papa hesitated for a moment or two before reacting; then he realized that the man's sudden departure posed a deadly threat to all of us. He ran into the bedroom and grabbed Kerry's rifle, then raced out to the tracks, but the German was already a long way off. I knew Papa well enough to be sure that he could have caught up with him, but first he would see if he could bring him back with a warning shot. But Kerry's rifle wasn't loaded. So Papa put it down, ran down cellar, and emerged moments later with a hand grenade. He drew back his arm, but then lowered it, and walked back sadly to the house.

"I've never killed anyone," he said, "not even a kraut. I just can't bring myself to throw this grenade at him with his back turned."

"You're right," Mama said in an effort to comfort him. "Just because they act like bastards doesn't mean we have to too." And then she added, under her breath: "God willing."

She had no idea how prophetic her words were. In any case, by nightfall we had put him out of our minds and were gathered around the fire making small talk. Kerry and Claude were playing their endless game of cards. Suddenly Papa cut in and said:

"Keep quiet, all of you."

Everyone fell silent, and I could see in the bedroom that George had propped himself up on one elbow. In the distance we heard the dull roar of a plane. That was all: nothing but an airplane. Mama went back to her sewing, and I continued rolling into little balls the strips of sheets that would serve as tomorrow's bandages. Papa returned to his post next to George's bed.

The roar of the plane grew louder, and I could see Mama and Papa exchange knowing looks. Without saying a word, they both got up. Mama turned out the kerosene lamp on the table. Kerry and Claude protested that they couldn't see to play cards, but Mama silenced them.

Papa snuffed out the kitchen lamp. Then he went outside and closed all the shutters. With a piece of blanket, Mama covered the door window that had no shutters. Papa came back inside and resumed his post beside George's bed.

"That plane, coming in low, smells of a rat," he said. "I have a feeling it's looking for something specific, and I have a feeling that something is us."

Just then the older German sat up in bed and began to shout: *"Kaput! Vous kaput!"*

So he knew that the plane was coming in search of us. Papa jumped up, strode over to where the German was sitting, and gave him a one-two slap across the face. The blond German suddenly awoke, saw what was happening, and demanded to know why Papa was abusing his comrade. The two Germans began talking a mile a minute in their own language; then the blond began to sob.

Papa came back to the bed. "The cases of ammunition in the courtyard," he said, "that's what they're after. There's no moon out tonight. With a little luck, they might miss their target. But let's not count on luck alone. No noise, and no light. Mama, you keep an eye out for the fires in the fireplace. They're just right the way they are: I looked outside, and there's no smoke. Just make sure you add the right sticks of wood."

Papa was right: small logs, neither too thick nor too damp. But Mama knew how to make a perfect fire as well as he did. Still, I thought, there was no way they could miss us: the house was painted an ocher color, which must have stood out like a bright spot in the darkness.

The seconds ticked away slowly; each seemed hours long. The blond German was still crying, knowing that death was stalking him, stalking all of us; and the irony was that his own people were trying to kill him.

A sharp whistle broke the silence, and a heavy explosion nearby shook the house. The first bomb. It had fallen in the marshes, but it hadn't missed us by all that much.

"One down," Papa murmured between clenched teeth.

"What's going on?" Claude asked him.

"A kraut plane is up there trying to find us, my boy. He wants to kill us dead. But don't worry. All your mother has to do is pray to *her* God and everything will be all right."

I couldn't tell whether he was joking or being serious. Was it possible that since George's miraculous recovery Papa was beginning to believe in God?

Silence. The only sounds were the menacing throb of the plane overhead and the sniffling of the German in the corner. Finally, the older German, presumably to lend courage to his cowardly comrade, stood up, thrust his right arm toward the ceiling and shouted:

"Heil Hitler!"

The savage cry rang through the silent house. That was too

much for Papa: he went red as a beet, walked over to the German, picked him up, and threw him down on the straw mattress.

"One more remark like that and I'll throw you down head first on the floor!" he snarled.

The German lay there rubbing his ankle, which had been on the mend till now, but which he must have hurt again when Papa threw him down.

A second bomb, then a third fell in close succession. I put down what I was doing and took little Claude on my lap. Every time another bomb exploded he buried his head in my chest. Several minutes went by without a bomb, and Claude raised his head and asked, his big blue eyes fixed on mine:

"Are we all going to die, Geneviève?"

I lowered my head and whispered in his ear, so that no one else could hear:

"I think so, my love. He may miss us several times but I think in the end he'll get us."

"Are you afraid?"

"A little bit. But it's not as bad as it might be, since we're all together."

"Hold me tight, Geneviève. I want you to be holding me tight when I die."

I hugged him as tightly as I could. Just then a bomb hit the tracks nearby, and the whole house seemed to lift from its foundation, and tremble as much as we were. Could it be that the house was afraid too?

"Tell me, Geneviève, do you think God's going to take both of us? Together?"

"Of course He is. He knows how much we love each other, so He wouldn't want to separate us."

"And Mama too? And the wounded soldiers? Even poor George, who's finally getting better? That's terrible!"

"Maybe He won't take any of us. That pilot up there seems to be dumb as dishwater, or blind as a bat, or both. He seems to be hitting everything but the house. Try to go to sleep now. Don't think about what's happening."

"Geneviève."

"Yes."

"Can I ask you to tell me what you were going to give me for my sixth birthday?"

"Claude! You know that's a secret. Your birthday's not till September 30th. You'll have to wait till then."

"But since we're all going to die . . ."

Claude knew that I had been taking numerous, secret trips to the cellar, and whenever he had asked to go with me I had refused, saying: "You can't come, Claude. I'm making you your birthday present." Birthdays were sacred, and presents only opened on the day itself, but under the circumstances I thought I'd better not deny him this one last pleasure.

"All right," I said. "I found a big, thick fir beam that fell off a freight train, and I've been making you a hobby horse out of it. Carving it myself. When it's finished, you can ride it either with or without wheels."

"Whatever gave you that idea?"

"Someone had drawn a beautiful horse on the beam itself: all I did was follow the drawing."

The roar of the plane warned us that it was back, and the whistle of a falling bomb warned us he was not far from the mark. Another bomb exploded close by, again right on the tracks, and again the house trembled. I hugged Claude even tighter. By the fireplace, Mama's head was buried in her hands, and I knew she was praying hard. Papa was sitting motionless beside George's bed, holding one of the lieutenant's hands in his.

The minutes passed, and no sound of the plane could be heard. Could it have run out of bombs? How many did those planes carry? The supply couldn't have been inexhaustible.

"Geneviève, what would happen if the bomb hit the stock of ammunition in the courtyard?"

"There'd be an enormous explosion," she said, "and all of us, the house included, would be blown straight to heaven. Where we are now there'd be nothing but a huge hole."

"Would the people in Sainte-Mère-Eglise hear the explosion?"

"Of course they would. Everyone for miles around would hear it. But don't worry: I think the plane has run out of bombs."

I was wrong. A burst of lightning tore the air, but it was further away this time, well down the tracks toward 103. Then another, followed quickly by a third, made me think that the pilot had given up and was letting his bombs fall more or less at random along the tracks. But now Mama, who had been a model of calm, began to tremble, and I couldn't figure out why till I realized she was concerned about Francis at the Sheepfold, which wasn't far from 103.

The sound of the plane's motor diminished little by little till we could hear it no more. But no one dared to go to bed. How did we know it wouldn't come back? So we stayed there, as if frozen in some strange tableau, throughout the night, until the first light of dawn convinced us that our nightmare was truly over.

Saturday, June 10, 1944

We had had our share of surprises over the past five days, but looking out the window that Saturday morning we could hardly believe our eyes. The bombs had knocked over telephone poles like matchsticks; the railroad tracks, both in the direction of 103 and of Fresville, were twisted and broken, rising from the scooped-out roadbed like so many crippled arms. In the marshes the bombs had traced a necklace of huge holes, and the water, normally so placid, made strange and constantly changing whirlpools. The wonder was that the bombs had fallen within a radius of less than a hundred meters from the house, forming an almost perfect circle of which we were the hub. How could he have missed us? And how could he have formed such a perfect pattern around us? It seemed miraculous. Papa, Kerry, Mama, Claude, and I gazed out at the pattern in silence. Claude and I exchanged looks. Then Papa said to Mama, shaking his head in undisguised wonder:

"You can tell your God that I take my hat off to Him."

"Nobody's keeping you from passing on the message yourself."

Papa shrugged and went into the house. The old German, for obvious reasons, kept even more to himself; and we made no effort to help him further. After yesterday's events, Papa had made up his mind to ask the American headquarters to send us an armed guard. He hopped on his bicycle and set off along the roadbed, zigzagging as he went to avoid the incessant fire from the Germans entrenched in the Château d'Amfreville. We watched him with our hearts beating fast, expecting at any moment to see him drop from his bicycle. But again, miraculously, he wove his way through the hail of fire until we could see him no more.

When he returned several hours later he brought with him bad news. The paratroopers were virtually out of ammunition, and in some places had had to resort to hand-to-hand combat. The fiercest fighting was going on at the Patte d'oie de Cauquigny. We were told that General Gavin and General Ridgway had set up headquarters not far away, but he and the men there knew they were goners unless help arrived very soon, in a matter of hours, in fact.

"Didn't the American officer who stopped in at 104 tell you about the ammunition and rations I fished out of the swamp?" Papa had asked them.

Apparently the officer had never made it through, killed by German crossfire before he could arrive at headquarters. The Americans found Papa's story hard to believe: ten tons of munitions and five tons of rations? But even if Papa's figures were slightly exaggerated, the results of his salvage operations would give them more food and material than they needed.

"They'll be here any minute to pick up the cases," Papa finished.

And indeed within minutes the stepped-up German fire announced the Americans' arrival. The soldiers gazed in wonder at the piles in the courtyard, and at the necklace of bomb craters circling the house. For most of the day the soldiers carried on their backs the contents of the cases. It pained us to see what those tall, smiling, happy-go-lucky soldiers who had first set foot in our house five days before had become; their eyes were circled with fatigue, their faces pale and sallow, covered by a several-day stubble. The laughter had been drained from them by the terrible days they had lived through. What was more, although they were determined to fight to the finish, they had to have felt that they had been abandoned, that the hoped-for reinforcements would never arrive. For the first time in my life I felt angry at being young, too young to help them. I would have loved to join them, to care for them and nurse them and, if necessary, to hold their hands when they were wounded or dying. But I knew there was nothing I or any of us at 104 could do to help them anymore.

Five P.M.

Up in my room, armed with George's binoculars, I could see in the distance an Indian file of soldiers walking along the high hedge that borders the Big Swamp, bent low, moving with infinite caution. Who were they and where were they headed? I strained, and as one of the last in line suddenly straightened up for a moment I shouted:

"Germans!"

They were doubtless coming from the Château d'Amfreville, and it looked as though they were heading towards Cauquigny. I knew that the soldiers transporting Papa's ammunition had not yet had time to reach Cauquigny, that they had stopped off at a farm not far from 103. The Americans occupying the Cauquigny Chapel were an outpost, and the Germans were heading for them. Unless they could be warned somehow, they would be massacred on the spot, for they had nothing but their knives and bayonets to hold off the German column.

What could I do? What could any of us do? Suddenly I had an idea: Papa Maurice. By using the back roads, he could ride his bicycle and, with a little luck, reach the chapel before the Germans got there. If he warned them in time, they could at least take some measures to receive the Germans properly, or perhaps abandon the chapel and retreat to safer quarters.

I had a moment's hesitation. I'd forgotten who I was, only a girl of eleven. Besides, if I called Papa, I'd be obliged to admit that I had borrowed the lieutenant's binoculars without asking permission. That was good for at least a slap across the face. Too bad! I raced down the stairs two at a time.

"Mama! Mama! Where's Papa?"

Without waiting for her to reply I ran down cellar and grabbed him by the sleeve. I dragged him after me without saying a word. Finally I caught my breath enough to say:

"Hurry!" I pointed out towards the Big Marsh, then repeated: "Hurry!"

We rushed up the cellar stairs and as soon as we reached the top Papa grabbed the binoculars and looked where I had pointed.

"Goddamn! The dirty bastards! They're going to attack our boys!"

"Let me go with you, Papa! There's going to be a battle, and the boys will need a nurse. I've learned a lot. I'll scrape up every last bandage I can find and bring it with me. But please let me go!"

He looked at me with a new interest. "All right, girl, go on. I'm going on ahead. But first you'd better ask your mother for permission."

"What if she says no?"

"Let your conscience be your guide, child."

"O.K. I'm going. I'll meet you there. Are you taking the bicycle?"

"Of course. It's my only chance. I may not make it to the chapel, but I'll try. Along the way I'll try to warn the soldiers stationed at the farm near 103. The ammunition is stocked in the barn there."

"Have they taken everything you fished out of the swamp?"

"Almost. There's still enough left for one or two more trips for those six-man crews."

"Shall we get started, Papa?"

"Yes. And along the way try praying to your God. You're going to need it, and so are the soldiers over there. And in case we don't see each other again, good luck, my girl."

"Good luck, Papa." I grabbed him and hugged him for the first time in my life with what I can call real pleasure. We both went downstairs and Papa, without saying anything to Mama, went directly outside, took his bicycle, and began pedaling furiously towards 103. I tried to stay calm, but I couldn't: I knew I had to tell Mama, and I knew it wasn't going to be easy.

"Mama, hurry up and give me everything we have left that can serve as bandages. I'm going to Cauquigny with Papa. There will be a lot of wounded soldiers there in a little while."

"What are you talking about, child?"

"There's a group of Germans making their way there right now, along the edge of the swamp. We saw it through George's binoculars. The Americans stationed at the chapel are out of ammunition. It's going to be a slaughter. Please now, Mama, hurry!"

"You're not setting foot outside this house!"

"Oh yes I am! Papa said I could!"

"Children have no place on battlefields. War is for grownups."

"You're afraid I might be killed? Is that it? Well, I don't care! I prefer to die over there with those soldiers than go on living in a family that treats me like a dog!"

I don't lose my temper very often, but when I do I lose it completely. Before Mama could recover from my outburst, I ran into the bedroom. George asked me what we were arguing about. I opened the closet, grabbed some sheets, and dashed to the door again.

Too late! Mama had shut it and was blocking it with her body.

"Geneviève, listen to me. Calm down . . ."

"I don't have time to."

"Please, Geneviève, listen to me."

"Mama, do you want me to get *really* angry?"

Mama knew that my temper tantrums were uncontrollable, although infrequent. And when I wanted to, I took on great strength, more than enough to push my mother aside. I made one last attempt to persuade her:

"Mama, what was the point of saving all those boys from drowning if we're going to abandon them now? If you had one sound reason for preventing me from going I'd obey you, but the fact is that you don't. Don't go telling me I'm too young. I'm as old as you are! That shouldn't come as any surprise to you, if you think about it: what have you ever done to try and make my life easier when Papa goes after me? All you do is cry in your corner!"

I knew I'd gone further than I should, and Mama's tears were flowing down her cheeks, but I couldn't help it; my anger filled my entire being. Even her tears didn't move me. The thought that our boys were going to die was breaking my heart, and there was no room for any other thought or emotion. I knew that I would gladly give my life to save theirs, and Mama couldn't understand!

"Geneviève, I have a very good reason for not letting you go over there. Let me tell you what it is, and after I've said my piece if you still are determined to go, you have my permission."

Her words had a calming effect, and as I stood there with my arms full of sheets I nodded that I was willing to hear her out.

"When you go out walking with your little brother," she said, "you have to keep a constant lookout for him, to make sure he doesn't go too close to the water. Did you ever stop to think that the soldiers will feel the same way about you? Instead of thinking about defending themselves they'll worry about whether you're all right. And that could cost them their lives. Is that what you want?"

I could feel my anger subside like the air going out of a balloon. My mother was right. I hadn't thought about that. I looked at her and said, terribly ashamed of myself:

"I'm sorry, Mama. For all those awful things I said."

"Don't give it another thought. I understand what you were feeling. It's the war that's to blame."

"Isn't there anything I can do?"

"Pray, child. Pray, and offer your sorrow, your anguish, your-self . . ."

"Myself! That's some offering. God would have a good laugh over the gift!"

Mama shook her head and told me a personal parable of hers:

"Have you ever seen Monsieur Froissard cut a diamond? In its raw state it's quite ordinary. It looks like a piece of plain glass. But with his hammer and little chisel and a great deal of skill and patience he turns it into one of the most beautiful and precious stones on the face of the earth. And if that diamond could speak, it would tell us that it was worth all the cutting and polishing it took to make it so beautiful. That diamond is you, Geneviève. Suffering polishes all of us. But all God sees is the result."

I wasn't sure I understood exactly what she meant.

"And don't forget that here on earth we are all little more than shipwrecks lost on an ocean of suffering. We have very few means at our disposal to alter the state of the world, but there are times when they can be effective."

I stared at her, still searching to understand the real sense of her words.

"Why don't you go up to your room and think about it," she said.

Again I apologized to her, set down the sheets I was still holding in my arms, and went upstairs. I had the feeling I was carrying the weight of the world on my shoulders. I sat down on my bed and tried to reflect. Still, everything Mama had said seemed murky to me. Offer my sorrow, my anguish, even offer my own life. Why? What good would all that do those poor soldiers I had so wanted to help?

My gaze landed on the binoculars that I had left standing on the windowsill. I was so lost in my thoughts that I didn't really see them. Why was it then that I suddenly got to my feet, walked over to the window, and picked them up? I couldn't say.

I could see that the Germans had surrounded the chapel. The Americans were filing out one by one, their hands over their heads. Their ammunition had run out hours ago, and all they had left to defend themselves with were their knives. The Germans lined them up in a double column, and I guessed would be taking them back to the German headquarters at the Château d'Amfreville. There must have been about thirty Germans in all, and as many American prisoners. Yes, the Germans were marching them off in that direction.

They had gone about three or four hundred meters when two Germans grabbed one of the prisoners and pulled him from the ranks. Pointing their rifles threateningly at him, they made him undress completely. They tied a rope around his ankles, then tossed the other end over the stout branch of a tree, and hoisted him up so that his head was hanging down a meter or so from the ground. My parents had told me that in wartime, prisoners and wounded soldiers were relatively well treated by their captors. So what did this awful hanging mean?

Suddenly one of the Germans stepped over, brandishing a knife, and began to slash away at the paratrooper, who twisted and turned at the end of his rope in a vain effort to protect himself. The German went on about his horrible business almost methodically, as though he had all the time in the world. I put down the binoculars and burst out crying. I had to do something to save him. But what? The scene was taking place a good kilometer and a half from the house. What if I asked Mama to help me carry the boat, which was tied up on the Little Marsh side of the tracks, over to the other side, so that I could pole it over to where they were? Maybe the sight of a little, unarmed girl might shame them into stopping their terrible torture.

But no sooner had I formulated the plan than I knew it was hopeless. It would take me more than two hours to get there by boat, and by then all the poor paratroopers would have been killed. Even if I got there, what made me think the Germans would listen to me?

I wiped away my tears and picked up the binoculars again, torn by the desire not to see and the need to know what was going on.

The American prisoners were helplessly watching their comrade, when suddenly several of them—or ten it looked like—threw themselves on the circle of Germans. The Americans were probably completely unarmed. There was a brief skirmish, punctuated by a burst of gunfire, and the Americans fell to the ground. I had the impression the Germans had aimed for their legs, though I couldn't be sure.

The Americans who had not taken part in the assault were made to come forward and drag their fallen comrades up against the hedges that bordered the marshes. Then they were ordered back into line. The Germans advanced on the wounded Americans and began to repeat their terrible torture, slashing away at the seated paratroopers, who tried as best they could to protect their faces. I could see the Germans' knives flashing in the sunlight as they raised and lowered their arms in painful rhythm. All I could see was the gleam of sunlight on the knives, and the backs of the Germans.

Mama has told me many times that I'm no ordinary little girl, and now I felt it myself for the first time. I felt a strange sympathy for those American soldiers: I lived their pain and suffering, their dying, as though I too were being cut and lacerated by those knives. Each slash that they received, I received too. The first two struck me in both forearms, just below the elbow. Then I lost track. All I knew was that I was sick, that I couldn't bear it any longer, that I fell to my knees.

And I prayed. I offered my pain, my anguish, my suffering; I offered my very life if only that horrible massacre would cease. But who would hear me? And who would answer my prayers?

How long did that butchery go on? Three quarters of an hour? An hour? I have no idea. The last image I had was of two Germans cutting the rope that had held the first American suspended. They dragged him over and tossed him into the swamp. Then, apparently pleased with their afternoon's work, they headed in the direction of Amfreville. So far as I could tell, they were taking no prisoners with them.

Night was falling, covering the murdered with a merciful blanket. I began to shake from head to toe. The battle of Cauquigny was over. Thirty or so American soldiers, unarmed, had been massacred. Suddenly my entire being was filled with shame, shame at being alive in a world where such atrocities were permitted. And I knew for the first time, with total conviction, that hell was not somewhere down below, not a place one went to after death: hell was right here.

I went downstairs. Kerry, Claude, and the American guard that had been dispatched to stay with us that morning were deep in a game of cards. They only glanced at me, and if they noticed that my face was filled with pain and suffering, and stained with tears, they must have thought it was because Mama had punished me: they had no idea what I had witnessed and felt during the past hour.

I tiptoed into the bedroom, intent on putting George's binoculars back without waking him up. But George was wide awake, and he looked at me closely.

"*Oh, Geneviève*," he said in French, "*vous beaucoup pleurer.*"

I nodded, unable to say a word, for I knew if I tried to talk I would burst into tears. I picked up the notebook that was on the night table and wrote in it, as legibly as I could:

"German soldiers very bad men."

I wished my limited vocabulary included an English word stronger than "bad," but it didn't.

"Why, Geneviève?" George asked, after reading my message.

I took the notebook back and wrote:

"Germans have killed 30 American soldiers."

George sat up suddenly, supporting himself on one elbow and looked at me closely.

"Where, Geneviève, where?"

"Two kilometers, George," I said, my voice little more than a whisper.

"Are they all dead?"

"Yes."

George took his binoculars from me, set them down on the night table and picked up the damp washcloth Mama always kept by his bed, to cool his brow. Gently, he wiped away my tears, murmuring:

"My little Geneviève, oh my little Geneviève . . ."

I felt old and tired, so tired I wanted to die. I kissed George. I decided I would straighten up the bed. Tonight Mama could take care of the patients without me. The guard would be only too happy to help. Kerry too.

As I crossed the kitchen, where Mama was setting the table for supper, I said:

"Don't ever talk to me again about God. I don't believe in Him anymore."

Mama, who didn't know what I had just experienced, thought that I was referring to our emotional scene of that afternoon.

"You're just saying that because you didn't get your way today.

Soldiers in combat, June, 1944. *Editions Robert Laffont: Service Iconographique.*

The battle of Sainte-Mère-Eglise. *Editions Robert Laffont: Service Iconographique.*

Perhaps some men were sacrificed this afternoon, but do you have any idea how many God's going to save? Of course you don't. So don't judge what you don't know."

I shrugged. I felt so sad that I couldn't bring myself even to say goodnight to anyone. Not even Claude would have his usual goodnight kiss. How could I wish anyone "goodnight" after what I had seen?

I couldn't go to sleep. Every time I closed my eyes I would see the torture and suffering I had witnessed a few hours before, and again my body was filled with pain and my soul was filled with sorrow. No prayers tonight. God, You're no longer my friend.

Later that night, Papa brought home the news that he had never made it to Cauquigny. By the time he reached the American lines, the fighting had already started. But the Americans had been warned that the German column was advancing toward the chapel; and they withdrew eight hundred meters back, into the ruins of the Leroux farm near the Merderet Bridge, leaving only sixteen men behind to cover their retreat.

My only consolation, hearing Papa tell the story, was that only sixteen Americans had been captured, not the thirty I had estimated. Of the sixteen, not one survived.

Sunday, June 11, 1944

My initial glance out the attic window made me realize that something strange had happened. First of all, I realized it was full daylight, the first time since the paratroopers arrived that I didn't wake up at the first faint light of dawn. That didn't surprise me all that much; since I hadn't fallen asleep for hours last night, haunted by the events of yesterday, my weary body had refused to respond to its normal clock. I saw that the waves were still as choppy as ever, the weather as gray and grim as always.

I couldn't chase the indefinable feeling that something strange was going on. I slipped into my clothes and dashed downstairs two at a time, the partly closed door at the bottom of the stairs hardly braking my fall, so that I burst into the kitchen and directly into the arms of the American guard. He apparently found my unexpected arrival rather comic, for he laughed and said something in English I couldn't make out. Papa and Mama seemed to find my collision with the new American visitor equally funny, for they were laughing as hard as he was. They seemed strangely relaxed, their faces beaming in a way I hadn't seen for a long time. Decidedly, something *had* happened. But what?

"Mama, what's going on?"

"Curiosity killed the cat!" she smiled. "First say good morning to everyone. Then I'll tell you, but not before."

I made the rounds as fast as I could, a kiss on the cheek for everyone including Kerry and George. When it came to Papa I hesitated a moment, but taking my courage in both hands gave him a noisy kiss on the cheek. The guard smiled and pointed to his cheek; so I obliged and gave him a polite peck, and then turned to Mama.

"So, now can you tell me?"

Without a word, Papa handed me the binoculars and led me outside, where he pointed in the direction of Amfreville.

All of a sudden I realized we were outside the house, standing right on the tracks in direct line with the château, and not a trace of a bullet. Silence. I adjusted the binoculars ever so slightly and then I saw—oh what I saw!—the American flag flapping in the breeze, flying proudly over the château. It looked so beautiful, all those stars and stripes that I recognized right away. One day in class, Mademoiselle Burnouf had drawn it for us on the blackboard, using the only colored chalk available. Then she had us draw it for ourselves at our desks. Never had we worked so hard to draw a flag; we wanted to get every detail absolutely right, for it was, we knew, the symbol of freedom. After we had all drawn it, she had gone around and picked up all the papers and burned them in the stove; she knew that anyone found with a drawing of the flag would have been in serious trouble.

She had also had us draw the English flag, and the Russian, and further promised that after the war she would teach us each of our Allies' national anthems, in its native language.

I lowered the binoculars, then raised them again to make sure I hadn't been dreaming the first time. No, it was true; the flag was still there. The Americans had taken the château, which meant that the Germans were gone. Soon the war would be over, or maybe it was already! Only now did I realize what it was that had so excited and intrigued me when I had first opened my eyes: it was the silence, the complete absence of any gunfire. We had grown so used to it in the past six days that now that the noise had ceased it seemed strange to us.

"What happened, Papa? When? And how?"

"The troops that we've been waiting for, those that came by boat, finally did arrive and hooked up with our paratroopers."

"Our paratroopers." At long last they were going to be able to rest and recuperate. How many of them had survived? All of a sudden I thought of yesterday's massacre, and tears came to my eyes. To think that they had been murdered for nothing! I handed the binoculars back to my father and went back into the house, without a word. I went up to my room and shook Claude, who was still asleep.

"Claude! Wake up! The war is over! The Americans have won!"

Rubbing his eyes and shaking his head in wonder, trying to figure out what had prompted me to awake him so abruptly, he said:

"What did you say?"

I took him in my arms and carried him over to the window. From that vantage point we had a clear view of the flag flying on the château roof. Without realizing it, I was hugging him in my arms more tightly than I intended.

"The war may be over, Geneviève, but if you keep on squeezing me that way I may die anyway."

I told him I was sorry, that I was so excited I had forgotten myself, and gently I carried him back and set him on the bed. His face was so serious that I couldn't help asking him what was the matter, why wasn't he happy.

"Don't you realize something?" he said gravely. "If the war's over, we have to thank God, and I think we ought to do it right away before we forget."

He got down on his knees and clasped his hands and began praying, his eyes closed. I was tempted to follow his example, but somehow I couldn't. My memory of yesterday's horrible events was too deeply etched in my mind. I was still outraged at God. Besides, I had something much more important to do: I had to learn how to be free.

I tiptoed out of the room, went downstairs and walked outside onto the railroad tracks. For five days I hadn't dared take a step along the tracks without fearing for my life. I gazed out at the silent marshes. I whistled for my friend the redheaded woodpecker. No answer. I tried again. Nothing, no one answered my calls. Just what I was afraid of: either the birds were dead or they were so frightened by the carnage of the past few days that they had lost their voices. And their love of life. I realized I was going to have to learn to live without them, and perhaps even without the sun. Again today the sky was covered with a thick layer of gray clouds, like a vast shroud. What if the sun had also decided not to reappear ever again? How could I go on living, without my birds and my sun? I felt a dark wave of sadness engulf me from head to toe. From the threshold where she was standing, Mama saw me lost in my sad thoughts, and came over and put her arms around my shoulders.

"You look as though the world has come to an end!"

I burst into tears and buried my head in her arms.

"There, child," she soothed, "you've been strong and courageous these past days. Now is no time to give up."

"I called the birds and they don't come. The sun is hiding too. Everything's so sad, Mama."

"The birds will come back. Give them a little time to forget how frightened they've been this past week. Don't forget, you didn't sing these past few days either. Yet you're still alive. As for the sun . . . the clouds are scudding. I'll bet you'll see the sun before the afternoon is over. And when we've all forgotten what has just happened, everything will be just as it was before. Everything will be normal again."

"I won't ever forget!"

"Yes you will. Time erases everything. Little by little memories disappear, first a tiny detail you can't remember, then an entire day. No matter how hard you rack your brain, you can't remember."

"No, Mama. I know I won't forget. When I'm very old, if I have grandchildren, I'll be able to tell them exactly what happened, down to the last detail."

"Well," Mama said, shaking her head, "maybe you will. Haven't I always said you weren't any ordinary little girl?"

Actually, my mother was wrong. In discovering war with its

endless succession of horrors, I had become an ordinary little girl. I had lost my innocence, and the birds must have known it. From that time on they never once responded to my calls.

Since the war was over, I asked my mother for permission to go to the eleven o'clock mass in Sainte-Mère-Eglise. I still had time to make it.

"Not on your life! No one has any clear idea of what's going on there. It shouldn't be long before we find out what the situation is, and whether it's safe."

"What about my first communion? It's only two weeks away."

"You're not going to change my mind, Geneviève, so stop trying. If you're good, I may let you go over to the Sheepfold this afternoon to visit Francis, but that's all. And you can take Claude if you promise to take good care of him. You should see how beautiful the glider is."

"That's true! We can see the glider. Wait till I tell Claude!"

I ran upstairs, while Mama was preparing breakfast, to wake up Claude. Glancing out the attic window, I saw that Papa was already out on the marshes, in his boat, heading for the Sheepfold.

Claude was kneeling at the foot of his bed, praying. I waited for a minute, then said:

"Claude, come on downstairs and have your breakfast."

It was as though he was so immersed in his prayers that he hadn't heard me. Finally I lifted him up and literally carried him downstairs. If he had had his way, he would have remained there, lost in prayer. I envied him his ability to pray with such intensity, such fervor. I couldn't. Whenever he asked me, I helped him say his prayers, because I was older, but I knew that he could teach me a lesson or two despite his tender age.

Downstairs, I set my precious package down at the table. While we ate, we discussed the latest events, but the refrain was constant: the château's in the hands of the Americans, the war is over. It was as though the news was so extraordinary we couldn't really believe it was true. A hundred projects filled my head, and I laid them out for Claude, who got more and more excited. When I told him we might make a trip to the Sheepfold that afternoon, his face lit up.

After breakfast I hoisted Claude up onto the chair between the old clock and the fireplace, and began to dress him. Mama was on her knees. diligently polishing the red tiles, as she did every Sunday.

Suddenly I heard something hit the floor and, turning, I saw that a hand grenade had fallen from the pocket of our American guard, and was rolling toward the kitchen door, which was closed against the cold. A quick glance told Mama and me both that the firing pin was still attached to the soldier's uniform, and that the grenade would therefore go off.

All I had time to think was: "How stupid! The war is over, and now we're all going to die because of a dumb accident right here in our house!" The guard who had been sent to save and protect us, whose first name I didn't even know because I had baptized him "our guardian angel," was actually going to be the angel of death.

I hugged little Claude close to me and turned my back to the room, hoping my body would act as a buffer against the explosion and perhaps save him. I could see Mama, still on her knees, and through the tears in her eyes I could read fear and despair. And through my head was running: "How stupid! How stupid!"

Claude must have seen it too, or became aware of the danger, for I could hear him murmuring: "Dear God, me if You want, but not Geneviève, not Mama."

The soldier, who till then had seemed paralyzed, finally reacted. He ran toward the grenade, which was still rolling because of the incline of the floor, picked it up, dashed outside, and threw it in the general direction of the swamp. Only a second or two later a loud explosion pierced the air. None of us dared breathe as the thunder went echoing down the tracks.

Mama was the first to react. She picked herself up and went outside. Our guardian angel was lying, face down, in the courtyard. Poor man, I thought. He sacrificed himself for us.

Claude followed me outside. Mama was kneeling beside him, and suddenly I saw that he was not dead. His face was buried in his arms, and he was sobbing like a baby. Mama caressed his tousled hair and murmured reassuring words to him, none of which he understood. But he must have known from her tone that she was trying to make him feel better, and at length he got to his feet. He towered above my mother; yet to me she looked twice as tall.

When he heard the explosion, Kerry hurried out to find out what had happened, and the guard explained the accident to him. George called him into the bedroom and at first seemed to protest; but when he heard the full story, how the guard had risked his life to save us, he patted him on the back and told him how pleased he was with the way he had reacted.

I tried to cut in and tell George that it was probably my fault anyway. When I came downstairs that morning I had run full tilt into the guard's arms and may have pulled the grenade loose from its nesting place above his upper pocket.

Even the old German, who with his companion had followed the course of events from their corner, showed a sign of humanity. He hobbled over to the American and warmly shook his hand, followed by the younger German.

When things calmed down, I asked Kerry if he would teach me how to shoot his rifle. I expected an argument, but he smiled his giant smile and said "Sure!" He told me to set up an empty K-ration can on the grade-crossing gate, and asked me to bring out a chair and put it in the middle of the tracks, so he could take it easy on his bad ankle.

The first time I fired the gun I was surprised by the noise it made, but I soon grew used to it, and on my fourth shot I managed to hit the target. From then on I rarely missed. Claude, who had been watching, asked if he could try too, and Kerry agreed, but the rifle was too heavy for Claude even to lift. Kerry stood up, laid the barrel on the top of the chair, aimed it in the right direction and let Claude pull the trigger. Bang! Bull's-eye for Claude.

Claude took out his board game and invited George and Kerry to play with him, and soon the house was filled with their laughter as they rolled the dice and moved their little, brightly painted horses forward.

I helped Mama clean the house and set the table, so that we could have lunch as soon as Papa came back. Claude and I gobbled down our lunch, since we couldn't wait to leave for the Sheepfold. For once in our lives, Mama said it was all right to walk along the tracks in the direction of traffic, something we had never before been allowed to do. But with the tracks broken like matchsticks in a dozen places, there was no danger of any train coming through for some time.

We left the house all bundled up, as though it were winter, and raced down the road toward 103. We couldn't quite believe, after the past few days, that we were actually free to run around and play again without fear. We stopped at each bomb crater, shaking our heads in disbelief at the power of the explosion that had taken those heavy rails and twisted them like supplicants' arms—rails that for years on end had supported the weight of the huge trains that thundered by, without ever breaking or bending. What power was there in those bombs for such awesome destruction? Why did adults have to spend so much time and energy inventing ways to destroy rather than to build? They were capable of making beautiful works and doing beautiful things at times. Why not always?

Among the most beautiful things I had ever seen adults do was harvesting a field of wheat. The men, each carrying his scythe over his shoulder, took up their stations at the edge of the field early in the morning, about four meters apart. Then, after passing the stone one last time or two over the gleaming blade, they set off, moving slowly forward with rhythmic strokes, as the wheat fell always in the same direction, off to the left. When the men had advanced far enough, the women moved in behind and began to pick up the wheat, tying it into big bundles and gathering them into groups of five. From a distance, the bundles looked to me like school kids cooking up some mischief. I often used to wonder what those bundles of wheat were really talking about as the sun set, after all the humans had left the field. Were they discussing the marvelous fate that would soon turn them into the basic food that fed the earth's people? Were they wondering which among them might end up as the holy bread passed out at communion? Were they estimating which among them would be chosen by men to serve as next year's seed? Yes, I was sure that they were talking about such kinds of things as the sun's rays, almost horizontal, bathed them in gold.

Our hearts filled with happiness, and we continued on our way. But our happiness didn't last very long. When we reached the bridge over the river we literally stumbled over two corpses lying in our path: huge corpses, swollen and smelling to high heaven. Claude looked up at me, his questioning eyes filled with distress. I wasn't much help, for I felt just as sick. What was more, I didn't understand. Mama took this route every day on her way to milk the cows on the farm adjoining 103. That meant she had to have seen these bodies. And that meant that she knew we would see them too, that she *wanted* us to see them. Why? Did she want us to see war in all its brutality, so it would remain engraved on our minds forever? Or did she simply want to make sure we saw the bodies in daylight, to avoid our finding them on our way home, when it was dark or growing dark, which would have terrified us even more? I still couldn't figure it out. All I knew for sure was that if she wanted to spare us this sight, she could have encouraged us to take the boat over to the Sheepfold. Later on I asked her several times why she had done that to us, but she always managed to skirt the question.

Those bodies stayed there for weeks, until finally one day later in the summer they were gone, either buried or thrown into the marshes by some charitable soul.

I'm the older sister, I thought, and it's up to me to take charge. I helped Claude over the awful obstacle and on we went, but all the happiness we had felt till now had evaporated. Still, I wanted to try to make Claude feel better, so I said:

"After all, they were Germans. Think of it this way: at least those two can't do us any harm."

Claude didn't respond, but simply gazed at me with those big blue eyes so filled with pain and sorrow that I had to avert my gaze.

Fortunately, the sight of the glider sitting in the middle of the field at the Sheepfold changed our thoughts and gave us both a lift. Good Lord, how beautiful that glider was! We circled it completely, touching it with our hands, examining each little detail. There wasn't a scratch on it! What could it have brought with it, men or cargo? I climbed inside and sat in the pilot's seat. For a brief moment I had the feeling that my dream had come true, that this was a real plane and I was the pilot. What if it didn't have any motor! That didn't matter.

Francis joined us and kissed us both, then said:

"Come here, kids, I have a surprise for you."

He took us across the field to where something round and metallic was sticking out of the ground. Someone had strung barbed wire around it.

"What is it?" Claude asked.

"Guess," his big brother said smugly. "Can you guess?" he said, turning to me.

"A bomb?" I said at length.

"One that didn't explode when it hit the ground," he nodded.

"What's the barbed wire for?" I wanted to know.

"To keep the cows away from it," he said. "It might explode if they nuzzled it once too often."

I thought it would be bigger. I still couldn't understand that something that size could pack the power to make those huge craters, or turn our rails into matchsticks.

"I have more news," Francis said. "Unfortunately, not good news. Blanchette is dead."

Our poor cow, dead! No more milk! Several other cows were also killed by the bombs or gunfire. However, the house itself was intact.

"You're lucky you weren't hurt," I said to Francis.

"You don't know how lucky," he said. And then he told us that the night when the plane had come looking for us, or for the ammunition in our courtyard, he had heard the sound of the motor and come to the door to see what was going on. He'd heard a whistling noise, then felt wind on his fingers. A bomb had exploded not far off, and a piece of shrapnel had passed between his thumb and forefinger, without touching him, and buried itself in the armoire behind him.

He told us, too, that on the night of June 5th, paratroopers had also landed at the Sheepfold; he had received them by taking them down cellar and offering them a welcoming glass of hard cider.

The afternoon passed quickly as we brought each other up to date about the events we had survived during the past week. Francis served us some *crème fraîche* with sugar and freshly picked apples, and then told us he thought we'd better get started home.

"I don't want you out on the road after dark," he said.

Before leaving, I went upstairs to my room and looked out to see if the steeple of the church was still standing. It was, but no flag was flying from it. I felt that until the French and American flags were flying from the church tower, we couldn't really say the war was over.

We made a detour on our way home to avoid the two dead Germans. Mama had been wrong: the sun had not come out, but it was less cold than it had been. We passed the lookout post where Papa had stood guard, and again my heart froze; inside were all the men and boys Papa had left behind the night of the 5th: dead, lying right where they had fallen. Poor Monsieur Touze: he won't be coming by anymore in the morning, he won't be pulling on my pigtails anymore, saying, after he's tasted my coffee: "Geneviève, I swear if you were a few years older and I were a few years younger I'd ask you to marry me. Any girl who can make coffee that good . . ." He knew as well as I that there wasn't a grain of real coffee in the pot, so his compliment was doubly appreciated.

I would have liked to make a detour to the farm, to see how our "boys" were making out. Now that the reinforcements had arrived, they would have a chance to rest and recuperate. We hadn't met a single one of them along the way, and I realized that now that the main invasion forces had arrived, our paratroopers would probably be moving on.

I resisted my urge, however, for Mama had made me promise that I would keep strictly to the itinerary we had agreed to. I had learned to live with my father's blows, but I think that if my mother had learned I had disobeyed, and slapped me across the face, I would have died of shame.

In any case, she seemed relieved to see us arrive. A good fire was burning in the fireplace, next to which Kerry and the guardian angel were seated deep in conversation. I went in to see George, who was propped up, with several pillows behind his back.

"Tomorrow," he said, "Kerry is going to teach you something."

"Can't you tell me now what it is?" I pleaded.

George pointed at the window, at the growing dark, and said: "No, tomorrow."

I knew better than to insist. Still, I couldn't help wondering: would it be a new shooting lesson? I hoped so.

Tomorrow, Geneviève, tomorrow.

Monday, June 12, 1944

Up at the crack of dawn, I helped Mama prepare breakfast. All five of our guests slept well, and the older German was no longer coughing. Mama's remedy had worked again. Kerry joined us at the table, so that I was seated between him and our guardian angel. Mama remarked that I looked tiny between those two giants, and it was true that our newest visitor was as tall as Kerry, though as dark as Kerry was fair, and just as nice. I told Mama that yesterday at the Sheepfold Francis had measured both Claude and me, and that we'd both grown.

"In fact," I said, "I meant to tell you yesterday: I'm now two centimeters taller than you!"

"You mean I won't be able to call you 'little girl' anymore? What do you mean by passing me so quickly!"

She smiled and said that right after my first communion we'd better get started on my trousseau.

"We'll use the white parachute that George arrived with as your wedding gown material," she laughed. "With all these handsome young Americans around, I'm sure you're going to fall in love with one of them. And the next thing I know he'll have kidnapped my daughter!"

"If you think you can get rid of me all that quickly," I said, "think again, Mama. The man I marry is going to have to be someone very special. You know how difficult I am."

She smiled and suggested that before I started sewing my wedding gown I'd better get busy with the dishes. While I washed I kept thinking about what Mama had said, but only half jokingly. I really was a big girl now, and she actually had begun to think about my trousseau.

Kerry called me over and asked if he could borrow one of my school notebooks and some colored crayons. I dried the dishes as fast as I could so I could look over his shoulder and see what he was doing. He was drawing, very quickly and skillfully, all sorts of strange-looking objects, none of which made any sense to me. Soon the whole page was covered with them.

While he drew he kept up a steady stream of conversation both with George and the guard, and though I couldn't understand exactly what they were saying, I had the impression they were referring to us, the children, and that the drawings had something to do with us. When he had finished the page Kerry turned it over and drew something I recognized right away: a grenade just like the one the guard had dropped yesterday.

I still didn't understand what Kerry was up to. Beneath each drawing he wrote something in block letters, then handed me the pocket dictionary and asked me to look them up. Claude joined me and tried to figure out what the drawings represented, but he didn't understand either. The dictionary wasn't too much help, but I found several of the words in French: "bomb," "anti-tank trap," "grenade," "mine." Finally it dawned on me that Kerry had been drawing various kinds of weapons: he had drawn a mine, the top of which looked like the bottom of a dinner plate; an incendiary bomb, which had pretty blue and white stripes and didn't look the least bit dangerous; little anti-personnel bombs which had little wings and resembled children's toys I had seen; and various caliber ammunition.

I made Kerry understand that I still didn't know what he was trying to accomplish. He scratched his head, then conferred with George in English for a minute before making a sign for the guard to lend him one of his grenades. Kerry went out into the courtyard, having motioned for us to follow him. I watched him put the grenade in the grass; then he pointed first to me, then to the grenade. Thinking that he wanted me to pick it up I bent down and reached for it.

"No, Geneviève, for God's sake don't touch it! Dangerous! Boom!"

Finally I understood: Kerry was trying to show us graphically all the possible kinds of weapons we might come upon, so that we would recognize them and avoid them at all cost. To show Kerry I understood, I pointed to his drawing of the mine, then gestured toward the grass at the edge of the embankment and shook my head vigorously: don't worry, we would never touch them.

We went back into the kitchen, where I explained to Mama the strange lesson I had just had.

"You see how kind and thoughtful they are," she said, nodding. "They know that when the marsh dries there will be lots of weapons you could come across. They want to make sure you'll never touch them."

To thank my Americans, I went around and gave each a big kiss on the cheek. They were all so tall! Even on my tiptoes I couldn't make it unless they cooperated and bent down.

That afternoon a jeep drove up to within fifty or sixty meters of the house—it couldn't get any closer because of the bomb craters—and two Americans arrived. They wanted to see Lieutenant Wingate, and Mama ushered them into his room. Apparently a field hospital was being constructed near 103, and tomorrow all our visitors would be transferred there. We were all overjoyed that at last George would receive proper care, but I knew that their departure—especially George's and Kerry's—was going to leave a big hole not only in our house but in our hearts. Noticing my depressed mood, Kerry invited us outside for another shooting lesson, which turned out to be even better than yesterday's.

"At this rate, you'll soon have your marksmanship medal," George told us. Since I didn't understand, he explained that soldiers had to reach a certain level of skill in shooting before they were qualified.

Papa had spent the day at the Sheepfold, digging trenches to bury the dead cows. It was hard, slow work, and when the Americans saw what he was up to they dispatched a kind of big tractor with a plow on the front, which they called a bulldozer, and within an hour or two it had dug a hole big enough to bury them all!

At dusk, Kerry took down his rifle again and motioned for us to follow him outside. Aiming the rifle upwards, he emptied it, and suddenly the sky was illuminated by a dozen lighted arcs, what I had always imagined fireworks to be.

"Tracer bullets," Kerry enunciated, and we repeated after him. We forgot, because they were so beautiful, that these nighttime bullets could also carry death.

For our last night together, Mama cooked a very special dinner. Both fireplaces gave off odors that made our mouths water. In the distance, we could still hear the rumble of cannons, off in the direction of Montebourg, beyond Fresville. We had tried to forget the war, which had moved scarcely ten kilometers farther on, but the constant boom of the cannons reminded us how close it still was.

Around the dinner table, I looked in wonder at this strange collection of people—Germans, Americans, French—who had never set eyes on one another a week before. I tried to guess what each of them was thinking. The Americans seemed to project a feeling of strength and *joie de vivre,* certain that tomorrow would bring them their dreams. I hoped and prayed they would not be disappointed. In my heart, I knew the war wasn't really over, that it was only beginning. Kerry's ankle would keep him out of combat for several weeks more, perhaps, but afterward, what would become of him?

Seated next to him was our guardian angel. I hardly knew him, but he too breathed life and hope: would he survive these horrors to realize his dreams? I felt for him, for all of them, even the Germans. The younger one especially, who was always civil; less for the older man, whose face remained a mask. And what feelings lurked behind that mask? Despair? Revolt? He was seated next to me at the table. I gazed down at his hand, which was lying there on the tablecloth, and all of a sudden, for some inexplicable reason, I overcame my fear and timidity and placed my hand over his. He looked at me in surprise, his face no longer a mask but clearly upset and angry. I smiled at him but said nothing. He searched my face, as if for a sign. Seeing how embarrassed he was, I simply handed him the basket of bread. He nodded in thanks. I would have appreciated a spoken word of thanks.

I wondered what was going through his head. The invasion that the German armies had feared for so long, and that we had prayed for just as long, was now a reality, marking the end of the German dream. Did he have any idea how crazy and criminal Hitler's dream had been? He must have been pleased that we, who were supposedly the enemy, had opened our home to him, had cared for him and helped nurse him back to health. I wondered what the German officer who had died in my arms would have thought of his colleague's way of thanking us for our trouble by conspiring to kill us all.

Several times during the meal Papa got up and went into the bedroom, to see to "his" lieutenant. What in fact would become of him? Would the doctors save his leg? I thought of his mother, back in America, learning that her son was being sent back home. How happy she would be, even if they had to amputate the leg. Better return home with one leg than not return home at all!

And the Germans. I kept coming back to the Germans. Tomorrow they would officially be made prisoners, first interned in the American hospital, then in some prisoner-of-war camp. After the war they would go back home too. Would they have learned anything from the experience, these Germans, who three times in less than a century had sown death and destruction throughout Europe, each time more bloody and awful than before?

My mother's voice drew me from my daydreams.

"Your father's made up his mind to move us all tomorrow over to the Sheepfold."

"When?"

"I said tomorrow. Didn't you hear me?"

I felt the blood drain from my face. Mama saw it and said:

"Don't worry, darling. You're a big girl now, you can defend yourself."

"Is there any special reason why we're moving there?"

"Your father thinks that the Sheepfold is less exposed than 104."

The notion of going back to live at the Sheepfold gave me a sinking feeling in the pit of my stomach. For one thing, Papa would again have ready access to his reserve of hard cider. For another, his drinking companions would be nearby. As for me, I could foresee that the intermission was over, and that Papa Maurice would once again begin using me as his scapegoat. Then, too, I wouldn't be able to take the boat out anymore, and my old friend the duck would no longer come and nestle in my arms. I felt as though the world had just collapsed around me.

My parents gave us permission to stay up late this last evening. I knew that all good things had to come to an end, but we still protested when Mama came into the bedroom and told us it was time to let George and Kerry alone. "Up to bed now, children!" she called.

"Please, Mama, just a little while longer!"

Papa's authoritarian tones put a swift end to our pleas, and Claude was asleep almost before he hit the pillow.

A few minutes later Mama came upstairs to tuck us in. She gazed down at Claude for a long moment before she turned out the lamp, then said to me:

"If I were you I'd pray especially hard tonight. I have a feeling that because of everything that's happened these past few days Papa Maurice will be nicer with you from now on. But I can't swear to it. You should ask God for special protection."

"Please, Mama, don't say anything more."

I knew there was no way she could help me.

Tuesday, June 13, 1944

This morning, nothing nor anyone—not even my father—could force me to stay in bed. I was the first one up, and I put the coffee on for breakfast—the last meal we would all share. I made up my mind not to worry about the future. We would see what the future would bring, but meanwhile what was the point of thinking about it? I was tying my pigtails when Mama joined me. The sentinel, Kerry, George, and Papa were all still fast asleep. In the kitchen, the two Germans were awake; yet I hadn't made a bit of noise. They were light sleepers, that was all. Mama set the bowls out on the table and called everyone to breakfast. This morning I beat my father to the punch and took George's coffee in to him before Papa was awake. It paid to be an early bird.

"Hello, George, how are you today?" I said in my best English.

"Very well, Geneviève, very well thank you. And you?"

In reply I went over and planted a kiss on the end of his nose, which always made him laugh.

After having fixed his pillows and helped him sit up, I gave him his steaming *café au lait*. He smiled by way of thanks, and I could see he was feeling on top of the world. The thought that he would be leaving us forever made me suddenly sad, and George must have seen the look that came over my face for he put his forefinger to my temple and said:

"A penny for your thoughts."

"I was thinking how selfish I am," I said in French. "I was thinking that for the past eight days your leg wound has kept you here, in need of love and care. I was thinking that I would have liked to keep you here longer, that's all, and it's not a very kind thought, is it?"

"What are you saying, Geneviève? I can't follow you."

"Nothing. Pure nonsense. Pay no attention."

Later that morning, Papa pointed out to us a group of men heading in our direction from 103. They were stretcher bearers, walking in single file along the tracks. They only had three stretchers for the three wounded. The Germans were the first to leave. The younger one, who seemed genuinely moved to be leaving us, smiled at me and said goodbye, but the older one, as dour and taciturn as ever, left without a word.

Given the seriousness of his condition, George was the third to leave. Mama wrapped him snugly in a blanket, for despite the fact it was almost mid-June, it was still very cold in "our" marshes, and she wanted to make sure, now that he was on the way to recovery, that he didn't catch cold.

As a present, George left Papa Maurice his paratrooper's knife and his binoculars. I was dying to go with the stretcher bearers as far as the hospital tent, but Papa Maurice's blunt "no" was final. If for no other reason, I had my work cut out for me, getting ready to move to the Sheepfold.

Leaning on his broom-crutch, which he seemed to have formally adopted, Kerry indicated that he didn't need a stretcher, that he would hobble on after them. I went out onto the tracks to stay with them as long as I could.

The stretcher bearing George passed me by.

"Bye-bye, Geneviève!" he called, blowing me a kiss.

I tried to respond, but a lump came into my throat so that I could barely whisper:

"Bye-bye, George. *Bonne chance!* Good luck!"

Kerry hobbled after them, hoisting himself up onto the tracks. He shook hands all around, his grip firm and strong. Only Claude received a big fat kiss.

I watched him make his way painfully along the tracks, his huge silhouette moving awkwardly. Then, suddenly, I took off after him.

"Kerry. Please!"

He stopped and turned back.

"What is it, Geneviève?"

"Please, Kerry, would you leave me something to remember you by?"

He fished in his pockets, and the first thing he came up with was a clip loaded with bullets.

"Thank you, Kerry. Bye-bye. And good luck!"

I dashed along the tracks, ran into the house, and up the stairs two at a time. I carefully placed the clip in the box that held all my treasures.

I went downstairs and walked back out onto the tracks, watching as the stretcher bearers and Kerry slowly retreated into the distance. You mustn't be sad, I told myself, you mustn't. But it was no use. It was over. I would never see them again in my life. Never. I knew that the tent hospital wasn't all that far away, but I also knew that Papa Maurice had already told me it was no place for children, and I was never to go there. Once he had made up his mind, there was no point arguing.

Fortunately, there was enough work to do to keep my mind occupied. I helped Mama pack our belongings, and we all loaded them into the boat. Papa poled the boat, loaded to the gunwales, across the marshes. On the other side, he and Francis would carry our possessions on their backs to the Sheepfold. Actually, it wasn't all that much, since we had a basic set of furniture over there, too, and only transported our personal things.

While Papa was gone, Mama and I removed the straw that had served as a mattress for the two German soldiers, for the American guard who had been assigned to our house, and for my parents.

While we were cleaning up, Mama confessed to me a plan she had been mulling over for the past several hours. We had neither the time nor the tools to dig a proper grave in the marsh waters for the poor German officer who had died in my arms. What we could do, she thought, was to give him some semblance of a decent burial by surrounding his body with a fence of sticks that we could secure in the muddy bottom, and then cover it with with a roof of sticks. But would Papa agree to let us use his precious firewood?

To our amazement, when he came back from the Sheepfold, not only did he agree, but he offered to give us a hand. He helped us carry the firewood, and drove the vertical sticks deep into the mud. In less than half an hour, my parents had built a little wall around the body. The idea was that the alluvial soil carried in the water would build a burial mound around the site where the poor man had died. Actually, when a short time later the floodgates were reopened, the rush of the escaping water took both fence and soil with it. But for some strange reason, the body stayed put. At that point some good-hearted natives of Amfreville came out and, now that the soil had dried, buried him right there on the spot where he had died.

I folded Lieutenant Wingate's parachute, thinking to take it with me to the Sheepfold. As soon as she had some free time, Mama would use it to make me the pretty white dress she had promised. During his final trip to the Sheepfold, Papa had come within a hair's breadth of killing himself, partly because he had overloaded the boat. For the past week or so, the waters of the marshes had diminished noticeably, and we were sure it was because someone had already opened one of the floodgates without permission. As a result the boat was harder to maneuver, for it scraped bottom in many places; but at least it was in no danger of sinking. But the river itself was another matter altogether: there the course of the stream was, if anything, swifter. Mama and I were both watching as Papa reached the end of the shallow marshes and began to cross the river. We could see that the water was up to the gunwales, and we could also see that Papa must have made some wrong move, for suddenly the boat began to sink. But like all good captains, Papa refused to abandon his boat. We could see him slowly going down, perched on top of his heavy cargo—and there was nothing we could do to help. But Papa Maurice was not one to lose his head in any situation, and the next thing we saw he was clinging to the wheelbarrow, apparently the only part of the cargo that floated, letting the current carry him to solid ground on the other side. Everything else was lost.

"It doesn't matter," Mama said, breathing a sigh of relief. "There wasn't anything in that last load of any importance."

"My wooden horse was in that boatload," I said, trying to hold back the tears. "The one I made for Claude."

"Don't worry," Mama said. "I promise I'll find you some chores to do on the neighboring farms over the next few weeks, and with the money you earn you can go buy Claude a real wooden horse for his birthday."

We went through the house one last time, to make sure everything was neat and clean, and that we had left nothing behind. As Mama closed and locked the door, I whispered:

"Goodbye, 104. Thank you for taking such good care of us these past few days."

Summer 1944

Day by day, the war moved away from us, and little by little we were able to resume our former ways, with fewer and fewer travel restrictions. At the Sheepfold, life resumed its normal course. Francis, who had taken advantage of the solitude these past few weeks had imposed on him to study night and day, passed his exams with flying colors. The day after the results were announced, he told me, his chest swelling with pride, that he had already found a job. I was impressed, and asked him what it was, but he refused to tell. A few days later I found out anyway: he, like many young men of the area, had been hired to bury the dead, who were being brought in big trucks. Lots of trucks, from all points of the compass. Two huge fields at the outskirts of Sainte-Mère-Eglise had been given over to the American authorities as military cemeteries. The numbers were such that all of us offered to help in one way or another. I was among those who fished out the remaining parachutes that were still floating on the marsh waters, which we cut and used as shrouds. But the supply of parachutes was soon exhausted, after which we all contributed anything we could: old sheets, blankets, random material, as an interim measure until the caskets arrived by boat from the States.

I was still a little girl, but I couldn't help reflecting, as we cut and stitched our awful shrouds, that even though the war had retreated from where we lived, it was still raging not far away, and the proof

arrived daily, truck after truck. All these fine young men cut down
in the full flush of their youth. My heart was filled with a sadness
such as I had never felt, and if I had the power I would have willed,
right then and there, for the world to stop, so that the butchery
would finally cease. I found myself sitting and talking to myself
aloud, talking to those young men who would never grow up to see
their own sons and daughters come into this world.

"Why," I would say, "did you give your lives to free us? I
wonder if we're worthy of the sacrifice? I wonder if we'll really
appreciate the freedom you've given us again? If it had not been for
that crazy man Hitler, what might your lives have been? If I ever
decide to sing again, it will be because I have learned from you, my
Americans, the lesson of courage and hope. A lesson I will never
forget."

As I should have expected, Papa did begin to drink again, and
again he took me for his victim. There was nothing Mama or
Francis or little Claude could do to stop him. But the good weather
appeared and that buoyed my spirits slightly.

One afternoon Mama asked me if I would go fetch some firewood. Maurice Salmon, who was supposed to deliver us a load,
needed his horse and wagon to bring in the new-mown hay, and
wouldn't be able to bring it to us for several weeks. I agreed, but
suggested to Mama that, rather than pick up deadwood from the
ground, I would cut it off the trees. The fact is, dead wood taken
from the ground gives a strange, sickening taste to the food that is
cooked over it; we call it "the taste of deadwood," or "smoky taste."
Soups and coffee seem affected most by it. For some reason, deadwood cut from the trees, or cut green and dried in a woodpile,
doesn't impart this disagreeable taste.

"You see," I said to Mama, "I always told you my tree-climbing
ability would pay off."

"It's fine with me," she said, "only for goodness sake be careful. I
know you've told me God doesn't want you, but even He may have
His whims."

"Don't worry. I'm on my way."

The hedges enclosing the Sheepfold had one peculiarity: they were planted in double rows, which made a windbreak of a good two meters. Whoever had taken the trouble deserved a medal; the first row broke the wind so that what force was left was completely blocked by the second, and the horses and cows could take shelter on the lee side of the second hedge. They were even able to spend the entire winter outside this way.

For the time being, these hedges also served another purpose: a whole regiment of American troops lay billeted right next to them. Beneath the nearby trees, the pup tents blended into the hedge itself, and were as hard to detect from the air as the trucks and tanks concealed beneath their camouflage. From a distance, or from the air, it simply looked as though the hedge, in certain places, was a trifle wider.

I climbed up a tree not far from the hedges, with a saw slung over my back. I was singing, as I generally did when I worked. When I had reached a high point of the tree, I sawed off a number of branches and let them fall to the ground below. When there were enough, I would climb down and tie them into a bundle to carry back to the house. Mama cooked everything over the open fire, for we had neither a gas nor even a wood stove.

After I had made my first bundle, I decided to gather a second, more for the fun of climbing a tree taller than the others than for any other reason. If they were too heavy, I was sure I could find some nice soldier to help me carry the bundles to the house. In fact, there was one standing at the base of the tree I had just climbed. He was watching my every move. Still, I kept on singing while I worked. He moved away and sat down a little farther away, to keep from receiving one of my branches on his skull. I paused for a moment, and heard him say, in French, and in an accent that I recognized immediately:

"Tell me, young lady, are you a squirrel or a nightingale?"

"Neither one, soldier. I'm cutting some dry wood to cook with."

I slid down the tree trunk and landed a step away from him.

"You ought to be a paratrooper!" he said, extending his hand. I smiled at him.

"My name's Geneviève. What's yours?"

"Marc Levesque."

"That's strange. That's my mother's maiden name! Are you French Canadian?"

"I am indeed. Do you mind if I ask you a favor?"

"Not at all."

"Would you mind singing again that song you sang up in the tree?"

"Certainly. If you don't mind my tying up my firewood while I do. Mama's waiting for it."

I repeated the song, and when I had finished both the song and the bundle of wood, the soldier—as I had hoped—asked me if he could help carry the wood back to my house.

"Have you been singing a long time?" he asked.

"Since I can remember."

"Who taught you to sing?"

"My mother. She has a pretty voice, too."

"Have you ever tried to sing anything else than these popular songs?"

I looked at him strangely, not understanding what he meant.

"Like airs from operas for instance . . . Would you like to learn how to sing some?"

"Sure. But who would teach me?"

"I would," he said.

"Are you a musician?"

"A singing teacher. I organize concerts."

"And you also drive a tank."

"Not by choice," he said, "by necessity. I joined up and they assigned me to this regiment. But as soon as things settle down, I'm going to be reassigned, to set up entertainment for the troops. Plays, concerts, that sort of thing. If your voice is as good as I think it is, I'd like to take you with me. If you want to, of course."

"I have parents, you know . . . Especially a father."

"I'll know how to handle him."

We reached the house, and as thanks for the generous provision of wood we had brought back, Mama offered us both a cup of coffee, and while we drank it he explained his idea to her.

"I'm here on a month R & R," he said. "In four weeks I can teach Geneviève several songs, and train her voice."

"But she can't read a note of music," Mama protested. "How can you teach her?"

The Canadian didn't have a ready answer for that one, but it was clear he was not about to give up the idea. He left, promising to return the following day.

True to his word, he came back the next afternoon, cradling under his arm a spring-operated record player and some records. I clapped my hands with pleasure.

"Oh, Marc, where did you find it?"

"I bought it. It's not the best-sounding machine in the world, but let's give it a try anyway."

"What do you want me to do?"

"Put the record on, listen carefully to the words and music. Then I'll see if you're really talented."

He carried the record player up to my room and showed me how to operate it. One of the records was from the operetta *Rose Marie,* and the other from Lalo's opera, *The King of Ys.* Marc returned to his tent and I put on the first record. It seemed to me easier than the other, so I set about trying to learn it. In less than an hour I had mastered both words and music.

Pretending I was out cutting some more firewood for my mother, I walked over to Marc's tent; I approached it stealthily, with the help of the double hedges, so that I arrived without his seeing me. As I bent down and began gathering stray pieces of kindling, I broke into the song.

Marc, who had been puttering near his tent, stopped what he was doing, stepped over the barbed wire fence along the hedges and came over to me.

"How did you learn it so fast?"

"It's not hard to learn something you really love."

"Sing me as much as you know."

I did as he asked, and sang the entire piece. When I had finished he called out to his friends who were either puttering near their tents or simply relaxing:

"Come here, you guys. I want you to hear this little girl."

The soldiers walked over and sat down in a semicircle around the front of Marc's tank, while he hoisted me up and set me down on it. My feet got tangled in the camouflage netting, and I had to hold onto the cannon in order not to fall off. It was in this strange, uncomfortable position that I sang an operetta for the first time in public. And what a public it was! Could I have dreamed of a better one? Not only were they soldiers, whom I loved, but most of those present were Canadians, who understood the words I was singing in French. When I had finished they were generous with their applause!

"Encore! Encore! Sing one more!"

They didn't have to ask twice. By the time I had finished the tenth song, Marc indicated that it was enough. I could have gone on forever, but the growing darkness, and the knowledge that I had better get home ahead of Papa Maurice, prevailed. Reluctantly, I left my new friends. Marc helped me carry the firewood home again, and on the way he revealed that he had made up his mind to talk to Papa about his plans for me. Tonight. No point waiting another day. He didn't know what he was getting into. Drunk as a lord, Papa Maurice seemed scarcely to listen to what Marc was saying, and then said "no." Categorically. Marc refused to take no for an answer, telling Papa how he would make me the little princess of his military theatrical company, but Papa remained unmoved. He had no intention of letting me go. Certainly not yet.

I wasn't surprised by Papa Maurice's attitude. But I was surprised to hear Marc say:

"You don't realize this girl's talent, Papa Maurice. A voice like hers is a gift, one you may find only once in a lifetime."

"So what?" was all Papa could respond.

Finally admitting defeat, Marc shook his head and headed back to his tent. I tried to cheer him up by promising to learn *The King of Ys* overnight and sing it for him the next day.

"The whole thing? That's impossible. All you should try to learn is the princess's part. The rest can only be sung by men."

"All right," I acquiesced. But I have my own ideas, and the next day I sang for my professor the entire opera, including the men's parts, passing from the firm low tones of the King to the gentle, dulcet tones of Princess Rozenn. Marc couldn't believe his ears. Again he called his buddies over, and again I sang for that very special audience. In fact, for the next three weeks I gave a daily concert for them. "Come and listen to God's nightingale," Marc would call out to them when I arrived; the name was given to me by Marc because of my decided preference for religious songs.

And then the day came when their long furlough was over, and it was with the same sinking heart I had felt when George and Kerry had left that I saw them go. I watched the long line of trucks and tanks slowly disappear, and suddenly I realized that, like Kerry and George and all the soldiers I had met since June 5th, Marc did not even know my last name. For him, as for the others, I was simply Geneviève, Papa Maurice's daughter. So I wouldn't take singing lessons, I wouldn't learn any operas or operettas by heart, I wouldn't ever perform in public. I sensed that I had missed one of the great opportunities of my life.

Some time later, on a glorious summer day, Mama took Claude and me to the feast day of Saint Marguerite. The offering of ribbons that year was more solemn and fervent than ever before, nor have I ever seen one to rival it since. While the rest of the assembled throng gave heartfelt thanks to Our Lady for having granted us our freedom, I found it hard to share their happiness: I felt sad and unhappy, somehow oppressed. Suddenly I burst into tears.

A priest, who turned out to be a missionary, saw my distress, and after vespers came up and asked what was troubling me so. We sat down together on the low wall that surrounded the cemetery of Neuville-au-Plain, and I opened my heart to him.

I explained how our first communion had been postponed till

the end of July, because of the Allied landing. I told him how hard I had worked to learn my catechism, and how much I had been looking forward to that day, which, I said, I expected to be the most beautiful day of my life. When the priest examined us on our catechism, I had come in second of all the class, which automatically gave me, as a prize, the right to stand up during the morning ceremony, and with the person who had placed first, recite publicly an act of faith. Only the first four communicants had this right, the winner and second place—me—in the morning, and the boy or girl who had placed third and fourth at vespers. But when my turn came, another girl whose name was also Geneviève got up and began to recite the act of faith in my place. I was sure there had been an error, since this other Geneviève had placed last in the examination, so I got to my feet too. But the lady in charge looked at me and shook her head, though I could see she was upset at having to deny me my rightful place. I was thoroughly confused. Why had I been replaced at the last minute without even having been told? The girl who had taken my place read aloud a short prayer. Then, on her way back to her place, she paused and whispered in my ear:

"I guess I fooled you, didn't I?" and she gave me a wicked smile.

I still didn't understand, and I looked at her blankly. After mass, the other Geneviève came over to me again as we were walking to the vestry:

"Father Roulland is a man of flesh and blood, you know. He likes the good things of life just like anybody else. So last night Mama took him two nice chickens, and presto! just like that, he let me recite in your place."

My anger, which was extreme, was nothing compared to my mother's. During the first-communion ceremonies the parents of the children participating were supposed to take up a collection. Everyone considered that a great honor. But Mama, to pay back the greedy priest, forbade me to give him the hundred franc note that the old lady had pressed on me when I had gone begging for candle money. My anger subsided almost as quickly as it had begun, and I took Father Roulland's defense. But Mama remained intractable. It was the first time I had seen her bear a real grudge against anyone, and she was so adamant that she also forbade me to enroll for my fifth and final year of catechism the following autumn.

The fact was, I had almost never enrolled in the first place. My first contact with Father Roulland had been a difficult one. At our first class, he had spoken to us about "Our Father in Heaven" who, he said, was like our earthly father, who looked after us and cared for us and protected us.

That was too much for me. I got to my feet, collected my pencil and notebook, and stalked out, carrying my coat. Father Roulland, completely taken aback, ran out after me.

"Why are you leaving like that?" he demanded.

"I already have one father, who does anything that comes into his head, and it has nothing to do with taking care of me or protecting me. I don't need another one like that, thank you very much!"

"But this Father does love us, Geneviève. He loves us more than anything in the world."

"He does?" I stopped in my tracks, dumbfounded.

"Absolutely!"

"Then that's a whole other story."

Since then, Father and I had been the best of friends. So how could he have done that to me? The traitor!

Having heard me out, the missionary did his best to console me, and indeed his words made me feel better. Claude popped up from somewhere, and I introduced him to my new friend.

"I know you," the missionary smiled. "I saw you offer a pretty blue ribbon this morning to the Holy Mother. In fact, I remember that your sister had to lift you up so that you could reach the statue's arm." Then, turning to me, he said:

"Isn't he very young to make a vow?"

"It wasn't his vow, it was my mother's."

"And were her prayers answered?"

"Yes. Otherwise George would be dead."

"Who's George?"

Since he seemed really to care, I poured out the whole story to him about the American soldiers who had landed in the marshes the night of June 5th, how they had come to our house, about Lieutenant Wingate's wound and how he had almost died, about the German officer who had died in my arms and how badly I had felt because I wasn't strong enough to carry him with Mama to the house. And I also talked to him about "J-Two."

"J-Two?" he asked, obviously puzzled.

J-Two was another newfound friend the war had brought me. I had baptized him by that name because he was, though a soldier, so young that had he been French he would have been classed, for the purpose of ration tickets, "J-Two"—that is, no longer a child but not yet an adult. His real name was James Kimble, and though he was eighteen he looked more my age. He had enlisted, and he had already proved himself in battle, having fought hard and long during the liberation of the towns of Montebourg and Valognes. He had been sent back for a rest period granted to his entire regiment, and in a few days would be leaving again for the front.

I told the missionary that a few nights before, J-Two had had a terrible nightmare. He had dreamed that he was trapped in his tank, which was on fire, and that he was being burned alive. In his dream, he saw it happening at the entrance to a town called Saint-Lô, which he had never heard of. The next day he asked me if such a town really existed, and when I told him it did, he was inconsolable.

From then on he was convinced his fate was sealed, and nothing I could do or say could change his mind. He was obsessed by the conviction that he had only a short time to live. Yet he was a real soul mate for me, and even for Claude, and he was clearly more at ease with us than with the adult world. We used to go for walks together and play together and do all the dumb and silly things that children do. Yet, unlike most children, J-Two had a huge, deadly tank as his toy, armed with eight guns of various calibers that spit fire and death.

One day J-Two asked me if I would like to go for a ride in his tank. He said he had to practice shooting that day, and if I wanted to I could watch. I was delighted at the idea, and of course, once J-Two began shooting I wanted to try too.

That afternoon I arrived home in tears. My mother greeted me philosophically and wanted to know what I had done now. In reply, I took her hand and led her outside, then pointed to the horizon where the tops of six trees were neatly shorn.

"I did that!" I sobbed. "All I wanted to do was practice firing J-Two's guns. I only fired each gun once."

"How many shots did you fire in all?" my mother asked.

"Eight," I managed to stammer between sobs.

Then to my surprise she started to laugh. "Six direct hits out of eight tries," she said, "is not to be sneezed at. But don't go bragging to your father. He'd treat you the same way you treated those poor trees. The only difference is that they'll grow out again, and you would never recover after he got through with you."

The poor missionary priest had got more than he had bargained for when he asked me what the matter was. But he seemed fascinated by all I had told him. On the matter of J-Two, however, all he could offer by way of comfort was the reassurance that dreams and reality are often very different. "A nightmare is one thing," he said, "but the future is quite another."

We shook hands and he headed off into the night, toward the festivities which were by now in full swing.

"Come on," Claude said, taking me by the hand. "Let's go there too, before it gets too late." It was, in fact, already dark.

We made our way among the various booths and stands, but at one point I made a wrong turn and ran into some barbed wire, which cut my face. That was the last straw. Mama did her best to clean the cut, but I was in a sad frame of mind as we made our way back to the house. Along the way, it was not my own hurt that bothered me nearly so much as my concern about J-Two. Suddenly, out of nowhere, Claude said:

"You know, Geneviève, I don't mind dying, but I can't bear seeing you suffer."

I bent down and hugged him as tightly as I could.

A few days later, J-Two and his regiment headed for Saint-Lô. He promised to come back after the town had been liberated, if he was still alive.

"Stop talking like that," I said, "of course you'll be alive. You shouldn't let a silly dream disturb you!"

"If I'm wounded, I'll send someone to let you know. I promise."

Days passed. Weeks. Months. J-Two, my friend, never came back.

October 2, 1944

This morning Claude asked if he could go to school with me, and I was happy to have him as company. But as we were walking along, he complained that he had trouble moving his legs. He couldn't take another step.

A few days before, he had hurt himself sliding down the wings of the glider, but no one thought anything about it. Now I carried him back to the house, where Mama sent for the doctor. When he came, the doctor could find no visible wound, but he suspected there might be a blood clot in the leg, and he said that Claude would have to be hospitalized immediately. He was taken to the hospital at Valognes, where it was determined that he needed an operation to remove the clot and a pocket of pus in the thigh. He would be in the hospital for several weeks.

Every Thursday we visited the hospital, which was several kilometers away. We walked there, following the railroad tracks, but often Claude cried with such despair when we left that on some days I couldn't bring myself to enter his room. Sometimes I watched through a window, where I could see without being seen. One day I was watching the nurse change his dressing, and it was almost more than I could bear to see her take the long pair of tongs and remove the old dressings, then insert the new. The rubber tube that the doctors had inserted to draw off the pus could not dry the wound completely, and I could see little Claude's closed eyes and clenched teeth register the pain that each change entailed.

Claude's absence from the house made Papa even more spiteful with me than ever, as though I were to blame, and I did my best to keep out of his way. The departure of J-Two's regiment put an end to the presence of Allied soldiers at the Sheepfold; none came to replace it, and apparently, as the armies moved inland, new places were found for soldiers to rest and recuperate.

Once again I resumed my long walks through the countryside, but without Claude life seemed dull and empty. And what if he were to die? I didn't hesitate for a second: if Claude died, I would throw myself in the river. I knew one spot where the water was really deep, and I'd do it there, knowing I'd have no possibility of surviving. I had never learned to swim. It was not an idle threat: I had made up my mind that without my little brother, life was not worth living.

Papa was a good part of the problem; he had reverted to his former ways, and often he would take advantage of Mama's absence to take out his rage on me. I never breathed a word to her about it, but there came a time when I could keep things to myself no longer. One night, as soon as she arrived from her chores, I sat her down and said:

"I've done something that's probably going to make you angry. The only thing is, I can't tell you why I've done it. But I had my reasons. Promise you won't get angry with me."

"Good lord," she said, "*now* what have you done!"

"Please understand that I did it because I had to."

"All right, what is it?"

In reply, I removed my kerchief from my head. "That," I said.

Mama brought her hand to her mouth. "You cut off your pig-tails! But why?"

"I warned you I couldn't tell you. Ever."

"All right, have it your way. After all, it's your hair. Actually, when it grows out a little it won't be all that bad." She got up and walked all around me, studying the results from every angle. "You know," she said, "it makes you look older. You look like an adult now."

"But I *am* an adult," I said. "I'm going on twelve, Mama. That's getting on!"

Mama laughed and said, "The only problem is, I won't be able to grab you by the hair anymore."

"Don't worry," I said, "there's still enough left for you to get a good grip!"

Friday, October 13, 1944

On this bright autumn day, the lovely colors of the Normandy countryside were washed in warm sunlight. Mademoiselle Burnouf had gone off to a teachers' meeting, and given us the rest of the day off. I knew that Papa was at the house, and since the idea of spending this sunny afternoon with him did not exactly enchant me, I decided not to go home. I would not show up at the house until the normal after-school hour, which gave me several hours to wander wherever I pleased.

As I left Sainte-Mère-Eglise, instead of following the road toward La Fière I opted for a shady, rarely traveled path that took me in the direction of the Irsa Bridge, which spanned the railroad tracks about a kilometer from Grade Crossing 103. It was a path I had almost never taken. I wandered along it, my mind filled with plans for spoiling little Claude when he came home from the hospital. For now we were sure: Claude was going to make it. A few more weeks of patience. "Two or three weeks," the doctor had said. Of course I missed him terribly, but the knowledge that he would soon be home was like a tonic; it was almost as though he were already back. I felt a surge of confidence and renewed courage flow through me, and in my mind I began planning all the walks we would take, all the places we would go, as soon as he could get about again.

As I turned a corner in the path, just before the bridge, I ran smack into an encampment of American soldiers. The "camp" consisted of a number of pup tents. In front of the nearest one a soldier was diligently washing his metal mess kit. I walked straight over to him. His back was to me, and I walked silently, as I always did.

"Good morning, soldier!"

He jumped, as though shot, and turned around. Obviously surprised to see a young girl all alone, so far from any habitation, he looked me up and down and then said, in French:

"Good morning, Mademoiselle. Have you lost your way?"

"Not in the least. I live only a few kilometers from here."

"And what may I ask are you doing so far from home?"

"And if I were to say that the Good Lord sent me here so I could give you a hand washing your mess kit, would you believe me?"

"I'm afraid I wouldn't."

"Well, you'd be wrong. Move off, soldier: this is woman's work."

"The woman strikes me as being a trifle small. But all right, on two conditions: one, the work is well done; and two, you tell me your name."

I was pleased to note that he had already abandoned the formal *vous* and lapsed into the familiar *tu* form of address.

"My name is Geneviève, soldier. And if you knew me you'd know that whatever I do, I do well. If I don't know how to do something, I ask someone to show me, and then I try my hardest to do it just as well. So you see, soldier, it's all very simple."

He was clearly surprised by my words—to judge by the way his eyes grew wider—and I must confess that I was too. I had time to size him up as we talked: he was tall, dark, and handsome. There was a kind of goodness and gentleness that emanated from him which I had almost never seen before. When he laughed, dimples appeared in his cheeks, his eyes shone, and a delightful series of wrinkles appeared at their corners.

I felt happy to be there. And as always happens when I'm happy, and busily working at some task, I broke into song.

J'allais cueillir des fleurs dans la vallée
Insouciant comme un papillon bleu
A l'âge où l'âme à peine réveillée
Se cherche encore et ne sait rien de Dieu

As I was singing, and washing his mess kit, I watched his reactions out of the corner of my eye, as he pretended to be fussing with his tent. I had the impression that he knew my song, and I suspected he was wondering how I was going to handle the final notes of the refrain, so deep and full-toned that only operatic tenors could approach them with confidence. But I intended to surprise him. I could handle my voice as though it were a fine instrument.

> *Je composais avec amour ma gerbe*
> *Quand au détour du chemin l'aspect noir*
> *D'un sapin vert trouant le tapis d'herbe*
> *Me fit prier ainsi sans le savoir.*

After the last note, the soldier whistled in obvious admiration.
"What a lovely voice!"
Pleased with the compliment, I smiled. After I had finished washing his mess kit, he inspected it carefully.
"As you promised, the work's well done," he said. "I was right to take you at your word. Now, what can I offer you as a reward?"
"Nothing. I didn't do it for any reward. Just for the pleasure of being here with you for a few moments."
"You're an odd young lady, all right," he said.
"I know . . . Do you really want to offer me something for helping you?"
"Yes. How about some chocolate?"
"No thank you. I want my own kind of reward. But I'm afraid you'll be angry."
"Try me."
With my forefinger, I pointed to my cheek.
"A kiss," I said. "Right there!"
Once again I saw his eyes grow wide in amazement. Poor soldier, just when he had managed to absorb one surprise, along came another! Still, without a word, he leaned down and gave me a kiss on the cheek. I stood there with my arms crossed, as proud as punch. I'd never met such an obliging man.
"What's your first name?"

"Robert. Isaac Robert actually. But everyone calls me Robert."

"A pretty name. Well, Robert, I must tell you that you're the first man who's ever given me a kiss."

"No . . ."

"Yes, it's true. I've given some men a kiss, but you're the first one ever to have kissed me."

"Don't you have a father?"

"Yes, unfortunately. But I don't have to worry about him ever kissing me."

"Why? You seem like a nice young lady."

"That's what everybody says. Except for my father."

"Tell me about it."

"Oh, there's not much to tell really. And besides, it's a sad story. I'm too happy to be here to ruin it by talking about him."

"All right. We'll talk about your father some other time. Are you hungry? How about a little snack?"

"If you join me."

"It's a deal. Why don't we put our provisions in your basket and take a walk together. You can show me where you live, your village, and the surrounding countryside."

"A great idea!"

Robert filled my basket with all sorts of good things to eat, and off we set, arm in arm, as though we were the oldest friends in the world. We stopped in a field near the river, and Robert emptied my basket and set out the food at the foot of a tree. I watched his hands, with their long, fine fingers, and thought how beautiful they were. The warm autumn sun flooded the countryside with a gentle, reassuring light.

Seated with his back against the tree, Robert handed me two biscuits covered with jam and said:

"A penny for your thoughts, Geneviève."

"I was wishing today would never end. It's so nice being here together, just the two of us."

He smiled, but I thought I saw a cloud of sadness pour over his face.

"Come over here next to me," he said. "I have a secret to confess to you."

Without hesitation I went over and sat next to him. He put his arm around me, pulled me closer to him, and said, in a voice filled with sadness:

"You know, Geneviève, I'm alone too. With no one in the world. Sometimes it's very hard. Yet I'm a man, and it's easier, I think, for us to bear loneliness than it is for you. You're too young to be so lonely. I'll tell you what: let's be friends. You can tell me all your secrets, all your worries, and I'll do the same with you. Is it a deal?"

I found it difficult to answer, so I simply nodded my head. But I was so moved I couldn't keep the tears from rolling down my cheeks. Seeing them, Robert took my head in both hands and gently kissed the tears away.

The notion that I might have a friend, a real friend, a kind and gentle person, a man who might really like me, was more than I had ever hoped for and more than I could handle now. It was the best gift anyone could have ever given me! I didn't dare believe it.

From that moment I formed an immediate and unrestricted bond, a deep attachment to this person whom fate had sent me. Like all children who have been deprived of tenderness at home, I knew instinctively when real feelings came along. Snuggled there in Robert's arms, I felt secure. It was a new and soothing feeling. Robert caressed my hair with one hand. I enjoyed every second of a happiness that I was experiencing for the first time. For me, it was a great discovery. Never had I felt such total surrender, such a feeling of complete peace. Under my breath I murmured:

"Dear God, please make this day last forever!"

I thought he hadn't heard, but clearly he had.

"It will, Geneviève, it will. We'll find some way of carving moments of happiness out of each day. Agreed?"

"You mean it? We'll see each other every day?"

"Of course. But on one condition. That you stop using *vous* when you talk to me."

I accepted on the spot. Robert was right. *Vous* was too formal. Robert smiled and leaned over me.

"Now then, just how will we go about seeing each other every day?"

"I have an idea. From Monday on, I won't stay at school for the evening course. As soon as school's out, I'll fly out the door and come to your camp. We'll have our snack together and then I'll go home no later than if I had stayed for the course. My father will never know the difference."

"How about your teacher? Won't she be angry if you cut her class?"

"Mademoiselle Burnouf? Not in the least. In fact, she'll be delighted. She doesn't like me going home at night alone anyway. I never leave school till seven at the earliest, and now that it gets dark earlier, she's even more worried. I'll still do the work; I'll ask Mama to buy me some candles and I'll do my homework up in my bedroom, after dinner."

"Candles? You don't have any electricity in your house?"

"No. Our house is a long way from town. We don't have any running water, either. Do you want me to show you where we live?"

"Good idea. That way, on Thursday, when you don't have any school, maybe I'll come and visit you."

"In principle, we spend Thursdays visiting my little brother in the hospital. He has a terrible infection in his leg. But he's finally getting better, and he'll be home soon. What I'll do is ask Mama if I can stay home to be with you. That way, she can ride her bicycle to the hospital rather than having to walk all the way with me."

"Is the hospital far away?"

"Twenty kilometers."

"And you walk there?"

"Of course. There and back in one afternoon. And you know what, we often go for nothing. Some days Mama doesn't even want to go into Claude's room. She's afraid he might cry, and she can't bear it."

"You strike me as two pretty courageous ladies."

"We both love Claude."

"I can't wait to meet him."

"You'll see, he's everything I've said he is."

"Careful, or you'll make me jealous."

"You couldn't be: a friend and a little brother are two different things."

We both laughed. We were headed towards Grade Crossing 103. As we passed the Fière Château, I told Robert about the events of that first long night, and the sad story of Bernadette's mother, who was killed by a piece of shrapnel. Just then Maurice Salmon appeared from the château and headed in our direction.

"Hello, Geneviève," he said in *patois*. "I see you have a new friend."

Answering in French, I introduced Robert, as though he were an old friend. The men shook hands warmly. We walked together for a bit, and Maurice took his leave, explaining he had to get into one of the pastures in search of a horse who'd broken out of the corral. After he had left, Robert said:

"What language was he speaking when you first talked?"

"That wasn't a language, it was our *patois*."

"You mean the dialect you speak among yourselves in this region?"

"That's right. Actually, I've only been speaking French properly for the past four years or so. And with my father, I never speak anything but *patois*."

"In four years you've really learned fast," Robert laughed.

"You're right. I fell in love with French," I said. "What I love most is the imperfect subjunctive. We almost never have a chance to use it, I know, but it sounds so elegant, so beautiful. If I had my way, I'd make everyone use it from morning till night."

"I agree it's beautiful. But don't you find it a bit difficult?"

"All a question of getting used to it. And that's the real problem: since we all speak *patois* around here, I never get a chance to practice it, except in class."

We went on talking a mile a minute. I had never talked so much to anyone, and I liked it. I told Robert how the children of the region managed to restock their supply of candy when they ran out. All they had to do, I said, was root around in the fields for all the scrap metal they could find, and then turn it over to the Americans, who apparently sent it back to the States to be melted down and used to make more weapons. A double ration of candy could be had for turning in empty jerrycans. I also told him how the kids at school went out looking in the fields for the metal nose cones used to protect bombs while they were being transported. Several of our seats at school were broken or missing, and these metal caps, with a cushion on top, made ideal—and indestructible—replacements.

We arrived at Grade Crossing 103, and I pointed down the tracks toward 104, explaining to Robert that we lived there for part of the year. Then we headed off toward the Sheepfold. When we reached the fence, I pointed out to him our second house, which seemed lost in the midst of its thirty acres of fields. I hid my basket in the fork of two branches of a big tree, then backtracked toward Irsa Bridge. I had thought, when I had first come upon Robert's encampment, that it was a group of soldiers back from the front for R & R; but it turned out that the unit had the task of guarding the bridge and the section of tracks that passed below it.

We walked along the tracks from 103 toward the bridge, and as we walked I asked Robert if he'd mind doing me a favor. Some American soldiers I had met earlier had taught me a song in English, and although I knew the words by heart, I hadn't the faintest notion what they meant. Would he mind translating it for me?

"Of course not," he said. "Go ahead and sing it, and I'll translate as you go."

Scarcely had I sung the first few words than Robert interrupted me suddenly.

"Geneviève, don't sing that song. It's a dirty, dumb song."

"It is? I hadn't realized it . . ." and I blushed to the roots of my hair. "I'm sorry," I stammered.

"Don't be silly," he said. "You don't have anything to be ashamed about. If anyone should be ashamed, it's the soldier who taught you that."

To make amends, I told him that I wanted to sing him something else, and after a quick inventory I settled on one I especially liked, a song in Latin that I didn't often sing because it was so solemn. When I had finished, Robert said:

"That was beautiful, Geneviève. I love Gounod's *Ave Maria,* but even more when you sing it."

"I can't surprise you with any songs, can I? You know them all."

"It's not surprising, really. France is my second home," he said. "I lived in Paris for several years."

Then he explained to me that he had been born in America, of Jewish extraction. Before the war he had come to France and opened a clothing store. But as soon as the Germans invaded France, knowing full well what the Germans had in store for the Jews of Europe, he went back to America and as soon as America got into the war, joined the army and volunteered to help liberate France.

For the first time in my life I felt totally happy. Robert took me in his strong arms and lifted me onto the brick parapet of the bridge, which was still washed in the warm October sunlight. The cold weather was slow in coming, and though the leaves on the trees had begun to fall, they fell singly, and lazily, as though they too wanted to take advantage, as long as possible, of the last remaining days of warm weather.

From that day on, I was the first kid out of school in the afternoon. Mademoiselle Burnouf couldn't get over the change, for I had always lingered after school till now. Robert came out to meet me along "our" path, and the minute I saw him my heart beat faster. To please him, I worked even harder at my studies, to Mademoiselle Burnouf's great satisfaction—though she didn't know why. Mama did, for I had taken her into my confidence, and while she had not raised any objection to my seeing Robert every day, she had not encouraged me either. All she said was:

"Be careful, child, and don't believe everything soldiers tell you."

A pointless warning: I had a blind faith in the friend that fate had sent me. Day after day Robert pressed to have me introduce him to Papa, a notion that didn't exactly enchant me. Papa Maurice, who had risen to the occasion during our longest night and whom I had seen in a new and surprising light, Papa Maurice whom I had begun to admire and love, had reverted to his old self. The exciting and tragic intermission that we had lived through had, finally, been nothing more than that. Routine, habit, and the inexplicable grudge he bore me reasserted themselves. So how could I introduce my friend to him, a man so completely different? How would he react to Robert? Still, I knew that I couldn't postpone the meeting forever, and finally I agreed that I would bring Robert home one day when I found an opportune moment.

Meanwhile, chance had it that Robert met Mama. One afternoon while we were walking through the marshes, which had been dry since the month of July, we came out onto the tracks at Grade Crossing 104. To our surprise, the house was open: Mama had come over to dust and tidy up, and to air out the house. She was as surprised to see us as we were to run into her, but without a further word she put a pot of coffee on the stove and heated it up for us, as tradition demanded.

Before our visit was over, Robert had won Mama over completely. Not only that, he told her of a plan that had been simmering for a long time in the back of his mind and that he was now determined to follow through: he wanted to adopt me.

I was as stunned as my mother, and in fact perhaps even more astonished. Yet, she seemed to share my joy. Perhaps she had not ever been able to forget my words, uttered in anger but deeply felt when, with my arms loaded with sheets, I had said: "A dog would be better treated than me in this house!" Which wasn't quite true anyway, since she and Claude were there, and I knew they loved me. But she also knew of that deep, smoldering hatred Papa Maurice bore me, that would doubtless never change.

"The only thing is," Robert said, "I don't want to start building any castles in the air. I wonder if you could ask the judge, next time you're in Valognes, whether or not there would be any legal problems in my adopting Geneviève."

On our next visit to the hospital, my mother and I went to see the local judge. I was especially impressed by the way he was dressed: I had never seen a man dressed in a black robe before, with ermine trimming across his chest, and such a strange-looking hat. He began by asking me some questions about my family life. My mother, who was there with me, encouraged me to answer freely and openly.

"First, are you in good health, young lady?" the judge asked. "You look a little on the skinny side to me."

I smiled and answered, without hesitation:

"During these past five years I've lived like everyone else. There were many times I went to bed hungry."

The judge shook his head.

"And won't it bother you to leave your mother?"

"I'll be living in Paris, Monsieur. It's not as though I were going to the end of the world."

At that point, the judge's secretary cut in and said, very coldly:

"Watch your words, child! When you talk to a judge, you address him as 'Your Honor.' "

I felt myself go red, as though someone had deeply offended my sensibility. In a barely audible, emotion-filled voice, I managed:

"I'm sorry, Your Honor. I meant no disrespect."

But that was the end of our open and friendly conversation. I was like a snail that had withdrawn into its shell. The judge was furious. Not at me, it turned out, but at his secretary.

"When I want your opinion on any matter, I'll ask for it," he thundered. "I'd appreciate your letting me conduct this interview in my way. If your work were on a par with this child's ability to express herself—which it isn't—I'd be very pleased—which I'm not!"

Bravo! I whispered to myself. That's the way to tell her. And then, silently addressing the secretary: I hope that will teach you a lesson!

Then I immediately felt sorry for my thoughts. The poor woman was shattered by the judge's words. She too had turned beet red, her lips were quivering, and I could see that she was having trouble holding back the tears.

I felt so sorry for her that, without asking anyone's permission, I got up, went over to her, and taking both her hands in mine, said:

"I'm terribly sorry, Ma'am." Then, turning to the judge, I said: "With Your Honor's permission, I think we'd better leave. I'm afraid things have gotten out of hand, and I don't feel right about going on with the discussion. If my parents decide to follow through on this matter, we'll come back to see you again."

I took Mama by the arm and led her toward the door. At the threshold I paused, turned back, and said:

"Good day, Sir."

As we left I could hear the judge's voice, filled with astonishment, saying:

"That's the first time in my career that a child has taught me a lesson in my own courtroom. *She's* afraid things have gotten out of hand? Well, I haven't finished with her yet!"

We had almost reached the exit at the far end of the courtyard when the sound of footsteps made us turn around. It was the judge who, leaving all dignity behind, was running toward us, holding up the skirts of his long robe with both hands to keep from tripping over them.

"Wait, young lady. Not so fast!"

We stopped and waited for him to catch up. I had the feeling that I had probably gone too far, and that he was going to give me a good dressing down. When he reached us he stammered, still out of breath from his run:

"I want you both to have tea with me in my chambers. I warn you, young lady, I don't care how easily offended you are. I won't take no for an answer."

I realized he was no longer using the *tu* form of address with me that adults use in addressing children, and was trying to figure out precisely what that meant, when he said, looking me straight in the eyes:

"Does your silence mean you won't accept? I really must insist. I was wrong to speak as I did and want to make amends."

"I agree on one condition," I said, hardly believing my own words.

"Name it."

"That you make peace with your secretary and invite her to join us."

"Agreed. Agreed. Now wait here while I go change my clothes and invite my secretary."

And he hurried off as fast as he had come, again holding his robe high off the ground.

"I think you've overstepped your bounds," Mama said. "There are some things a girl your age just shouldn't do or say."

"Mama, I've been through a war and an occupation, and it seems to me I've earned the right to speak my mind. The man acted unkindly. And yet I know he *is* a charitable person. There are such pretty colors around his head."

"What in the world are you talking about?"

"Nothing."

The judge took us to his apartment, which was near the courtroom. An elderly lady served the four of us tea. We told them about my little brother Claude, who had been languishing all these weeks in the hospital, and more about Robert. We learned that adoption laws in France are really tough, and that in case the slightest infirmity of body or mind is detected, adoption is out of the question. We talked so long that by the time we left it was already dark. Twenty kilometers on foot might normally have been a discouraging prospect at that late hour, but we were buoyed by the double news we had learned that day: Claude would definitely be discharged from the hospital in a few days, and nothing seemed to stand in the way of my becoming Robert's legally adopted daughter. The only remaining obstacle was Papa Maurice . . . and Robert said that he'd take charge of that problem. Assuming of course that I could one day work up the courage to introduce them.

The longed-for opportunity came one evening from a most unexpected quarter. My parents were trying to figure out how they could bring Claude home from Valognes. There weren't any ambulances, at least in our part of the world, and no one we knew owned an automobile. There was Maurice Salmon, of course, who they were sure would be glad to lend his horse and buggy, but forty kilometers was a long trip, even for the horse. With a straight face, I said:

"A jeep and chauffeur, that's what we need."

My mother chimed in, right on cue:

"Do you think your friends from the Irsa encampment would accept? Really?"

"What do we have to lose? What do you think, Papa? May I have your permission to go and ask them?"

Thinking only of his son, and how badly he wanted to see him home again, Papa readily agreed.

"Of course, child, go to it. And be quick about it. Can you ask them tomorrow?"

Robert was delighted at the turn of events, and immediately requisitioned a jeep and driver. I took them both back to the Sheepfold to introduce them to Papa Maurice. I was trembling slightly as we drove up to the house. How would Papa receive them? And how would he react when I informed him that Robert wanted to adopt me? Perhaps, after all, he'd be happy to get rid of me, and all my worries would have been in vain.

Robert was so charming, and so nice, that he immediately won over the whole family. My sister Denise, who happened to be there and to whom I had confided everything, took me aside and said:

"You've made a good choice, Geneviève. He's really adorable." And then she added, with a deep sigh: "Lord knows, you've earned your happiness."

She went on to tell me her plans for the future, and said in passing:

"Of course, when I get married I'll only come home to visit once in a very great while. A married woman has to live with her husband."

"And leave her parents behind?"

"Of course, you ninny."

There wasn't room enough for everyone to go in the jeep, so Robert gallantly offered to let Papa Maurice take his place. Papa demurred, fearing that he would be depriving Robert of a pleasant drive through the countryside.

"Don't worry, Papa Maurice. Geneviève will keep me company until you get back. Your little boy will be so happy to see you; don't deprive him of that pleasure. While you're gone, I'll help Geneviève with her homework."

Papa did not have to be asked twice, and he climbed into the jeep, together with my mother and Denise, whom they were dropping off in Neuville-au-Plain.

We waved at them until the jeep had disappeared, then turned back inside, happy to be alone together. The only problem was that whenever we were together time sped by unbelievably fast. I tackled my homework, and Robert helped me tend the fire. He liked an open fireplace as much as I did, and I suspected he was as addicted to daydreaming as I was.

We heard the sound of the jeep, and ran to the door. There indeed was Claude, all scrubbed and smiling and happy to be home. My parents were overwhelmed with joy at having their long-lost son back again, and in their euphoria invited both soldiers to stay for supper. As we had agreed ahead of time, the driver begged off, on the pretense that he had guard duty coming up, while Robert accepted. Our little drama was unfolding right on schedule. I had to admit that I was trembling slightly, now that the great day had arrived. For I knew that Robert did not intend to waste any time and planned to talk to Papa tonight. I grew more and more worried as the evening wore on, until it became almost impossible to hide it any longer. What if Papa were to react negatively? What if he got mad and forbade me to see Robert again?

After dinner we went over to sit by the fire, except for Papa, who remained at the table with a glass of Calvados in front of him. Claude and I had our regular positions on either side of the huge fireplace, right where Mama always set the newborn chicks to warm. Robert, who was seated next to me, leaned over and whispered:

"You think I can mention it now?"

"Why don't you try. We won't gain anything by waiting."

Robert turned around to Papa and said, with a broad smile:

"Papa Maurice, there's something I'd like to ask you."

"Anything you like, Monsieur Robert, anything in the world."

I could see that Papa was in a good frame of mind. If only it would last! I had the feeling that if my heart beat any faster it would explode!

"You see, Papa Maurice, I've known your daughter Geneviève for several weeks now. I'm a bachelor, I don't have any children, and after the war I'd like to adopt her and take her with me. She'll live with me, and I'll see to it she gets a good education. She'll have everything she wants, I can assure you. I own a clothing store in Paris, and as soon as the war's over I plan to take charge of it again. What do you say?"

Silence. Yes, my heart *was* going to explode. I glanced over at Mama. I could almost hear her heart pounding too. Only Robert seemed to retain his composure. There was a smile on his lips.

Finally Papa raised his eyes, looked straight at Robert, and said:

"If you're a Parisian, what are you doing in the American Army?"

"It's very simple. When the Germans invaded France, I turned my shop over to some friends and left. I'm Jewish, and I don't have to tell you how the Germans treated the Jews." And he went on to tell Papa what he had already told me.

Papa shook his head slowly as Robert went on. Yes, he knew all about what the damn Germans had done to the Jews. But for him, the fact that Robert was Jewish was of no importance. Here where we lived, anti-Semitism did not exist.

"What part of America do you come from?" Papa asked.

"Guatemala. That's in Central America. My parents live there."

"But you intend to settle down in France?"

"Of course. I plan to reopen my store in Paris, and if you agree I'll take Geneviève there with me. What do you say?"

My father lowered his eyes for a moment, folded his hands, and seemed to be pondering the question. The seconds ticked by, each an eternity. Would he ever look up and reply?

At last he raised his head and again looked Robert straight in the eyes.

"All right. I consent."

My anxiety, which had built up all evening, ran out as though a dam had broken. It was replaced, almost immediately, by a feeling of joy I could not contain. But then all of a sudden everything was reversed, as I heard Papa say:

"On one condition."

"Which is?"

"That you promise me she'll finish school. I'd be too ashamed to give you an ignoramus."

A broad smile filled Robert's face.

"Not only high school, Papa Maurice. When I said I'd see she received a proper education, I meant university studies as well. I feel very strongly about it, and agree with you that education is all-important."

A further silence. Then:

"So what do you say? Is it yes?"

"In that case, yes." Papa said, and he looked over at me and winked. "You can take her whenever you like. She's yours."

I felt like jumping up and dancing around the room with joy, but I remained seated next to Robert, who put his arms around me and squeezed me. He was as happy as I was: we had done it!

"One more point, Papa Maurice. I'd appreciate your taking care of Geneviève for me till the war's over. I'll come and fetch her as soon as I'm demobilized. Till then, I count on you to take care of her for me. Anyway, the war can't last much longer. I'll ask Mama to initiate the adoption procedures as soon as possible. And I ask you, Papa, to make sure that no one does anything to harm or hurt

Geneviève from now on. No one, do you understand? If she does something wrong, let me know and I'll punish her. Can I count on you for that?"

"You have my word," Papa said.

"Geneviève may be coming home after dark. We've agreed that she'll come to see me at the camp after school, and if some evenings she's a little late, I don't want anyone to scold her, is that clear?"

"Don't worry, Monsieur Robert. She can come and go as she pleases. Now she's your responsibility. From now on, that's your concern."

Papa had given his word. And for him, his word was his bond. No more sudden rages, no more beatings, no more brutality. I was free.

I decided to test my new freedom.

"Is it all right if I walk with Robert partway back to his camp? You won't lock the door on me, Papa, even if you're in bed when I come home?"

Almost gently, he responded:

"Don't worry, child. The door will never be locked again, even if you come home at dawn."

My eyes filled with tears. I almost felt like hugging him. I slipped into my coat, and tied a woolen kerchief around my hair. Robert said goodnight to my parents, and off we set in the direction of his camp, without my even having taken time to tiptoe upstairs and plant a kiss on the cheek of little Claude, who was long since fast asleep.

There was a full moon out, and it seemed almost as bright as day. The countryside was bathed in silver. I remained strangely silent, so much so that Robert grew worried.

"Cat got your tongue? What's the matter, Geneviève? Or are you too happy to talk?"

Without replying, I snuggled closer against him and, holding his hand tightly, stroked my cheek with it, and covered it with kisses. We reached the bridge and I still hadn't opened my mouth. Astonished and upset, Robert picked me up and set me on the brick parapet.

"All right," he said, "I want you to tell me what's bothering you. Remember, you promised that you'd never hide anything from me. Ever."

"You're going to be angry," I said.

"Why? You know I never get angry at you. Go ahead. Speak your piece."

"All right, here it is. I'm happy that Papa has agreed you can adopt me."

"Great. So what's the problem?"

"But I don't want to be your daughter. Ever."

"What a crazy idea! Why not?"

I was thinking about what Denise had said, and her words had kept running through my head all the while we were walking here. "When I get married," she had said, "I'll only come home to visit once in a very great while. A married woman has to live with her husband." Which meant that sometime, maybe even soon if I had a fiancé, I would have to leave Robert! I would have to go live with a man I didn't yet know and abandon the only friend I had in the world? Never! I could never do it!

I had no clear idea about just what went on between husband and wife, but one thing I did know for sure: a wife did not leave her husband. Therefore, in order not to leave Robert, to spend the rest of my life with him, I had to be not his daughter but his wife. It was very simple.

Simple perhaps, but difficult to say.

"Why not?" he repeated.

"Can't you guess?"

"No, I really can't."

Then, putting my head against his chest, frightened to death by what I was about to confess to him, I murmured, so low I was not sure he could hear me:

"Because I love you. I want to be your wife."

I said the sentences calmly enough, I think, but my heart was pounding so loud I was sure he could hear it. If he had been struck by lightning, Robert could not have been more surprised. But his reaction was not one of derision; it was gentle and tender. He lifted my head and looked at me for what seemed like a very long time.

"Don't you see, my sweet Geneviève, that it isn't possible. I'm far too old for you."

"What difference does that make? That won't keep you from making me happy. Sure, I'm still very young. But here in Normandy girls mature quickly, like the summer wheat. As soon as I'm fifteen we can get married. By then, the war will surely be over and we'll be together forever and ever. You'll see, it's not only possible, but wonderful!"

"I can't marry you. We're from different backgrounds. Different religions."

"That doesn't matter. Your God and mine are one and the same. You know that as well as I."

"Have you loved me, I mean this way, for a long time?"

"Ever since I first laid eyes on you."

"And you never let on."

"I was afraid you'd make fun of me. I'm still very young."

"You can say that again!"

"There, you see, you *are* making fun of me. Are you angry?"

"No, but I am surprised. Put yourself in my shoes. It's the first time anyone's asked for my hand in marriage. And the fact is, you are young. So very young . . ."

"I love you. I'll never love anyone else. If you don't love me, tell me right away. It will hurt, but it's better I know the truth. I'll still love you."

"I love you too, Geneviève. More than you know. If I didn't, do you think I would have gone to such lengths to adopt you, to ask your parents to allow me to take you with me to Paris?"

"But I don't want you to love me like a father. When children grow up they leave their parents, and I don't ever want to leave you, even when we're both old and gray. Even after we're both dead, I'll still go on loving you. Do you understand that?"

"Yes, I do. But before making any decision, we have to think long and hard about it. A whole lifetime: that's a long period you're talking about. And the age difference between us is a real problem."

"I prefer being happy with you than unhappy with a younger man. But since you want to think about it, let's sleep on it. Think about it between now and tomorrow. If you agree with me, come and meet me on our path tomorrow afternoon, the way we always do. If you're not there I'll understand that you don't want me and I won't come again. We won't see each other any more. I'll suffer, but so what? Anyway, it's very late, so I ought to be going home. I want to be in good shape tomorrow so I can be worthy of you at school. You'll see: if you do agree, you'll never be sorry. Kiss me."

He kissed me. My first grownup kiss. It lent wings to my feet as I sped home. Never had I felt so happy, and I only wished that my heart had been twice the size it was to contain all the happiness that was flowing into it that night.

My father had kept his word: the door was unlocked. I took off my shoes and tiptoed through the kitchen, past the alcove where my parents were sleeping, up the steep staircase to my bedroom, where I dropped on my knees and prayed. With all my heart I prayed that the Good Lord would look down upon us and protect us, both Robert and me, no matter what the future held in store.

The following morning my mother didn't have to call up to me more than once to rouse me out of bed. I downed my breakfast in record time and dashed off to school. Today I had a rendezvous. A very important rendezvous, which might well decide the rest of my life. I hadn't slept all night. Slowly, insidiously, doubt had crept into my thoughts. What if Robert didn't come? What if he decided that I really was too young? What if he not only didn't want me to be his wife but his daughter either? My only reason for living would vanish, and it would have been my own fault. All day long these and other similar questions crowded into my mind, and tormented me unmercifully. When the bell rang signaling the end of classes, I was out the door like a rabbit. I ran as fast as my legs would carry me toward the path leading to the Irsa Bridge. There I forced myself to slow down and walk normally, but my heart was beating uncontrollably. With each step I took along that path, my anxiety grew, until it became unbearable. The tall trees that flanked the path made the relative darkness seem all the more ominous. If Robert did come, I assumed he would be waiting for me, as he usually did, at the outskirts of a tiny village not far from the camp.

I passed through the village, which consisted of no more than a few houses, and then my heart, which was heavy, took off as on a pair of magic wings: just beyond the last house I caught sight of a tall silhouette. He had come.

Thinking I had not seen him, he called out:

"Geneviève, I'm here."

I ran over and threw myself into his arms. He held me close against him.

"Did you think of me today, Geneviève?"

"Only of you. Despite all my good intentions, there was no way I could concentrate on my studies. Mademoiselle Burnouf noticed, and thought that my father had been picking on me again. She tried to comfort me. And do you know what I did to thank her? I burst into tears like a baby."

"Why? Were you afraid I wouldn't come?"

"More than afraid. I was afraid all last night and all day today. I've been shaking like a leaf since I left you yesterday."

"You see, there was no reason to. I did come. It is really me, in the flesh. Are you happy?"

"I wish I could tell you how much."

He stepped back a bit and looked at me.

"And now what, my darling?"

My darling! I was a woman. He had called me "my darling"!

"Now, my love, it's very simple," I said. "You get your war over with, I'll concentrate on growing up, and when you come back we'll get married."

"Not so fast, young lady. Somewhere in that sequence you left out something very important: your studies. I feel strongly about that, you know. As soon as the war's over and you're ready, I do want you to pursue your studies, go to the university. Yesterday I said to your father that I didn't want an ignorant daughter. Today I repeat that I don't want an ignorant wife. If you don't pursue your higher studies, I won't marry you. Is that clear?"

"I'll do whatever you want. I'll be a good, attentive student: you'll be proud of me."

"I'm counting on it. This afternoon I went over to see your mother and we had a long talk. She was a little taken aback by the news, but not all that much really. She had had some suspicion of what was going on in your little head. She has no objection, but she doesn't want your father to know, at least for several months, for fear he might not let you leave. As for the rest, nothing else is changed except for the fact that now we won't proceed with the adoption. So you have your way, you little tigress, I'm going to marry you. Hurry up and grow! I'm looking forward to marrying not only the youngest but the sweetest girl a man ever dreamed of!"

"Pinch me!" I cried. "I'm sure I'm dreaming some wonderful dream. Oh! Robert, don't ever let me wake up!"

He laughed and hugged me.

"One more thing," he said. "Your mother wants you to make your own trousseau. Which means you'll have to learn to sew. I gather that's a chore that doesn't exactly enchant you."

"I'll learn. I could learn anything to please you."

"Something else, Geneviève. Why did you cut off your pigtails?"

"Was it Mama who asked you to find out?"

"Yes."

"Then I'm sorry, I won't tell you."

"All right."

We had reached the bridge. Robert, as he had done every afternoon for a month now, lifted me up and set me on the parapet. Standing there in front of me, he stared at me, and it seemed that his beautiful dark eyes were filled with sadness.

"You're always hiding things from me? Don't you trust me?"

"Of course I do. But I don't want to hurt Mama."

"I'm sorry, but I'm afraid I don't understand."

"Let me try and explain. But first swear you won't tell anyone."

"I swear."

"All right. In the kitchen at the Sheepfold there are big cross-beams, and in the beams are big nails used to hold Papa's hunting rifle."

"And what does all that have to do with your pigtails?"

"You'll see in a minute. The night before the first time I took this path and met you, my father had been drinking. More than usual, in fact. Claude's being in the hospital had made him angrier than ever. Anyway, he tied my pigtails in a knot and hoisted me up and hung me by my hair to one of those nails. He kept me there for half an hour. My head hurt so much that I didn't dare move a muscle. I had the feeling that my scalp was going to come off. Luckily, I don't weigh very much or it might have. Anyway, as soon as he let me down I cut my pigtails so he could never do it again. That's the whole story. Now do you understand why I didn't want Mama to know? She had enough worries of her own with Papa without my adding to them."

Robert pulled me close to him and held me for a long time in his arms, without saying a word. The moon had risen, and when he moved back I could see that my soldier's eyes were filled with tears.

"From now on I'm taking care of you. I promise you'll never have to go through anything like that ever again," he whispered. "Don't worry: your life is going to be different."

I pulled his head close to me. Now it was my turn to kiss his tears away.

Several soldiers appeared and invited us to join them for their evening meal at the tents. I had been adopted not only by Robert but by the whole group. And as Robert had promised, my life at home changed too, immediately and completely. Papa no longer beat me. I was no longer his daughter; in his eyes I belonged to somebody else. And whatever else his failings, I had never seen that rough, uneducated man go back on his word. Since Robert had asked him to look out for me until he returned, he did. For the first time in my life he worried about me, asked if I had had enough to eat, advised me to dress warmly when I went outside, spoke to me respectfully, without a trace of his old hatred or brutality. I actually found him rather funny, but I carefully refrained from showing it. He was proud as a peacock, and bragged incessantly about his youngest girl, about the marvelous man who was going to adopt her, and about the endless studies she would pursue thanks to him. In the whole equation, I think it was the studies that made him most proud; in fact, that was really the one thing that mattered to the poor man, who to the end of his days would never get over the fact that he had never had the chance to become educated.

December 24, 1944

Christmas eve. For the first time in my life, a real Christmas tree, and a real present. The most unexpected, yet most dreamed of, present a girl can have.

After we had taken our customary places on the brick parapet, as we had done every afternoon for almost three months, Robert suddenly asked me to close my eyes and put out my hand. I did, and I could feel him slipping on my finger what I supposed to be a token ring of some sort. But when I opened my eyes I saw, to my surprise, that it was in fact a real engagement ring! For a moment I simply sat there and stared at it dumbly, unable to find any words to express what I was feeling. Then, as always happens when I'm happy, I began to sing. This time the only song that came to mind, which seemed appropriate:

> *When I felt your golden ring*
> *Slip upon my finger*
> *My heart was filled*
> *With happiness*
> *My lips were stilled*
> *But nonetheless*
> *I knew I had to sing.*
> *In happiness or sorrow*
> *We'll be together, one*
> *today and one tomorrow,*

Down the rocky road of life,
Man and wife
Into the setting sun . . .

Robert listened enraptured, then shook his head in disbelief. "I'm now convinced that no matter what the occasion, you'll always have one ready for it."

"I do know a lot," I said. "But my favorite one hasn't yet been written."

"Ah?"

"It's a song I dreamed about called *Geneviève,* that will tell the story of a girl my age. The story of her life, all her joys and sorrows, and when people hear it they'll be moved to tears."

"If you want to sing such a song, you'll have to write it yourself," he said.

"I know. But the problem is that I wouldn't know how to go about it. I don't know the rules for writing songs."

"Like anything else, they can be learned."

"Where? There isn't a library at Sainte-Mère-Eglise. And I rarely have a chance to read poetry. I've read some Lamartine, but I find him so gloomy."

"I think you'll find most poets rather gloomy, Geneviève. They tend to see life's darker side. But enough of this small talk. Let's go show your parents your new ring."

I jumped down off the parapet, and together we made our way to the house. Mama had a fire going, over which she had roasted a turkey. We all had dinner together. Papa had not been out for three days, and for three days had not touched a drop of drink. A new record. As a result, we spent a pleasant and harmonious evening, and after dinner we exchanged presents. For Robert I had embroidered six handkerchiefs, which I had been working on for several weeks. I had sworn that before I was through I'd learn how to sew and embroider properly.

A day or two before the New Year, Robert announced that his outfit was being transferred. He wouldn't be going far, just another post in the neighborhood of Sainte-Mère-Eglise. During our last evening on the little bridge that we now thought of as ours, he made me promise never to come back to it.

"Why?"

"Because another unit will be coming to replace us here," he said. "You might as well know I'm the jealous type, and the idea of your being here with other soldiers is more than I can take."

"Don't worry," I assured him, "however fond I am of this bridge, you can be sure I'll never come here again."

The day after Robert's departure, Mama and I went into Sainte-Mère-Eglise on some errands. On our way home I asked her if she'd mind taking a new route, "as a favor to me." Without inquiring why, and although the alternate route was a good two kilometers longer than the customary path, she immediately consented. I had asked her that favor because I had a strong feeling that Robert's new camp was somewhere along that route.

My intuition proved correct. Half a kilometer from the village, we came upon a military installation in the process of being set up. It was a much larger encampment than the one at the Irsa Bridge. Without a moment's hesitation I walked into the camp and looked around. A number of pup tents were already erected, but the soldiers' faces were unfamiliar. Then, suddenly, I found myself looking straight into the face of one of Robert's buddies. He broke into a big smile and called out to his companions. Within seconds, several of the Irsa soldiers had gathered, and they lifted me triumphantly onto their shoulders, while Mama looked on approvingly. Drawn by the shouts, Robert soon arrived, but his buddies didn't release me immediately from my lofty perch. When finally they did I rushed over to Robert, but he turned his back to me and I heard him mutter to my mother:

"I know Geneviève loves me, Mama, but then I have the feeling she loves all the soldiers!"

I was upset. How could he think such thoughts? Of course I loved all the American soldiers. How could I not, after all we had gone through together during those long days and nights back in

June? I had thousands of reasons to love them, but I realized, too, that I had never told Robert of that period. Why should I have: it would have sounded as if I were bragging, and whatever other faults our family might have had, bragging was not one of them.

Yes, I did love all the American soldiers. But there was only one with whom I was *in love*. I was so happy to have found Robert again. Was it possible that such a silly suspicion could in one second annihilate so much happiness? I took Robert aside and tried to talk to him. I wasn't responsible for his friends' exuberant reactions, was I? They were simply expressing their own happiness at seeing me again, knowing how much we loved each other. There was no reason whatsoever for him to be jealous, although, I added, I was secretly pleased to see how jealous he was. For wasn't it true that one was only jealous if one were in love? It didn't take much to convince him, and his solemn face soon broke into a grin. He offered to escort us back to the house, and we readily accepted. Robert couldn't get over the fact that I had come directly to his new camp. There were, he pointed out, several new camps going up all around Sainte-Mère-Eglise, and yet I had honed in immediately on his. The fact was, I could have found it with my eyes closed.

For the first time in several months, my little brother went to school with me after the Christmas holidays. His leg was completely better, and his impatience to return to school was touching.

The New Year also brought us a reminder that the war, which we had almost forgotten, was still very much with us. Our house was empty during the day, since Claude and I were at school and Papa, Mama, and Francis were outside working. One evening Papa returned home to find the front door smashed to bits—the work of a pickax to judge by the marks. One of my uncles who lived nearby told us that he had seen two men knocking on our door earlier in the day, and since he hadn't liked the looks of them he had called the Americans, who were stationed not far from us. They had responded quickly and captured the two men, who had by then broken into our house and put on some of Papa's clothes. Both were German prisoners who had escaped from a nearby camp.

That evening we were sitting around the table discussing the event. Mama got up to light the fire before starting to cook dinner when she noticed that the ashes had overflowed the hearth and spilled out on the floor. She asked me to bring her a dustpan and broom. As she was sweeping up the ashes, her broom struck something hard, which made a metallic sound.

"Maurice! Francis! Come over here. I have a feeling our escaped prisoners left us a little present before they were arrested."

With infinite care, Papa brushed the ashes away to see what the object was. Mama was right: they had left an anti-personnel bomb. I felt shivers run up and down my spine, and I'm sure the others in the room did too. We realized that if Mama had lit the fire, we'd all have been blown sky high. Thank God she had noticed the overflow of ashes!

That night we had a cold supper. First thing in the morning, Papa would go and fetch the American bomb-disposal unit to rid us of that awful souvenir.

When we were in bed, Mama came up and made us say an extra prayer of thanks. And like two angels we fell asleep. It was not until the following day, when she made our bed, that Mama discovered two more souvenirs: hidden between the sheets, at the foot of each bed, were two more bombs, one which would explode on contact. Mama usually put a hot water bottle at the foot of our bed, to warm our feet, but for some strange reason the night before she had not. Still, it was a miracle that neither Claude nor I had touched the bombs during the night. In Claude's case, his size had saved him, for even if he stretched out full length, his feet did not touch the bottom of the bed. As for me, pure luck; that night I had slept curled up in a little ball, which I almost never do, and had barely moved. After such events as these, doesn't one have to believe in destiny?

When Robert learned what had happened he went into a blind rage. He demanded that a report be drawn up of the incident, and that the two prisoners be immediately transferred to the military police, and a trial held. They should not be tried for escaping but for attempted murder. Can you imagine such a thing! Trying to kill two innocent little children. Robert went on and on, and everyone in the house was very serious and solemn, until I chimed in:

"Didn't I tell you the Good Lord wanted no part of me? As long as I'm within striking distance of any of you in this room, you obviously have nothing to fear. God's simply afraid that if I arrive in heaven I'll sow disruption and disorder all over the place. So He prefers to keep me down here where I'll cause less trouble."

I said it sincerely, but also in an effort to dissipate some of the tension that had been building, and within minutes my own good humor had spread to the others, and we all relaxed visibly. The "incident" was forgiven, if not forgotten.

Men's justice, however, is not so simple, nor forgiveness so swift. The suspicion was that, once the authorities learned of the two Germans' attempted murder, their lives would not be worth very much.

April 9, 1945

My birthday. Robert went up to Paris. A surprise. He brought me back a beautiful blue dress. He also had made for me, in utter secrecy, an adorable bracelet consisting of several English silver coins, with George V's face upon them, joined together by the master silversmith Monsieur Fossard. I've never been so spoiled in my whole life. I'm now in my thirteenth year. In two years I can get married. That's the only thing that matters.

May 1, 1945

Robert, whose camp had been moved once again, still paid me daily visits. He was now stationed at Blosville, which was not all that far from Sainte-Mère-Eglise, and we still managed to see each other whenever we had a free moment.

The first of May is a holiday, and so school was closed. When I awoke that morning I looked out the window, and to my amazement the ground was covered with a blanket of snow. It was still snowing, in fact, in big, lazy flakes that floated to the ground. I have always loved snow. I suspect that my love for snow dates back to a punishment my father inflicted on me when I was about eight months old. I am convinced that I remember the incident, though my mother told me the story, and therefore what is hers and what is real memory is difficult to separate. In any case, like all babies I was cutting teeth at eight months, and my crying kept my father from sleeping. One night, in a fit of rage, he picked up my cradle and carried it outside into the fields. Despite my mother's tears and pleas, he remained intractable, and to make sure she didn't try to bring me back inside, he locked the door and grasped the key tightly in his hand. Mama cried and begged and threatened to call the gendarmes, but nothing moved him. Despite my age I remember the clouds moving in the sky, a bright moon, and snowflakes falling. I watched them, followed them with my eyes, then reached up with my hands and tried to grab them as they fell. I would have loved to sit up, the better to catch the pretty white flakes, but I was tucked in too tightly, and couldn't. I remember a cow coming over and peering into my crib at this strange intruder, and later a colt. But more than anything I remember watching for the longest time those pretty snowflakes. I also remember moments of fear when the scudding clouds shut out the moon. Finally I fell asleep. And ever since I've cherished moonlight and snowflakes, and had a certain fear of darkness. Much later, my mother told me that at dawn she rushed outside, fully expecting to find me frozen. My crib was covered with a thick blanket of snow but when she scraped it off she found her baby with hands and face blue with cold, but so well tucked in that she had not been able to work free of her covers, and so reasonably warm and apparently little the worse for the experience.

On this May first, Robert and I took a long walk through the snowy countryside. The apple trees, which were already in bloom, were covered with snow, and the juxtaposition of white and pink was indescribably beautiful. After we had walked for a long time we were tired and sat down on the trunk of an apple tree that had been blown down in a recent storm. My soldier took me in his arms and said:

"I have some bad news for you, Geneviève. You must show me how strong and courageous you are. I have to tell you that I'm in bad shape myself."

"Don't say another word," I said. "You're being transferred."

Robert nodded. I felt a lump in my throat, and tears welling up in my eyes. To hide my distress, I picked a daisy and shook the snow from its petals. One by one I began to pick off the petals: he loves me, he loves me not, he loves me, he loves me not . . .

And then I began to sing:

> Tell me, darling daisy,
> Tell me, daisy mine,
> Tell me true
> As I love you

Let him love me too
Let him, darling daisy
Let him, daisy mine . . .

Tears were running down my cheeks. Robert took me in his arms and tried to comfort me.

"Don't cry," he murmured. "I can't bear to see you cry. I'll write you every day. And besides, I'll have lots of furloughs and I'll come to see you as often as I can. The war will be over in no time at all. They're talking about a matter of days. In six months I'll be out of the army and I'll come to fetch you and take you away forever. Be brave, my darling Geneviève. Promise you won't forget me."

"Forget you! I'd never forget you, even if I never saw you again. Will you really write me often?"

"Every day, cross my heart. And don't forget: I may show up here at any time. I'll come when you're least expecting me, and you'll look up and, presto! there I'll be. Will that make you happy?"

"How can you even ask such a question? What you deserve is a snowball smack in the face."

And suiting the action to the words, I picked up a fat snowball and rubbed it on the tip of Robert's nose, then took off as fast as I could run, with him in close pursuit through the thick blanket of snow.

There are days that ought to go on forever.

It was coming up to dusk. After a long, lingering kiss, the man I loved, the man who would soon be my husband, climbed into his jeep and drove slowly away, turning back dozens of times to wave and cry out: "Bye-bye, Geneviève . . . Bye-bye, my love."

Time passed. Each day the postman brought me the promised letter, which I awaited with love and fear. As soon as I had a free moment, I would withdraw into some private corner and read it alone, or sometimes in the company of Claude, seated on the parapet of the

Irsa Bridge, where I often spent hours dreaming of the happy days I had spent there, and of the happy days to come. The war was indeed over, Robert would soon be discharged, and, as he had promised, would come to fetch me.

Robert-Geneviève: I carved the two names a hundred times in the stone of the bridge.

One evening, when I had arrived home from school, my mother said to me:

"Be a good girl, go up to your room and bring me down some chestnuts. I need them for supper."

I didn't wait to be asked twice. I love chestnuts, and I knew that our supply was running low and would never last till the new harvest this autumn. I went up to my room, carrying an empty basket in my hand. At the top of the stairs my heart stopped, and I dropped the basket.

"Hello there! Guess who's here?"

It *was* Robert, yes, it really was! He had been hiding behind the door. I ran and threw myself into his arms.

"My, how you've grown in two months!" he said. "And you've put on some weight, too. You're also getting prettier by the day."

"I told you I'd hurry up and grow up fast," I said, "and I kept my word. When did you arrive?"

"This afternoon. I didn't want to go pick you up at school. I decided it would be more fun to surprise you this way. Are you happy to see me?"

"Of course I am. How many days' leave do you have?"

"Three full days. Every minute of which I intend to spend with you. Since the school year's almost over, your mother said you could ask permission to stay out of school while I'm here. That way we won't be separated even part of the day."

He was right: the very thought that even a crumb of happiness might be lost was unbearable. Claude volunteered to lend my soldier his big bed and to sleep during the three days in his baby bed downstairs. For the first time, Robert and I were going to share the same bedroom. That evening, I got ready for bed first and slipped into my bed. I pulled the covers up over my head and pretended I was asleep. But beneath the covers I was having terrible trouble controlling the laughter I felt rising inside me. I sneaked a look at Robert as he climbed into bed. He started to snuggle down, then with a look of mock anger turned to me and said:

"Tell me, Geneviève, who made this bed?"

"I did. Why?"

"In which case, my little chickadee, get over here and remake it! Unless you want me to sleep on the floor. I'm not used to being short-sheeted, and I'm not going to let you get away with it!"

Laughing so hard tears came into my eyes, I threw my covers off and started to remake his bed, while Robert went over and sat on mine.

"Boy, is your bed hard," he said, pressing down on it with both hands. "Can you sleep on it all right?"

"Sure, I'm used to it. It's a straw mattress."

"You're the only one in your family who has one of these, aren't you?"

"Yes, the others have inner springs and feather mattresses."

"Why don't you?"

"I don't know. Mama calls it my penance bed. She says that monks in their cells don't have one any harder. But I don't mind. Sure, if I had my way I'd prefer a softer bed like yours. There: it's all remade. Come and climb in. To make up for my sins, I'll tuck you in."

Robert slipped down between the sheets, this time without any trouble. I tucked in the blankets, then whispered in his ear:

"This bed is big enough for two, you know. Why don't I climb in beside you?"

Gently but firmly he said:

"No, you little devil. That's just not possible."

"Why not?"

"Because. You'll sleep with me after we're married, not before."

"But it would be so nice to snuggle in your arms all night. You just said my bed is too hard for anyone to sleep in. And you admit there's room for two in yours. So give me one good reason why you should refuse me. Just one!"

"There is one, actually, and it's both important and serious: because I love you."

"Oh la la! Now I don't understand a thing. You tell me you love me, and because you love me you refuse to please me. That doesn't make any sense to me. It's just what I thought: grownups are crazy. And you're a little crazy yourself. But I don't care. I'll love you the way you are. But you have to admit you're a little hard to understand."

Robert took me in his arms and held me close.

"Listen," he said. "Trust me. I want you to know that I'd be even happier than you if you were next to me in this bed tonight. Grownups aren't necessarily what you think. But sometimes they have to put their duty before their happiness or pleasure. And there are times when the duty part is very hard indeed. So please don't make it any harder for me than it already is. Go climb into your own bed without trying to understand. Think of it as a favor to me, something you're doing because you love me. Agreed?"

"Agreed."

His voice was so filled with emotion that I hardly recognized it, and I could see by his face how upset he was when he said that to me. Without another word, I went back to my bed of straw and climbed in.

As a solitary child, living in harmony with nature, and despite my natural curiosity about almost everything, I had never posed any question, really, about how the human species reproduces. I hadn't any idea, even the vaguest, of the physical bonds that united man and wife. Luckily for me, I might add, for given my curiosity, I would have wanted to try it out immediately—the same way that, as a little girl, I wanted to show my friend the pike that I was just as bright as he and jumped into the water, even though I didn't know how to swim. Poor pike, when I think of it: I was so angry at him after that experiment that for two weeks I deprived him of the goodies I had been feeding him every day.

In any case, Robert was a gentleman, and even if I had known and wanted to try it, I know he would have refused.

I awoke before him in the morning, sneaked downstairs, and brought him up breakfast in bed.

"Come on, lazy bones, the sun's up. Finish your breakfast. I'm taking you out for a walk."

"Where are you going to take me?"

"Three guesses."

"Tell me."

"The Irsa Bridge, of course."

"I thought I'd made you promise not to go back there. You mean to tell me you disobeyed?"

"You told me not to go there as long as the army encampment was there. There hasn't been any for a long time."

"And how would you know that if you hadn't gone there your-self, young lady?"

"Because," I said, my temper rising, "my father works over in that area every now and then. He told me. And there's something we better get straight right away," I added, hardly repressing my anger. "I always tell the truth and I always keep my word. If you don't remember that, you and I will have trouble getting along, I must warn you!"

I could see that my words had an immediate effect.

"I'm sorry," he said. "Please excuse me. Come over here." Then, seeing that I didn't move, he added: "You may remember that I'm the jealous type. It's only because I love you so much. Sometimes I can't control it."

"Promise me that you'll never hurt me again."

"Cross my heart. I'll be a model husband."

"You'd better be! Otherwise, I'll eat you up."

I removed the breakfast tray from the bed and threw myself on him, nibbling his ears with mock savagery. He laughed and fought me off and kept calling me his little Normandy savage.

Every detail of those three days remains engraved on my mind. Three fleeting days of happiness. How fast they went; how perfect they were; how few such perfect days are given any of us to live in the course of our long lives.

August 14, 1945

Nine o'clock in the morning. My little brother and I were already on the Irsa Bridge, my favorite place. After a while we decided to climb down to the railroad tracks below, and to the bed of stones that flanked it, where we had often gone with Robert and his buddies when the camp had been there. It was an ideal spot for target practice, and the soldiers had set up all sorts of makeshift targets there, and even taught us to try it ourselves. Claude had even practiced firing one of their machine guns there one day.

I'd neglected my little brother these past few weeks, but he didn't take offense. On the contrary, he was overjoyed to see me so happy. He was also pleased to see the change that had taken place in Papa Maurice, who no longer mistreated me. Claude used to shake his head in wonder and say to me:

"Even if you had married the lord of the manor and become the lady of the village, Papa would never have treated you with more respect."

And it was true. Tough old Papa Maurice had mellowed, at least so far as I was concerned. And I owed it all to Robert.

Robert. Soon we would be joined together and live happily ever after. The war was over, he would be discharged in a matter of months, and come to fetch me.

Claude's voice called me from my daydreams.

"Geneviève, come here. Help me, I've taken a tumble."

About thirty yards away he was lying flat on his stomach almost in the center of the stone pit. I ran over as fast as I could.

"What happened, sweetheart?"

"Nothing really. A piece of wire caught in my shoelaces and tripped me up."

"Did you hurt yourself? Don't cry, it's not serious. I'll free your foot."

I tried to work the piece of wire free, but I couldn't. Finally I stooped down, to get a better angle, and pulled on the wire with all my might.

A tremendous explosion broke the silence. Much later on I learned that the wire had been attached to a land mine, and in pulling it, I had set it off. In fact, it turned out that the whole area under the bridge was filled with land mines, and it was a miracle that none had exploded the many times that Robert and I had gone there when he was still stationed at the bridge.

The explosion propelled us both into the air, but in different directions. I landed not far from the railroad tracks, and by some miracle managed to struggle to my feet. By sheer willpower, I made it the few meters to the roadbed of the railroad track, even somehow crossed the little stream that served as drainage ditch at the base of the bed itself. My intention was to cross the tracks and reach the telephone that I knew was on the pole of the semaphore on the opposite side. But I had overestimated my strength: I couldn't make it any farther. Despite my enormous efforts, I couldn't get beyond the first track.

During all this, I remained completely aware of what had happened to me, and almost clinically examined myself as I lay there. I was completely naked: my clothes, as well as my shoes, had been blown from my body. I could see that the blast had ripped me open in several places. On my right side, a gaping wound revealed my intestines, that spilled out onto my thigh. My hands were burned and broken in a dozen places. The little golden ring that Robert had given me had melted and was encrusted in the flesh of my finger. With my broken hands, I reached down and tried to stem the descent of my intestines. I managed to hold them, pull them back up a trifle, and was amazed as I examined them to see that they were blue, almost purple. But there were other even more amazing revelations to come: my legs were also broken in several places. The tibia of my right leg was sticking straight out, as though an arrow had struck my leg and remained embedded there; the kneecap of my left leg had simply disappeared, a gaping hole marking where it had been a few minutes before. I had the feeling that my right eye had been gouged out, but actually it had only been pierced by shards of the mine blast. My face and hands were horribly burned, the skin virtually vanished. I knew I must have had a terrible wound in the throat, too, for every time I opened my mouth a flow of bright red blood spurted out. And yet I was not suffering. I tried to think.

I heard a train whistle from the direction of the Chef-du-Pont Station. I still had enough presence of mind to realize that if I remained where I was on the track, the next train through would finish me off. Therefore I absolutely had to move. My mind gave the order; but my body failed to respond. I had lost too much blood; there was no way I could make it to my feet; I was just too weak. With all my waning strength, I fought fiercely against my declining forces, which I could feel ebbing away second by second. Seeing that I had no chance of succeeding, I leaned over and let my own weight pull me down, till I was lying on the roadbed; then I let the force of gravity take over as I slid down into the drainage ditch below. It was dry, and its steep sides protected me from the rays of the sun. My mind was still alert, and as I lay there I tried to figure out what would become of me. The idea came to me that if Robert were to see me in this condition he would no longer love me. Therefore, I had to die. No question. Without him, I couldn't go on. There was no other solution: I had to die. Suddenly I realized that tomorrow would be August 15. The idea that I would be arriving in heaven on the birthday of the Virgin Mary made me smile. I hoped that my soul was not as damaged as my body. If it were, the Good Lord would have trouble recognizing me. I was overwhelmed with a sudden feeling of high spirits at the thought of the expression on Saint Peter's face as he saw me arrive in that frightful state. In his deep voice he would say to me:

"*Now* what have you got yourself into, you little ninny?"

I felt like falling asleep, but I knew I had to fight against it. I couldn't fall asleep. I wanted to live my death as I had lived my life, by scrutinizing every second of it.

I still felt no pain whatsoever. I knew that in this condition I ought to be screaming with pain, and yet I felt relaxed and almost cheerful. I knew I was going to die, but that didn't bother me. It might be several days before they found my body, and even that struck me as quite unimportant.

All I could see from my strange vantage point was the little bridge where I had spent so many happy hours. It was beautiful, bathed in bright sunlight. I tried to remember the last song I had sung for Robert. What was it anyway? I couldn't for the life of me remember. Come on, Geneviève, put your mind to it. Yes. It was a song from a Lalo opera. My darling soldier had been amazed by my ability to move, almost without transition, from the voice of Princess Rozenn to that of the King. "You have gold in that voice of yours," he had told me. "Someday you'll be rich and famous." I had laughed and said: "I'll never sing for anyone but you. That way you'll never be jealous."

Since it was written that my life was to end today, I was happy that fate had brought me to this spot I loved so much. I couldn't have chosen a better place. Silently I thanked God for His choice.

I lost consciousness for several seconds. I woke up trying to remember what Robert had told me one day: what the words "bye-bye" came from in English. But I couldn't remember. "Take me close to You, God." Something like that. But that wasn't it. "I'm going to Thee, God." No, not that either. I couldn't remember. I felt like singing. I began to sing the opening notes of *Ave Maria,* but a flow of blood drowned my song. Too bad. I'd never sing again.

Suddenly I thought of the German officer I had held in my arms more than a year before, also on the edge of the railroad tracks. I was less lucky than he. He at least had a last moment of happiness on earth: he had listened to and loved my song. I wouldn't even have that. It was finished. I had to give up even that. I lost consciousness again for a brief moment, or so it seemed to me. Suddenly a man was bending down over me.

"What happened, child? Did you fall off the train? What's your name?"

"Geneviève, Monsieur. I'm Papa Maurice's daughter. My mother is the grade crossing guard of 103."

Every time I opened my mouth to talk, another stream of blood spurted out.

"Don't talk anymore, child. I'm going to telephone for help," he said. He seemed more upset than I was. "We'll get a railroad handcar down here right away for you. Don't worry. Everything's going to be all right."

I heard him run up the slope and call from the phone on the other side of the tracks. I found him strange. Why did he tell me not to worry? I wasn't worried. I was going to die, that's all. It was very simple. I knew one thing at least: it wasn't hard to die. Those who are mortally wounded didn't suffer at all.

The man came back to where I was lying and covered me with his blue worker's jacket: "I'm going to 103 and let your mama know, child. I won't be long. Is there anything you want me to tell her for you?"

"Yes. Tell her that I want to be buried in a French flag and my casket covered with an American flag. Tell her to write Robert; I want him to know that I died thinking of him. And tell her to ask him not to cry. And you shouldn't be crying either, Monsieur. Dying's not all that serious. What's your name?"

"Maurice. Maurice Friouze. Don't talk anymore, child. You're hemorrhaging every time you open your mouth. Please don't talk anymore. I'll be back before you know it."

I was thirsty and so tired. So very tired. The man promised to come back very soon. But Mama won't be able to come with him. The rules of the railroad were very strict. She was not to leave her post for any reason whatsoever, even a matter of life or death. Such as was the case now. Even if her children were dying. It was better that way. I didn't want her to see me in this state anyway.

The August heat caused my blood to coagulate on my wounds almost immediately. The only place where I still bled was my throat, and then only when I opened my mouth. I felt fine. I had no notion of time. Had I been in the ditch for a long time? I felt so sleepy. I fought fiercely to stay awake. I wanted to hear the final beat of my heart.

I had forgotten to tell that man something! But it didn't matter, really. Mama would surely remember. I wanted to make sure she put all my mementos in my casket, the souvenirs all my soldier-friends had given me: the little leather cap; the insignia of the 82nd and 101st Airborne Divisions; Robert's own insignia, the winged horse; Kerry's cartridge clip; George's metal cigarette lighter; a button from J-Two's uniform. Yes, Mama would surely remember all of them. I was sure she would. I fell asleep again.

I was awakened by the sound of voices. My father was there, leaning down over me, as well as the man who had found me. Papa's thick voice came to me as through a wall:

"Do you understand what we're saying?"

The question struck me as so absurd that I hesitated before replying. Then:

"Of course I do! What kind of question is that? I'm not dead yet!"

"Then tell me where Claude is."

"He's over there, in that pebbly area under the bridge. Go and fetch him right away. It's too late to do anything for me. You can see that I'm dying, but there may be a chance to save him. Please, hurry and see to him!"

Two of the men busied themselves lifting me out of the drainage ditch. Drawn by the smell of blood, swarms of flies had gathered on my body, laying their eggs everywhere in my open wounds. I must have been a gruesome sight; one of the men had to turn away and throw up.

They placed me on a stretcher and lifted me onto the handcar

stationed on the tracks. When they had lifted me, my body was
pierced from end to end by the most horrible pain I had ever felt.
Why hadn't they left me there in the ditch to die? I had felt so
comfortable there, with no pain at all.

Impossible to leave me on the handcar. Each time its wheels
came to a break in the rails it shook me so that I couldn't help from
screaming, and each time I screamed, another stream of blood
flowed from my mouth, in frightful little spasms. The men were
afraid to see me die there on the handcar, so they made up their
minds to carry me on the stretcher to the Chef-du-Pont station.
Throughout the endless trip, I kept begging them to set me down
and let me die, to go back to the Irsa Bridge and help find my little
brother. Monsieur Pottier, the kindhearted stretcher bearer who was
at the head of the stretcher, walking backward and therefore facing
me, was sobbing like a child. In our neck of the woods there were
no longer any private cars, let alone ambulances. The war had seen
to that.

An American army truck was commandeered to take me to the
hospital at Cherbourg, and with some difficulty my stretcher was
hoisted up onto the back of the truck and placed in the middle. I
was having more and more trouble seeing, but I was still able to
follow their every movement. I was sinking into a state of semi-
consciousness, but I was aware of that too. Still, I was able to hear
them discussing what to do next; they made the decision that the
men who had brought me this far should return to the Irsa Bridge
to take part in the search for little Claude. The county chief asked
two men I knew, Monsieur Legoupillot and René Lemaire, who
happened to be there, to join his search team. The more searchers
there were, the better chance they had of finding the boy. I could
see Papa Maurice sitting on the bench of the truck, huddled beneath the canvas cover. On the other side of my stretcher a young
American soldier was also seated. He had said he wanted to accompany me to the hospital. I was still holding my intestines in my
hands. I wanted to let go of one of them, in order to make a sign to
the soldier to come closer, but I couldn't: it was as though they
were glued to my stomach. But the soldier saw that I was strug-

gling to make some kind of signal and he knelt down beside me, right next to my stretcher.

"You're a very brave girl, Geneviève."

With a voice that was no more than a mere whisper now I said: "What time is it, please, soldier?"

The soldier glanced at his wristwatch.

"Ten past one, Geneviève.

"Thank you."

Ten past one. Let's see now . . . I was wounded about nine thirty. I have a feeling . . . What? I don't remember. Oh, yes. What I do remember is what "bye-bye" used to mean: "God be with you." That's it.

I felt very pleased that I had finally remembered.

I hurt so much now, so very much. How unhappy Robert would be if he knew. I was glad that he didn't. Over on his bench, Papa was crying silently. Did that mean he loved me, even a little bit?

The jolts of the truck as it drove along the country roads toward Cherbourg brought an endless series of moans from my lips, despite my efforts to suppress them. The pain was unbearable, more than a human being should be made to endure. The young soldier was still kneeling beside me, bent down low over me, watching. I looked up at him one last time and managed:

"Geneviève is dying, soldier. Bye-bye."

I could see that tears were streaming down his cheeks. I wanted to console him, to tell him not to cry, but I couldn't. I had held out as long as I could. I was aware that the end was near. I still had time to think:

"Adieu, Robert, adieu, my love. Don't forget I love you for now and for all eternity."

And then everything began to grow dark. I heard, close beside my ear—unless I heard it only in my heart—his gentle voice, his tender voice, say one last time, as he had said so many times before:

"Bye-bye, Geneviève."

And then nothing. Darkness.

I slipped into a coma that was to last for the next nine days.

August–December 1945

When I came out of my coma the first person I saw was a tiny nun who was dressed entirely in white. I often used to complain about being so small, but she seemed to be even smaller than me. The room I found myself in was enormous, containing about twenty beds, occupied by girls more or less my own age. Seeing from her post a few meters away that I was awake, the tiny nun hurried over to my bed. I looked at her open-eyed, still amazed that a grownup could be so small. She placed a finger on her lips and said:

"You're awake? Good. But you mustn't speak under any pretense. You have a bad wound in your throat, and the slightest word might start it hemorrhaging again. Simply shake your head if you understand what I'm saying."

I nodded. She smiled.

"That's good. Very good. Relax and don't move. I'm going to get the surgeon. He wants to talk to you."

And with those words she turned and hurried away on tiny feet. I was surprised at how fast she could move. In a few moments she was back, accompanied by a man of fifty or so, also dressed all in white.

"I'm glad to see you awake," he said. "I must warn you, though, that you mustn't try to speak if you want me to save your voice. Not yet anyway. You must be patient. In a few days we'll give it a try. Do you understand?"

Again I nodded. The surgeon then asked me a whole string of questions, which I tried to answer as best I could.

"Are you still going to school?"

I nodded.

"Did your teacher teach you fractions?"

Strange question. Of course she did. Again I nodded.

"Therefore, if I talk to you about a ten percent or twenty percent chance of something, you'll know what I'm talking about?"

More and more intrigued, I nodded once more.

"Good. Now, here's what I wanted to say. You've been badly wounded."

I wondered if this doctor had all his marbles. Of course I'd been badly wounded. You'd have to be blind not to know that. But fortunately, the good doctor couldn't read my thoughts.

"You *can* get better," he went on. "But on one condition only. Listen to me carefully. Eighty percent is up to you and you alone. My science will be worth about ten percent. And I'm leaving another ten percent in the hands of the Good Lord. How does that strike you?"

With my right hand, the only one that was free, I made a signal indicating that I wanted to write my reply. The girl in the next bed was writing on a slate, which the surgeon borrowed, together with a piece of chalk. He helped me sit up by fluffing up the pillows behind my back and adding another pillow to those already there. I took the chalk and grasped it as tightly as I could with my fingers. But I couldn't manage to hold the slate in place and write at the same time. The surgeon leaned over, held the slate for me, and I wrote:

"I understand. My getting better will be long and hard, but it's a challenge I accept. I'll do whatever you tell me to do so I'll get better as soon as possible. Okay?"

He looked at what I had written, then glanced down at me with a mixture of surprise and admiration.

"You're going to be here a long time," he said, "but I have a feeling you have the toughness and courage to make it. With both of us giving our best, we'll succeed."

This time I shook my head and pointed to the enormous crucifix the nun was wearing, then held up three fingers. The nun laughed wholeheartedly.

"She's right, Doctor. Not the two of you, but the three of you," she said.

She handed me the rosary, with its silver Christ a good fifteen centimeters tall, and as I brought it to my lips I couldn't help thinking: "Well, You've done it again, Jesus. You've shown me You still don't want me up there with You. Once again You've slammed the door in my face." Those thoughts made me want to laugh, but the thick bandages that imprisoned my head kept me from any such display. All I could do was bite my lips. The doctor and nun saw it.

"Why are you laughing?" he said.

I wrote on the slate: "That's a secret between Jesus and me."

They both smiled. Then I wrote:

"I want to know a number of things. First, where's my little brother?"

"I don't know," the surgeon said. "Ask your mother. She'll be coming to visit you every Thursday afternoon."

"Do you know whether Robert is aware of what happened to me?"

"Who's Robert?" the surgeon asked.

"He's her future stepfather," the nun chimed in. "Her mother told me that she was going to be adopted by an American soldier. The adoption papers are being processed now."

The surgeon shook his head. Given my condition, the notion of adoption struck him as highly improbable.

The nun left and went into the cubicle that served as her office and bedroom, then returned, still trotting, bearing a letter with a postmark from the north of France. She handed it to me and asked me if I wanted her to read it to me.

I shook my head, took the letter, covered it with kisses, and slipped it into my nightgown, next to my heart.

"He means all that much to you, this soldier of yours?" the surgeon asked.

Nodding, I wrote: "He's my only reason for wanting to live."

"That's not very nice for the Good Lord," the nun observed.

I scribbled on: "The Good Lord has no cause to be jealous. He is and will remain my sole reason for dying."

The surgeon burst out laughing.

"Geneviève," he said, "anyone who's just gone through what you have, and has not only survived but still retains a sense of humor, has every chance of recovering. I must confess that I wasn't sure whether your intellectual faculties might have been affected. Needless to say, I'm reassured."

"That would be all I'd need, for my mind to go," I wrote. Then: "Am I in such bad shape?"

"Pretty bad," the doctor said with a grimace.

"Can you give me a rundown?"

"No, not today. You need rest more than anything. I want you to sleep. Don't you agree, Sister? We've already talked more than we should today. Later on, I'll answer all your questions. Meanwhile, remember what you told me: 'It's a challenge I accept.' You must get better."

"All right," I wrote, "I'll get some sleep. But can I read my letter first?"

"If you want my opinion, I think you'd be better off reading it after you've had some sleep."

I acquiesced, and handed him back the slate and chalk. Under the covers, I placed my hand on the beloved letter, then closed my eyes. The nun straightened up my pillows and I heard the surgeon say to her:

"The child is really quite something. I think she's going to pull through. If willpower has anything to do with it, I'm sure she will!"

The compliment went straight to my heart. I tried to make my mind go blank, to repel the thousands of questions that were trying to crowd into it. I promised to get some rest, and I would. I must have fallen asleep within minutes.

———

When I awoke, the tiny nun was leaning over me, a finger on her lips.

"Don't forget," she said, "no talking. At least not for a while yet."

I nodded, to reassure her that I remembered. The surgeon, who was with a little girl a few beds away who had been operated on for appendicitis, hurried over.

"Well, Geneviève, I must say that when you do something you do it all the way. You've been asleep a full twenty-four hours. Which pleases me no end. You must be feeling much better. I've brought you a thick notebook and a pencil. Now you ask me any question you'd like."

I wrote: "First I'd like to read my letter if you don't mind."

"Of course. Give it to me and let me open it for you."

I extracted it from beneath the covers. The envelope was all crumpled. The surgeon smoothed it out as best he could and clipped off the top of the envelope with a pair of scissors he was carrying, attached to his waist by a thong. He handed me two pages covered with the strong, firm handwriting that I recognized and loved. The letter was dated August 22, 1945.

My darling little Geneviève:

I've just learned from your mother the terrible tragedy that has just happened to you and little Claude. I can't find words, my darling, to tell you how sad I am at the news, and to know how you must be suffering. Yet I want you to know, my angel, that you have to keep on hoping and know how much you have going for you. Modern surgery is making enormous strides these days. We'll make you well again, of that I am sure. As soon as I received your mother's letter I asked to be discharged from the Army as soon as possible. The paperwork is now going through, and I'm assured that I'll be out in three to four months' time at the latest. As soon as I'm

out, I'll be there as fast as I can make it and I'll stay with
you forever. You'll see, my darling, with time and patience we'll make you as good as new. Meanwhile, make
sure you do everything the doctors ask, even if it's sometimes painful. You must be brave and obedient. Don't
forget that everything the doctors are obliged to do is for
your own good. Always remember, too, that your future
is at stake. You must accept everything, however difficult
it may seem at the time. Remember, most of all, that I
love you more than anything in the world, and I want
you better as fast as possible. *You must do everything in
your power to that end.* If you can write me, please do as
soon as you can; if you can't, because of what has happened to your hands, ask your Mama to write a letter for
you. But above all, darling, don't leave me without any
word of you. Hurry and get well. I must end this letter
now, but I'll write more soon.

With all my love,
Your Robert

P.S. As soon as I can get leave, I'll be there to see you.

I closed my eyes for a few minutes. So . . . despite everything that
had happened to me, Robert still loved me. That was the best
reason in the world to recover. The doctor made no attempt to
interrupt my silence. Then, suddenly, he said:

"Come, come now, Geneviève, don't cry. I trust the news in your
letter is good."

I nodded, trying to wipe away the tears that were spilling down
over my bandages. Then I took the notebook and wrote in it:

"My soldier is trying to get leave as soon as possible, so he can
come and visit me. I think the time has come to talk about everything I've broken, don't you agree?"

"What do you want to know?"

The pencil raced across the paper.

"Will you be able to save both arms and legs, or will you have to amputate anything?"

"I'm pretty sure we can save everything. Your arms are fine. If you can't move your left arm, it's because that's the needle in your arm at the end of that rubber tube. As soon as you can eat normally, I'll unhook that machine and you'll have full use of your other arm.

"As for your hands, despite a few broken bones, there's nothing we can't put back together as good as new."

"And what about my legs?"

"The right seems to be coming along fine. I had to do away with a bit of your tibia when I set it, but it won't affect the length and I see no real problem. As for the left leg, I can't be so positive. I had to put it in a plaster cast from the foot to the top of the thigh, whereas for the right a splint sufficed. To plaster over open sores or wounds is always a problem, but I had no choice. In any case, we're going to watch that leg like a hawk. If you notice anything abnormal, please let me know right away, even if it doesn't strike you as very important. You'll have your fair share of beautiful scars, but you'll get better. You'll walk again, if you really set your mind to it. As I said before, your recovery depends more on you than on anything else. Are you still game?"

"Yes." Then: "What about the rest of me?"

"Of all your wounds, the one in your midsection will be the first to be completely normal again."

"Which part of me will take the longest to be better?"

The surgeon hesitated for a moment.

"Please level with me, Doctor. I'll cooperate, don't worry, but I need to know. So?"

Slowly, as though the words were being dragged from him, he said at length:

"Your face, Geneviève. We're going to have to call on plastic surgery to restore your face, and that, I'm afraid, is beyond the scope of my competence."

I raised my hands to my face, which was covered from neck to forehead, with only my eyes and lips visible, and patted it, trying to feel through the bandages. Then I took the notebook and wrote:

"Please take off my bandages right away and give me a mirror."

"No, Geneviève. It's too early. You're not strong enough yet. In a few days, if you still want to, but not now."

I sat up on one elbow, almost pulling the needle from my arm, and wrote:

"I want to see now. If you don't, I'll remove the bandages myself."

"You really want to?"

"I'm more solid than you think," I wrote. "Don't worry, I can take it. The sooner I know, the better it will be. That way, I can plan my campaign to get better–with your help, of course."

"All right, if you insist. But first I want you to know that plastic surgery has made enormous strides over the past few years, and you're going to be the beneficiary of that progress. Furthermore, an English scientist discovered a new drug, about ten years before the war, that's now being fairly widely used, and it can work miracles. Through the American Red Cross I'm going to obtain some, which we can use to combat the infection in your legs."

"What's this drug called?"

"Penicillin."

"Fine. I'll remember that. Now can you remove the bandages and show me my face?"

With obvious regret he complied.

"Above all," he said, "I don't want you to cry out when you see yourself, however upset you may be. If you want to save your voice, you must not speak or utter a sound now. Do you understand?"

I nodded, then wrote: "Will I be able to sing again?"

"Of course. There's no reason why not. Your vocal cords are intact. A piece of shrapnel struck your throat and sliced a bit of it away inside, but it's healing nicely. But don't set things back by talking or crying out, all right? Next week we'll give your voice a tryout."

Gently, he unwound the last bandages. I couldn't keep my heart from beating faster and faster. The nun brought me over a little mirror. The doctor leaned over me.

"Remember now, no using your voice no matter what your reaction. Keep telling yourself: I'm going to get better. Promise?"

I nodded. If I hadn't realized it before, now I knew that what I was going to see would be awful, shocking. For a moment I hesitated. For a moment I thought: maybe it's better if I don't look. I took a deep breath, then another. I thought of all the soldiers who, over the past several months, had found themselves in a similar situation, and faced up to it. Was I going to be less brave than they? They showed me the path, and I was going to follow it. I had no right to turn back now. I seized the mirror and looked. What I saw *was* horrible. It bore no relation whatsoever to my adolescent features. The burned and swollen and bruised flesh that I saw was not me; it was not even human. Only my lips and chin had escaped more or less intact. The worst part was my cheeks; the skin as it mended was beginning to attach itself again to the bones. I looked so frightful it was all I could do to keep from throwing up.

The doctor took the mirror away from me and said:

"You're a brave, brave girl, Geneviève. You handled that like a true soldier."

I wrote: "Thank you. That's the nicest thing you could have said. And I *will* get well. I want to with all my might. There's only one request I must make: I don't want Robert to see me in this state."

"Why?"

"Because he'd stop loving me. And if he did I'd prefer to die."

But I was also thinking: and I also couldn't stand to know that he was feeling sorry for me.

"We should be able to handle that," the doctor said. "When he comes to see you we'll put the bandages back on."

"It's a deal."

The doctor turned and walked over to the cubicle where the nun was. I could hear them discussing something, and then the doctor walked back to my bed.

"We're going to give you a little something to swallow," he said, "to see how it goes. To see if your throat will take it. Do you have a preference?"

"A little light coffee, if that's allowed."

The nurse disappeared, to return a few moments later carrying a little covered bowl, the top of which looked like a beak.

"We call this a 'duck,' " she said, "because of its beak, which will make it easier for you to drink lying down."

The name made me smile. I thought back to my duck in the marshes, my friend Mister Duck, whom I hadn't seen in over a year. I wonder what had become of him? Would I ever see him again? We'd had such good times together, Mister Duck and I. I smiled again. The nurse mistook my smile, and said:

"So you like the bowl, eh? You'll see, it will be a big step toward feeding yourself again. Do you want to try it yourself, or shall I help you?"

With my finger I made her understand that I preferred she help me this first time. She slipped the beak in between my teeth and gently raised the bowl to let a little of the warm liquid flow into my mouth. Scarcely had the first drops reached the back of my throat when I let out a scream of pain. Surprised and upset, the nurse let the bowl go, and it fell and broke on the floor. The surgeon, who had been attending the girl in the next bed, rushed back.

"Geneviève," he said. "Please! You mustn't scream!"

And yet it hurt so. I sobbed uncontrollably, and the thought ran through my mind: "What a great start!"

The doctor opened my mouth and examined the interior. I wasn't bleeding, but the pain was so unbearable I was convinced that I must have torn something open. It took me several minutes to regain my composure. Finally, I took my notebook and wrote:

"Do I have to try again?"

"That's enough for today," the surgeon said. "Try to get some sleep. We'll try again tonight when you're feeling a bit stronger. Only," he added, gesturing to the bottle stationed above my head, "I don't want to keep feeding you with that thing too much longer."

I nodded. I knew then, if I had doubted it before, that my path back to health was going to be long and rocky. What pain and suffering still lay in store for me? Would I be strong enough to endure them? All of a sudden my future looked horribly bleak. For several minutes I felt sorry that I hadn't died. It's so easy to die, and so hard to go on living. I envied the little girl in the bed next to me. I had gathered from the nurses' conversations that she was not going to make it. Her appendix had burst, and there was nothing more they could do to save her. She was ten years old, an only child, as pretty as a picture, and had parents who adored her. Why did she have to die, and I to live? It made no sense. Life just wasn't fair. To try to give myself a little courage, I reread Robert's letter. Robert, my only reason for going on, for fighting to get better. How I wished he were here with me, that he were with me forever. He promised me: by late autumn he'd be out of the army and free to take care of me every day. Ten weeks, ten long weeks to wait, and then we would never leave each other again.

Suddenly I realized that I didn't even know what day it was. I wrote something in my notebook and handed it to the little nun who was bending over sweeping up the pieces of broken bowl on the floor. My question amused her, I could see, for she smiled and said:

"It's August 28th. You've been here for two weeks now. Is that all you wanted to know?"

I shook my head and took back the notebook.

"Could you tell me what you did when you saw me arrive here in such a state?"

"What struck me as most urgent. I called for a priest and told him to make it fast, so that he could administer the last rites to you. But as you see, you didn't need them."

"I could have told you you were wasting your time," I wrote. "God doesn't want me."

"How do you know that?"

"It's very simple. I had a dozen chances to be killed and each time God shook His head and said 'No.' He's afraid I'd foul up His paradise. Just as soon have me down here. Too bad for me."

"Why?"

"Because life down here isn't much fun. If I had my way, I wouldn't waste another day down here; I'd go straight on to paradise."

"I know what you mean," the nurse murmured. "Considering the state you're in. But life is a gift of God, and we must take it as it comes."

"For me this gift has been more often than not a great burden, I assure you. And," I wrote, "I have a feeling there's more to follow."

"Don't despair, Geneviève," she said, "everything will work out in the long run. If you don't keep your spirits up you'll never get better. And I don't want to see you delirious ever again the way you were."

I wrote: "To make the doctor happy, I'll try to get some sleep."

I closed my notebook, having then and there made the resolution to treat my body like some machine that needed repair, to do my best to get it back in working order. I also made up my mind not to let myself get depressed, or to think such thoughts as I had just expressed, about preferring to be dead. I fell asleep.

The nurse woke me up and asked me if I felt strong enough to try and take another sip of liquid.

I nodded, but indicated I'd prefer to try a spoonful rather than resort to the bowl.

The nurse brought me a spoonful, and I tried to lap it up the way I had seen kittens do. The result was less painful than the previous attempt, but it still hurt almost unbearably. I didn't try to swallow any more, but I still felt I had accomplished something: I hadn't screamed.

The doctor, who was at the bedside of the girl who had appendicitis, came over to me.

"Bravo, Geneviève," he said. "I'm proud of you. That's victory number one, and I'm sure there will be many more."

He examined my throat, then explained to me what had happened. At the moment of the explosion, I had probably screamed, by reflex reaction, and at the same moment a piece of the land mine had struck my throat and sliced everything on its way through. It would be some time before I could eat by myself, and I would probably have to learn to use my vocal cords again, too. The internal wounds were long and deep, and it would be some time before they were completely healed.

In the middle of the night I heard the little girl next to me call for the priest. She must have sensed she was dying. The priest arrived in great haste and administered the last rites. Her parents had been called, but they were too late: the little girl was gone, and I saw that her face was wreathed in a lovely smile.

Seeing I was awake, the priest came over to my bed.

"I'm a very light sleeper," I wrote. "The little girl died, didn't she?"

He nodded.

"She's lucky. Why her rather than me?"

"I don't know, Geneviève. We propose; God disposes. Perhaps He has such difficult plans in store for you that He is preparing you by the suffering you've been made to endure these past weeks."

"Not these past weeks," I wrote. "It's been going on a long time. And, honestly, I don't see what He is getting at."

"It's not for us to understand His ways," he said. "Let Him do as He sees fit. As often as you can, try to say to yourself: 'His will be done.' You'll see, it will make things easier."

"Really?"

"Try it for a few months and then let's talk about it again."

Our conversation was interrupted by the arrival of the girl's mother. The mother's sobs brought me suddenly back to those days over a year ago when my soldiers were dying, and the pain and horror of it all. Was it always so difficult to die? I wondered.

In early September, Dr. Blanchard, the surgeon who had been treating me, came into Room 17 one afternoon, before nap time, and sat down on my bed.

"I'm going away on vacation," he said. "But before I go I think we ought to try a little experiment. What we're going to do is let you use your vocal cords for the first time. I want you to say a single word. Raise your head, so that you are stretching your neck, and say 'fine.' " He placed his fingers on my throat. "All right, say it."

"Fine."

The sound that emerged from my throat was thick, harsh, and crude. But Dr. Blanchard smiled and said:

"That's good, Geneviève. Let's try it again. But without forcing."

I took a deep breath and said:

"Fine."

Then, for good measure, I added:

"Everything's fine."

"That's enough out of you, big mouth! When I want you to improvise I'll let you know. Now, open your mouth and let me take a peek inside, to see what effect those sounds have had. Good . . . It looks as though my little repair job is holding up. Did you drink any coffee this morning?"

I nodded.

"Try to tell me your answer, but if at any point it hurts, then stop."

"I . . . drank . . . a little . . . coffee . . . this . . . morning . . . and . . . at . . . noon. . . . Two . . . tea . . . spoons."

The sounds that came out of my mouth surprised me. And upset me. The doctor saw it and said:

"Don't let that worry you," he said. "That will take care of itself. More important, does it hurt?"

"When I drink, yes; when I talk, no."

"I'm sorry it still hurts you to drink. I had hoped to take you off that bottle before I left."

"When are you going?"

"Tonight. I'm a tired old man."

"I'm sure you must be tired. You stayed up all night with that little girl who died, and then you were on the floor all day as well."

I was speaking very slowly, and very strangely, and I wasn't sure whether he could understand me. But at least he wasn't telling me not to talk.

"How do you know all that?"

"I have eyes."

"One, Geneviève, only one."

"I only use one now. But I still have two."

"Geneviève," he said softly, "I'm afraid that your other eye will never see again. It was filled with shrapnel. Dr. Cau did all he could, but to no avail."

I was stunned. "You mean, I'll never see again with that eye?"

"I'm afraid not."

"You simply forgot to tell me!"

"Geneviève, there was so much wrong; I simply forgot to mention that detail."

"How many other details have you overlooked?"

"None of any importance."

"Name some of the unimportant ones."

"Well, I haven't told you, for instance, that for the rest of your life you'll be a walking iron mine. You have hundreds of pieces of iron in your body."

"You can remove them, can't you?"

"Not all of them. There are far too many. I'll remove those that are painful."

"You mean to say I'm going to walk around the rest of my life with all that iron junk in me?"

"Yes. And if what they say is true, you'll grow up stronger than Popeye."

"What do you mean?"

"They say iron is good for children."

"Very funny. And besides, Doctor, I'm not a child. I'm a young lady."

"I was joking, Geneviève. Just because you have your voice back doesn't give you license to start griping. Otherwise I'm going to regret I gave you permission to talk."

"Is there any danger I might lose it again?"

"Actually there is. With all the cuts inside your throat, it's a miracle you're talking at all."

"Did you remove all the pieces of metal?"

"Not all. There are still a dozen or so tiny pieces lodged in your gums. But I was afraid if I removed them I might ruin your beautiful teeth."

"I'm glad you didn't. That's about the only beautiful thing I have left."

He must have detected my note of bitterness, for he said:

"No regrets, Geneviève, for that leads to depression, and depression prevents you from getting well."

"All right, Doctor," I sighed. "I'm tired anyway, so I'll try to get some rest. Have a good vacation. And thank you for everything." Then, after a moment's pause: "Why did that little girl with the appendicitis die, Doctor?"

"Because her parents brought her to me three days too late. They kept thinking her stomach ache would go away, as it usually did. Peasants are hard people, Geneviève. They don't generally respond to a child's cries. And you can see the results."

"And now all they can do is cry," I murmured. "How very sad."

"It is indeed. I did everything in my power." He shrugged. "There are days when I wish I'd never decided to become a doctor."

"Now who's talking of regrets? Please, Doctor, no depression. We need you. *I* need you. What would have become of me without you?"

"There are other surgeons. I'm not the only one here."

"Yes, but it was you whom fate chose to save my life."

"I admit it was a tough job. When I first laid eyes on you I couldn't quite believe what I saw."

"I know. I was lying out in the sun for four hours before they found me. I was covered with flies and fly-larvae, I know. It must have been awful. What did you do first?"

"I gave you a warm bath, to get rid of the larvae that were beginning to eat you. Then I had you carried over to the operating table. I didn't know quite where to begin."

"You're terrific, Doctor. The proof is that I'm still here."

"My only mistake, perhaps, was repairing your vocal cords."

I looked up at him in horror, but I saw he was smiling. "You find I talk too much."

"You're pretty good at it."

"You haven't heard anything yet. Wait till I start singing again. Then you'll have something to complain about."

"Why?"

"I have a range of six octaves, and I sing all the time. From morning till night, and from night till morning. I hold every world record. Just wait!"

"I wasn't complaining, by the way. Besides, it would liven this room up. You really enjoy singing all that much?"

"Put it this way: I'd prefer to lose my eyesight than my voice."

"Don't say such stupid things! Your eyesight is terribly precious, too. How do you know, by the way, that you have a six-octave range?"

"One of the American soldiers was a former music teacher. He heard me and wanted to take me with him as part of a troop entertainment group. But my father wouldn't hear of it."

"Then how come he allowed your friend Robert to adopt you?"

"That was different; he's only allowing Robert to adopt me after he's discharged from the army in December."

"Aren't you happy with your parents?"

"Not really . . . You see, my father drinks a lot. And as you can guess . . . I'm lucky, I guess, that a soldier wanted to adopt me. He loves me as though I were his real daughter, and I love him too. So it works out just fine. He wrote me that it didn't matter to him that I'd been wounded and disfigured; he still loved me just as much. But I know that I'll be all well again someday, as good as new, so he won't have to be ashamed of the way I look. As long as he still loves me, I know I can get well; but if he ever changes, I wouldn't give two cents for my life."

"I don't know whether I ever mentioned it, Geneviève, but I have a little girl just about your age. Ever since I met you I've been telling myself how lucky she is. You're the bravest person I've seen since I've been taking care of this war's victims. We're all going to work together to make sure you get well again. There are a lot of people in this ward who love you, Geneviève."

"Will I be able to sing again soon, Doctor?"

"When I get back from vacation, we'll give it a try. We'll start with some simple melodies, without any very high or very low notes. If that first step is successful, there's no reason you can't go on from there. Does that make you happy?"

"More than happy! Oh, I'm sure everything will work out. I have a constitution of iron."

"For the moment, Miss Iron Constitution, you look a trifle pale and tired."

"But in good spirits, Doctor. Didn't you say that meant everything?"

"I did indeed, and believe me, I've noticed it."

The little nun opened the door a crack.

"Doctor," she said, "your replacement is here. He'd like a word with you in your office."

"I'll be there in a moment, Sister."

"Before you leave, Doctor, do me one favor. Please unhook me from that machine," I said, pointing to the bottle that nourished me. "That way I'll have to start feeding myself normally."

"And what if you can't?"

"I'll manage somehow."

He looked at me skeptically, shook his head, and then without a word went over and unhooked the infernal machine; he gently withdrew the needle from my arm and nodded at me knowingly.

"I know you'll manage, Geneviève," he said. He turned to leave.

"Thank you for everything Doctor," I said. "And have a good vacation."

After that long conversation, I was exhausted and wanted only to sleep, to sleep for a full day if necessary. I was happy to have found my voice again, even if it did sound strange to me. In another month, he had said, I could sing again, too. But would I be able to wait for a month? On these thoughts, I sank into a sound sleep.

I was awakened by a new doctor, who at first glance seemed as nice as Dr. Blanchard. Considerably younger, I noted. But the initial impression did not last for very long.

He began by removing the drain from my right leg, then unwrapping the thick bandages that swathed it, and the cotton underneath. There was a piece of fine gauze covering the open wound at the top of my thigh, which he pulled off. I winced, but that was nothing compared to what followed. With a quick pull, he snatched away the gauze that was covering the various cuts and wounds up and down my body, and with it came whatever poor skin I still had, including that which had begun to reform. I gritted my teeth, but I couldn't bear it. I let out a blood scream. My wounds began to bleed again. The little nun, who was present, tried to reassure me, reminding me as well that I shouldn't scream or I might ruin my voice forever, but I was suffering so her words fell on deaf ears. Meanwhile, the new doctor was cleaning, scrubbing, pushing, pulling each of my open sores with heavy hands, and by the time he was finished I had almost fainted.

Next he came to the plaster cast on my left leg. What was the cause of that foul odor emanating from the leg? he wanted to know. The nurse explained to him that the portion of the kneecap that the explosion had torn away had made a gaping wound that was still suppurating: that was probably the cause of the odor.

The doctor stood there scratching his head for a moment, then ordered the cast removed. A male nurse arrived, bearing an enormous pair of shears, like those used to cut sheet metal. He slipped one blade of the shears beneath the cast, and to make the incision had to lean with all his force on the upper handle, at the same time pressing down on my wounds. Worse, the lower blade, in progressing down the leg, entered the hole where my kneecap had once been, and the pain was so great that I fainted.

When I came to, the nurse was washing my wounds, very gently, and though it was painful, I knew I could bear it. The doctor was gone. As it turned out, there had been an emergency in another ward, and instead of returning later as I had feared, he was tied up there for several days. Meanwhile it was the nurse who changed my bandages.

The afternoon of the new doctor's first visit, Mama came to see me. She seemed pale and thinner than I had remembered, and she was dressed all in black. The sadness on her face vanished when she saw that I was awake. She held me gently in her arms, and we stayed there for a long time without speaking.

"Where is Claude, Mama? Tell me how he is."

"At the Valognes Hospital," she said without hesitation. "Same ward as last year. He's still on the critical list. I'm afraid he's in even worse shape than you, Geneviève."

Without another word, I tore a page from my notebook and wrote him a letter, which Mama promised to deliver on her next visit to Valognes. In my letter I asked Claude to be patient and brave. I promised to get better fast so that I could come and take care of him as soon as I was back on my feet.

The new doctor's second visit almost turned into a catastrophe. The bandages of my left leg were covered with pus when he arrived, and on the spot he announced that he would have to amputate the leg. The nurse tried to reason with him, explaining that if the bandages were soiled it was because I had been a bad girl. She made the accusation coldly, and I started to protest when I caught her eye and realized that she was trying to cover up for me. What a poor liar she was, the dear little sister! Her lie had made her blush to the tip of her ears. But she had won the day: she had made the doctor give me a day's grace before amputating.

"If the leg is less pus-ridden tomorrow I won't amputate. Otherwise . . ." Then he turned to me and said: "As for you, young lady, I suggest you try to be a better patient, If not, you're the one who will have to pay for it."

The nurse accompanied him from my bedside, but reappeared a few moments later.

"I was afraid you might give me away," she said. "I hope you weren't too surprised by what I said, but that doctor will amputate at the drop of a hat. I've heard tell that for a corn or bunyon on the foot he'll take the leg off below the knee! No, I'm exaggerating. But we must do something. I'm sure that Dr. Blanchard can save your leg. The only thing is that it will take a long time. Here's what I suggest we do, Geneviève, while waiting for Dr. Blanchard's return. Dr. G —— always makes his rounds at the same hour every day. Half an hour before he comes, I'll remove your old bandages, clean the wounds, and put on new bandages. What he doesn't know won't hurt him."

"He's bound to ask you some questions, though, and you'll be obliged to lie."

The idea that a nun might lie struck me as so incredible that I couldn't refrain from making the remark.

"Your leg is worth a few lies," she said, shrugging her shoulders. "The chaplain will give me absolution. Lies do exist; we must only use them, though, to help those around us. Now, let's talk about your leg: my only concern is that when I replace the bandages it may hurt so much you'll cry out and the other patients will hear and perhaps give our little game away. So when I come I'll bring you an ether mask. If you take a few whiffs you'll hardly feel a thing. That way, no one will be the wiser."

"How about the other girls in the ward? Are you sure they won't notice something and tell the doctor?"

"I doubt it, but to make sure I'll let them in on the secret and pay them for their silence. I have a huge stock of sweets that the American Red Cross gave us, and that should be perfect legal tender." Then, with a worried look, she added: "And how about you, Geneviève? You won't say anything, will you?"

"That's a crazy idea!"

"The only reason I mention it is . . . you do talk a lot."

"Only with people I like. And, believe me, Dr. G —— is not among them."

We put our little game into play, and it worked beautifully. The month of September actually seemed to go by fairly fast, perhaps due in part to the fact that I wanted to save my leg so badly that each day our little game worked seemed to speed by. When one day Dr. Blanchard walked into the ward again, we all breathed a sigh of relief. The first thing he did, after examining my left leg, was to order that a new cast be put on. There was no chance that the few fragments of bone that had once been my kneecap had any chance of rejoining without a long stay in the cast, even if the price we had to pay was at the expense of my other leg wounds.

One day I let slip, while talking to Dr. Blanchard, that I was sad and distressed that I was missing the entire school year. As always the good doctor was filled with good ideas.

"I have a suggestion," he said. "What if I brought you my own children's school work every day? That way you could keep up with your class."

I was so excited by his offer that I reached up and grabbed the surprised doctor around the neck, pulled him down, and gave him a big kiss. I think the dear man was more moved than he was willing to admit.

From that day on, he thought of me as his own daughter and couldn't stop doing things to make me happy. Knowing how much I loved flowers, he made sure the tiny vase he had given me was constantly filled with flowers of one sort or another, and as soon as one bouquet showed signs of fading, another would arrive. Better yet: with the complicity of my friend the nurse, he concocted a scheme to draw the birds to the window at the head of my bed. Our rations were fairly meager, but between the bread crumbs we salvaged and the sacks of grain the doctor came up with upon occasion we kept the windowsill outside scattered with improvised bird food. I still couldn't move my legs to watch my feathered friends, but by arching my neck I followed their movements as they came and went.

One day a teacher from Sainte-Mère-Eglise paid me a visit, and she brought with her as a present a big doll stuffed with straw. How was she to know that I hadn't played with dolls for years? Anyway, Dr. Blanchard put the doll to good use. He said I ought to use it as a kind of doll-diary: each time I had to be operated on, I would make an appropriate incision on the doll's body, and later I would sew it up as carefully as possible. That way, when I left the hospital, I would have a complete record not only of how many operations I had had, but just where and what they were. It might have struck some people as rather ghoulish, but in my situation any diversion helped.

I continued to write Claude every day, and each Thursday Mama collected my mail. She mailed my letters to Robert and personally delivered Claude's. Since Dr. Blanchard's return, time was moving more quickly. Each day I did my school work, which he brought back next day all corrected. It was now nearing the end of the year, and I was counting the days until Robert would arrive to take care of me. Each day I could feel myself getting stronger. My legs were still prisoners—one in a cast, the other still being drained—but they hurt me less than they had. My face was perhaps not pretty yet, but it had become at least acceptable. I was told that two grafts might be required, but that was not certain at this juncture. I decided to let Robert make that decision. The grafts would be done in Paris. Robert would have returned to his old store, but would manage to take time out of his busy day to come and visit me at the hospital. Despite everything, the future looked bright.

And, to top it off, Christmas, the happiest season of all, was just around the corner.

December 22, 1945

From my room I could hear Christmas carols floating up from the chapel on the floor below. The choir was rehearsing. Despite his promise, Dr. Blanchard was still refusing to let me start singing again. He kept postponing the day, time and time again. But when I heard the voices from the chapel I could not bear it any longer. He had to allow me to go down and rehearse with them. I could easily be taken down on a stretcher, and even though I was lying down, I could still sing. But when Dr. Blanchard heard of my request he flatly refused. I began to suspect that he was keeping something from me. I asked him to tell me the whole truth. Right now.

I could see that he was flustered and upset, but he finally stammered out that, indeed, my voice—so far as singing was concerned—was a thing of the past. Despite all his efforts—past, present, or even future—my former singing talents could not be restored. I refused to believe him. From my earliest memories, singing was the thing I loved most in the world. My reason for living. It just wasn't possible. I began to cry and soon was sobbing, as though that would help. Dr. Blanchard was visibly distressed, and he tried to comfort me by saying that perhaps, after all, if I put as much courage and tenacity into learning how to sing again as I had into regaining the use of my legs, then who could tell . . . I clung to that tiny shred of hope, but my instincts told me it was false. Somehow, though, the hope, however vague, made me calmer, and I decided not to waste another minute but to make an initial try right then and there.

Alas! the sounds that emerged were not those sweet and vibrant notes that had once come so effortlessly, but scratchy and discordant, and terribly unpleasant. I was stricken, thoroughly and hopelessly stricken. I caught myself thinking: it was all in vain. I might as well have given up. I wish I were dead. I wish I were dead. And with these dark thoughts coursing through my mind, I tried that night to drift off to sleep. But try as I would, sleep would not come.

December 23, 1945

Today I was expecting a visit from my mother, who would be bringing with her not only a Christmas present but, I hoped, news of Robert's impending arrival. I was counting the minutes. What would she say when she learned I would never sing again? Would she understand the depths of my distress? Would she find words that would somehow comfort me, give me a slim ray of hope?

When visiting hours began, I had the shock of my life. Despite my inability to move my legs, I bolted upright in my bed, into a sitting position, something I normally couldn't do myself. The man walking across the room with a heavy step, fingering his cap nervously as he came, I had not seen for more than four months: it was Papa Maurice.

He was dressed in his Sunday best. He was wearing a black ribbon in his buttonhole, and his new shoes made a crackling noise with every step. He paused at each bed and peered, then moved on until he reached mine. I didn't even dare open my mouth and ask him what had brought him here, for I sensed, rightly it turned out, that he had come to make me suffer.

Struck dumb by his arrival, I sat there motionless, and he seemed equally at a loss for words as he gazed at my bandaged head. For several moments we stared at each other. Then he opened his mouth and a torrent of words poured out. I noticed that he was still fingering his cap as he talked. Seemingly not having any notion of the pain he was causing me, he spoke not loudly but as fast as a jack rabbit.

"I'm fed up with the little games they've been playing with you here. Your brother Claude is dead. He didn't survive his wounds. Your mother didn't want you to know. After all, you're responsible for his death. You were told to take care of him. So you're responsible for what happened. That's the way I view it. I don't see why I should spare you. If you were to live a hundred years, and your life was that of Job, it wouldn't be enough to wash away the sin of my son's death. Your punishment begins today: your soldier won't be coming back for you. In the physical state you're in, you can't be adopted anyway. I've forbidden him to ever lay eyes on you again. He tried to protest but I wouldn't listen. I've sent him packing and said if he persists I'll have him arrested. Do you hear me? You'll never see him again!"

I looked at my father as though I were seeing him for the first time. He was no longer the cruel and mean man I had once known, but a poor broken father who was stricken to death by the loss of his beloved son. His coming to see me was simply an effort to try and make his own broken heart feel better. I felt sorry for him. I wanted to say something comforting, but I couldn't utter a single word. A welter of thoughts pounded through my brain. "Claude is dead. It's your fault he's dead." It was true: by pulling on that metal wire I had set off the explosion. I couldn't have foreseen what was going to happen, but the fact is *I did it.* And my little brother was dead. And Robert would not be coming back. Ever. Yesterday I learned I would never sing again. Today I had lost Claude and Robert. It was too much. The thread of life to which I had been clinging desperately for over four months suddenly abandoned me. I fell back on my bed. My neighbor saw it and called the nurse, who was busy a few beds away talking with another nurse from the next ward. Both nurses raced to my bed. The tiny one, my friend, searched for my wrist and felt my pulse. Through a wall of cotton, far away, I heard her murmur thickly:

"Good Lord, the poor child's dying! Sister Augustine, run and find the chaplain! And Dr. Blanchard! Hurry!"

I could vaguely hear sounds around me, but thickly and darkly. Yet I had the clear impression I heard Sister Augustine's footsteps hurrying away. Dr. Blanchard arrived almost immediately and examined me.

"What happened?" he asked the girl in the bed next to me.

"A man came to see her a few minutes ago. He told her that her little brother was dead, and that her stepfather would never come to see her again."

"Who was the man?"

"The man who was carrying his cap in his hand. You must have passed him when you came into the ward. He wasn't talking loud enough for me to really hear, at least not everything, but I had the impression he was suffering himself. He was crying as he left."

In my semi-conscious state I remember taking note of that detail: *He was crying.*

Then I heard the tiny nurse saying:

"Shall I put up the screens, Doctor?"

"I'm afraid so, Sister."

The screens . . . That meant I was going to die. At long last! Far from frightening me, I found the news comforting. It was done, done at last. My suffering would be over. The screens. They only brought them during the day, when the patient was close to breathing his last. I felt the doctor injecting me with some kind of liquid, into my left arm. Intravenous, they were called, and they were the only kind that didn't hurt me. The reaction was quick to follow: I opened my eyes. Kneeling on the edge of my bed, the nurse was cradling me in her arms, my head against her chest. The big silver crucifix she wore hung down and touched my chest. I gazed at it fixedly. And then, suddenly and much to my surprise, I heard myself saying:

"Oh, Sister! Of all the Golgothas in the world, do you know of any more cruel than those where they crucify children?"

And then everything began to grow dark again. I could scarcely make out the chaplain who was administering the last rites. Sister was crying. I could feel her warm tears dropping onto my hands. I heard her say to the chaplain:

"It's over, Father. Poor little Geneviève will suffer no longer."

And that was the last I remembered as I sank into the darkness, into the comforting night where memories that break your heart do not exist. A night from which I would have been happy never to emerge. But have I ever had the choice?

Epilogue

Again, death would not have me. But to say I recovered from that last crisis would be an exaggeration. When I came to, I was completely blind. Later, when I could be transferred, I was sent to the Cochin Hospital in Paris, in the care of the renowned eye specialist Dr. Offret. After months of care, this great man restored the sight of my left eye. I had no memory. What I took at first to be amnesia turned out to be a reduction of my intellectual faculties due to the destruction of brain cells which had occurred on that December day when my heart had stopped beating. The fact is that I have never really fully recovered the alert intelligence that I had possessed as a child.

But here I must pause and thank Papa Maurice, who, when my case seemed hopeless, still forbade the surgeon in charge of my case to either give me electroshock treatment or to perform brain surgery, as he would have liked. He maintained that time alone and my strong constitution would prevail in the end. And he was right.

It took me months and months of hard work and self-discipline before I could learn again what I had lost. But at the end of that time I managed to put back together some semblance of order in my head, which the shock of that autumn and winter of 1945 had turned upside down. I undertook this re-education process after I had left the hospital, and I did it alone, without the help of anyone except Mademoiselle Burnouf. At the age of fifteen I passed my *Certificat d'Etudes* at Sainte-Mère-Eglise.

Today, thirty-five years after my accident, I have spent a total of five years in hospitals. I have undergone thirty-three operations. Actually, there's still another operation to come, though no French surgeon dares perform it: the operation on my right eye. Too bad: if it were to succeed, my vision would be almost normal again.

My body is, as Dr. Blanchard predicted, a walking iron mine; more than three hundred fragments are still imbedded in it, ranging from the size of a pinhead to that of a walnut. Plastic surgery has, indeed, restored my looks to something at least acceptable, although I have, to my great dismay, lost my ability to express myself normally by my facial reactions. As a child, so I am told, that was one of my chief assets. As predicted, too, I can no longer sing: my singing voice is lost forever. There are times, too, when for long periods I lose all use of my vocal cords—for no apparent reason—so that I cannot even speak. But then, again inexplicably, my voice returns.

Cruelest of all, I lost my Robert. Papa Maurice had indeed forbidden him to see me, but he had persisted until my mother too, after that December 23rd, had told him of my further medical complications and convinced him my case was hopeless. Then and only then did he give up, not only on me, but also on his plans to stay on in Paris. He returned to Central America and, a few months afterward, married a local girl. It was the only reasonable thing to do. I still shudder today at the thought that he might have seen me in the condition I was at the time. I had wanted his love; I could not have endured his pity.

To occupy the endless hospital hours, I wrote to a number of pen pals around the world. Just receiving a letter, even from someone I had never met, made life a bit easier. Among them was a Frenchman of Polish extraction. In the course of his correspondence he revealed that, several months before, a woman had broken his heart. He in turn learned from my letters of my concern about returning home to my parents once I had been discharged from the hospital.

He proposed; I accepted without hesitation, and without ever having laid eyes on him. I was seventeen years old.

From the start we both knew that our hearts would never wholly recover from the wounds they had received. But we nonetheless determined to make ourselves a solid, if not a sentimental, couple. The birth of our first child with a stomach defect brought us momentarily closer together, but when after two months of agony, the baby died, something in our relationship broke as well. We struggled on together for several more years and five more children. But then one day my Polish sailor pulled up anchor and left his home port behind, never to return. I was left with the task of supporting and bringing up the five children.

I think it was at this time that I finally understood what my father had been trying to tell me years before, when we had been perched at the top of the tree at twilight. He was not there to lighten my burden but to prepare me, without knowing it, for the Job-like misfortunes that lay ahead. Without that Spartan preparation, I would never have survived. And I can now say that my childhood, which I have described not unfairly here, was despite all its trials and tribulations the only time in my life when I remember moments of happiness.

Today, Papa Maurice has mellowed in his later years. He drinks less. However, after thirty-six years of marriage, he and Mama finally decided to go their separate ways. Of all his children, I'm the only one who pays Papa occasional visits. Now it is he who cries when he sees me arrive. I do my best to surround him with comfort and tenderness, but the past is too much with him, and he can never put it far from his mind. Time is said to heal all things, but I have learned that that is not wholly true, that certain things cannot be forgotten. Engraved in my mind forever are the deaths of those I knew and loved, not the least of whom were those American soldiers, who had come to free us from the Nazi yoke and who died there in the fields and marshes close to our house. Were we worthy of their sacrifice? It is a question I still ask myself.

Robert, too, will never be forgotten, as he has never forgotten.

Some twenty years have passed since he wrote telling me that he, like me, had a daughter named Stephanie, and asking if he could be my Stephanie's godfather. Today, as I write, both our Stephanies are grown and married.

The wounds in my heart, like those in my body, will never completely heal. The man whom I have never stopped loving is happy, and that brings me solace and a measure of happiness, as do his letters posted from a country in Central America. I think of how little time we spent together and marvel that so deep a love could have been forged in so short a time. Fortunately, we still have eternity to look forward to.

On Christmas Eve 1945 God once again showed that He did not want me. I traveled to the gates of paradise, only to be turned away. Despite all this, I have done my best to make sure that those around me enjoy a happiness I have so rarely known. Depression may stalk me, but it has never conquered me. In the big, handsome house that I built with my own hands there is no lock, and anyone who walks in is always welcome. I have seen people arrive there exhausted and cynical, people whom very often I have never seen before in my life; they join us for family dinner, and leave with the conviction that the qualities of love and charity are not completely dead.

When the weather changes, my scars, my countless old wounds, act up and make it painful for me to move. But I still suffer even more from the wounds I did not receive, I suffer hell whenever I think of the tortures of those American soldiers I saw massacred beneath my eyes on June 10, 1944, tortures that I suffered with them at every stroke. I have never found any rational explanation for that strange affinity that links me forever to those martyred soldiers—to such a degree that on certain days of inclement weather there are times when for hours on end I cannot move my arms. A complete paralysis. Surely there is some explanation; it's a matter of finding it. Perhaps, quite simply, it lies beyond our powers to understand.

I am still waiting, with a certain degree of impatience, for the day when, sooner or later, the reluctant God up there will be obliged to nod rather than shake His head. That kind of remark upsets my children. Stephanie frowns at me as if to say: "Will you never learn to be serious, Mama?" Perhaps it's simply that I've never grown up. I'm still as prone to ask questions as I was when I was a child.

One of the questions I ask myself, over and over again, each time I reread this poem that moves me so is: who was it, Monsieur Lamartine, that hurt you so, of what indelible wound were you referring when you wrote these lines:

> *The Book of Life is the highest book*
> *It can neither be opened nor closed as we choose;*
> *For the parts we love there is no second chance*
> *Not even a peek, not even a glance,*
> *While the page of death turns itself.*
> *No matter how hard or often we look*
> *To relive that moment of glory, we lose.*
> *While the page of death turns itself . . .*

WITH GRATEFUL THANKS FROM THE MAJOR GENERAL

Dear Maurice and family,

Thirty-three years have passed since the night that began the liberation of Europe. In that interregnum several generations of soldiers have passed through the ranks of this Division. Those of us who follow the men who spearheaded the liberation continue to look to that night as the epitomization of the airborne spirit. Their sufferings and successes are our heritage, and we jealously continue to share them.

We know, just as they knew that night, that our successes were to no small part the result of the help we received from many French men, women and children who risked and gave their lives with us in pursuit of the common cause. Many of you were not known to us at the time; and the Duboscq family, although long known to us by deed, has only recently been identified by name. We knew that you collected, sheltered and led our soldiers to their comrades. We knew as well that you told us of the land and where the enemy lay. We knew that in your small boat, Maurice, you collected our supplies. Only now can we offer thanks to all of you for that help. We suffered then your anguish over the loss of your son and the wounds of Geneviève; only now are we able to say so.

The invaluable aid that the Duboscq family provided on the nights of 5-6 June, 1944, and the sacrifices you made, are a part of the heritage of the 82nd Airborne Division.

ROSCOE ROBINSON, Jr.

Papa Maurice receiving the Medal of Honor and Geneviève America's
Guard of Honor. Philippe Jutras is at the far right. *Author's Collection.*
Editions Robert Laffont: Service Iconographique.

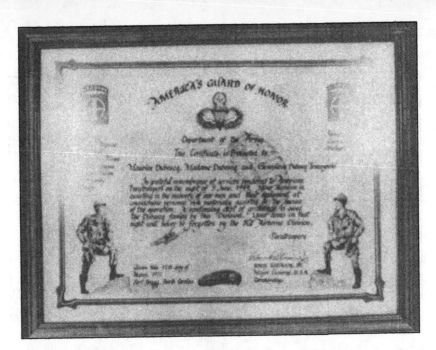

Certificate of America's Guard of Honor. *Author's Collection.*
Editions Robert Laffont: Service Iconographique.

Pen-and-ink drawing of Grade Crossing 104 the night of June 5, 1944,
given to Papa Maurice and Geneviève with the compliments of U.S. Major
General Roscoe Robinson, Jr., and Philippe L. Jutras, Curator of the Sainte-
Mère-Eglise Museum. *Author's Collection. Editions Robert Laffont: Service
Iconographique.*

To Geneviève Duboscq (in 1944)
whose gallant spirit made possible
the passage of the equivalent of two
battalions via the secret passage through
the flooded marshes of La Fière in order
to join forces on the other side of those marshes
as stated in "Night Drop" by S.L.A. Marshall
chptr 12.
A more courageous person, I ever got to meet!
Best personal wishes
Always,
Philippe Jutras
Sainte-Mère-Eglise
10 September 1977

To Geneviève Duboscq from Philippe L. Jutras, note dated September 10, 1977. *Author's Collection. Editions Robert Laffont: Service Iconographique.*

In the center is Papa Maurice; and on the right Philippe L. Jutras. *Author's Collection.*

Papa Maurice today, standing by Grade Crossing 103. *Author's Collection.*

Geneviève returning from a walk to Grade Crossing 104, holding freshly picked water irises and wearing two medals: one awarded to civilians wounded during the war, and the other (the smaller one) awarded to her in Israel. Her children are behind her. *Author's Collection.*